HV
15
.R34

Rapoport, Lydia.
Creativity in social work : selected writings of Lydia Rapoport / edited by Sanford N. Katz. -- Philadelphia : Temple University Press, 1975.
xxvii, 228 p. ; 23 cm.

Includes bibliographical references and index.
ISBN 0-87722-043-3

1. Social service--Addresses, essays, lectures. I. Title.

HV15.R34 361'.008

75-13637
MARC

Library of Congress
04313 572494 B 6223

Creativity in Social Work

Creativity in Social Work

Selected Writings of Lydia Rapoport

Edited by
Sanford N. Katz

Temple University Press
Philadelphia

Temple University Press, Philadelphia 19122

Published 1975
Printed in the United States of America

International Standard Book Number:
0-87722-043-3
Library of Congress Catalog Card Number:
75-13637

Contents

Acknowledgments

This book could not have been possible without the encouragement and support of Mr. Emanuel Rapoport, Lydia Rapoport's brother, of Kenneth H. McCartney, Dean of the Smith College School for Social Work, and of Dame Eileen Younghusband and Dr. Carol Meyer, who were Miss Rapoport's friends. I am more grateful to them than I can say.

Assisting me in the work of collecting Miss Rapoport's papers and choosing selections for inclusion in this book were Dr. Meyer and Elinor Zaki. The latter worked with me in editing the papers and in planning the order of their presentation. They have my sincere thanks and deep appreciation.

To fill any gaps in my information about Miss Rapoport's life and career, I relied on the clear memories of Mr. Emmanuel Rapoport, of my wife, Joan Raphael Katz, of Dr. Charlotte Babcock, and of Miss Harriet Bloomfield. I wish to thank them most warmly.

Melba McGrath, my aide, has been, from the moment this book became a possibility, an enormous assitance, not only with her splendid editorial talents, but with her support beyond the call of duty. She has heard my sentiments before but I should like to repeat my appreciation.

We are indebted and grateful to the journals and publications which permitted us to reprint the articles included in this volume: *Smith College Studies in Social Work; Social Service Review; Social Casework; Comparative Theories in Social Casework; Social Work; Handbook in Community Psychiatry; Social Work Education Reporter; Family Planning: The Role of Social Work;* and *Journal of Education for Social Work.* In the interests of clarity and consistency, minor changes and deletions have been made in the articles, but there have been no alterations of sense or fact.

Royalties from the sale of this book will be added to the Lydia Rapoport Endowment Fund at Smith College, Northampton,

Massachusetts. The Fund was established by Miss Rapoport's friends and relatives to perpetuate her name, which is identified the world over with the highest achievement in social work.

Foreword

Eileen Younghusband, DBE, JP

This volume contains articles written by Lydia Rapoport over a period of time. Each article was produced for a specific purpose, a conference or a seminar, or to describe a given piece of work, yet they illustrate a consistent body of concepts derived from research, wide study, and experience of practice. The theoretical underpinning is the psychoanalytic theory in which Lydia Rapoport was steeped. Over the years, however, she became increasingly interested in cultural and sociological concepts and the contribution that these, in combination with psychoanalytic insights, could make to a better understanding of human behavior and its modification.

Although her highly intelligent and creative mind drew her to an interest in psychosocial theory, as in social philosophy, she always wanted to discover what light these shed on the current reality, and how theoretical knowledge could be used to give practitioners more precise tools for assessment and action, for more finely differentiated and goal-focused professional practice. She was constantly brought up short by the plethora of untested assumptions in social work, by small islands of knowledge floating in seas of ignorance. Hence the plea throughout these articles is for more research, and for more controlled experiment to validate or contradict accepted assumptions in social work practice.

Unlike some social work theorists, she made actual practice an integral part of her professional development. It was her work with Gerald Caplan on the reactions of parents to the crises created by the birth of a premature baby, in which she herself undertook much direct casework, which lies behind the articles in this volume on the application of crisis theory in social work. These articles and those on family planning especially illustrate the richness of her theoretical formulations, her tough-mindedness about testing out and giving evidence for their application in practice, and the imaginative humanity which made her so sensitive to people's feelings under stress or their aspirations for a more satisfying family life.

Lydia Rapoport was a brilliant teacher—as many readers of this book will remember with nostalgia. She was highly organized in her knowledge of a subject but she also endowed her teaching with creative imagination and an ability to set alight the enthusiasm of the group.

My friendship with her goes back to 1953–54, when she came to the London School of Economics as a Fulbright Scholar. We saw each other constantly and stimulating professional discussions slid into, indeed became inseparable from, a friendship which was fresh and full of zest whenever and wherever we met. The last time was in London in the spring of 1971, when she was on her way back from Israel to New York. She was very ill then—indeed she died not long after—but she was undimmed as a person. It was typical that when I told her about some work being done on separation at the Tavistock Institute she immediately realized the connection with her interest in crisis theory and next day rang up Dr. Murray Parkes for an appointment.

Somehow she knew then that we should not meet again and that her United Nations assignment on family life, which she had been enthusiastically anticipating and planning for, would not be carried out. Great opportunities for future achievement lay ahead of her. She was indeed one of the few creative and disciplined thinkers in social work education who was well known and respected internationally as well as in the United States. These articles show the quality of her mind and her rich humanity, and this book has been produced by her friends in the hope that social workers in different parts of the world will gain fresh insight from reading them.

Introduction

Carol H. Meyer, DSW

This collection of the most significant writings of Lydia Rapoport can be viewed through many lenses.

For some it will provide an intimate view of the creative mind at work. Lydia Rapoport was an artist who sought and always found the mot juste; she was a scholar whose wide and eclectic reading constantly enriched the development of her ideas; she was a professional who discovered the correct balance between theory and practice; and, not least, she was a humanist whose deepest concern was that the outcome of her study, practice, teaching, and writing should be effectual service to people.

Others will be interested in the substantive contribution of these writings, the sheer impact of the knowledge to be gained from them. They will open vistas for students and beginning practitioners, but the experienced social worker will also find new ideas, new connections among familiar ideas, new implications to be drawn from research findings or clinical experiences. Above all, readers will repeatedly experience that "shock of recognition" when what may have been only an intuition for them is suddenly a coherent and clarified truth.

Perhaps the most important contribution of this volume is its implicit presentation of a role model for the professional. Obviously a social worker would feel the closest kinship here, but in these days of ephemeral fads in academia, working styles unsupported by experience, and dubious mandates, many other professionals would welcome a model, a "way to be if it were possible." Viewed as a whole, these writings of Lydia Rapoport present a method for becoming an effective, intellectual professional practitioner, aiming toward high standards, maintaining relevance to the current social realities, and aware of future possibilities. Despite the fact that these papers were written in the recent past, they reflect the immediate concerns of today. A true professional is always one step in advance of the actual present.

The four parts of this book suggest the precise components that comprise the best kind of professional for these times. First, in "The Creative Mind at Work," we find the observer. The ability to stand at a certain distance from one's profession, to assay it and to know its history and its strains, and still to care for it intensely and personally—this combination of objectivity and subjective commitment make possible a healthy self-criticism that reaches out into greater achievement. A person with a philosophic view of the meanings, values, and purposes of his profession can be relied upon to be nonpartisan and will earn the trust of students and colleagues. And a profession to thrive needs a good share of observers.

In the second part, "Crisis Theory and Preventive Intervention," the theoretician appears—the professional who moved outside her own discipline to that of public health in order to test the validity of her ideas through the interchange. This theoretician utilized formal research, clinical evidence, the wisdom gained through practice, and personality theory, placed her results in a social work framework, and presented them to the professional community. The combination seems necessary in order to breathe life into good practice theory. All practitioners will not achieve this high degree of theoretical contribution, but each should address some aspect of theoretical development—formal research, clinical evidence, articulation of practice wisdom, or selective use and testing of a range of theories. It takes a special person to combine these parts into one coherent whole, as Lydia Rapoport did in "Crisis Intervention as a Mode of Treatment" but one or more of the parts is available to every thinking professional.

The third part of the book, "Consultation, Supervision, and Professional Education," presents that "something extra" the observer-theoretician–practitioner can accomplish. To extend knowledge, but also to extend the boundaries of the practitioner's skills through indirect practice modalities, Rapoport was among the first to define these extended roles and to specify the necessary skills. It has become more difficult in recent years to confine the concept of help, in any professional terms, to the immediate "bedside" of the patient or the client. For example, in the mental health field, which was Rapoport's specialization, it has now become axiomatic that mental health must be a consideration in all social institutions with which people intersect. Whether the site be a school, a family, an industry, a church—whatever the setting, the principles used in the development of mental health must be woven into the fabric of an individual's social ecology. Rapoport presented approaches to consultation in mental health as a method of influencing that ecology toward the prevention of illness.

A profession grows through continuous development, discovery, and communication of its theories and practice principles. Rapoport as the compleat professional addressed herself to supervision and advanced education. There is always a new cutting edge in her approaches to direct and indirect practice in social work, and the chapter on advanced education displays her original stamp on the plan to educate for practice in community mental health. Again, awed by the wide range of Lydia Rapoport's interests and abilities, one can read these essays simply for what can be learned from their content.

"Social Work and Family Planning," the fourth part of the book, represents Rapoport's most advanced work. It demonstrates once more that though she belonged to her time she could see beyond it. In this section we find social work practice joined with an area of social policy. Rapoport matured professionally, as did social work itself, in discovering how practitioners can be engaged in the formulation of social policy. The area she chose here was family planning, a new field riddled with contention and misinformation. The professional task was to define the problem, to assess the social policy issues and their underlying politics and economic determinants, to find the population at risk, to study the sociology of the problem, and finally to carve out a professional social work role in the area. This movement into a subject of vast significance but of unknown parameters required a professional retooling. It demanded familiarity with interdisciplinary materials, intellectual rigor, and a clear sense of role in order to define the appropriate professional terrain for the social worker. This final section of the book can serve as a guide for the social worker who hopes to extend her knowledge and skills in any new field, or as enlightenment in the cloudy field of family planning. In either case the impact of the contents is powerful.

So here is a book, a collection of articles that reflect the engagement of the professional, Lydia Rapoport, with the ideas, issues, and problems of social work. It is a book that will offer knowledge and provoke new debates within the profession.

Times of Changing Expectations

Rapoport identifies craftsmanship as "beautiful work, with a visible and articulated sense of purpose." To achieve this level of professionalism social workers need not only a full repertoire of skills but also the background knowledge to support their understanding of the human phenomena with which they work, the rationale for differential use of their skills, the consciousness of values and social purpose that give the skills meaning, and the sophistication about society's structures, functions, and policies that will enhance or restrict the application of these skills. Craftsmanship, in short, demands personal aptitude, versatility, and high intellectual competence.

It is conceivable that the expectation of craftsmanship cannot be fulfilled. In the mid-seventies, American society is less concerned with craftsmanship than with pragmatic solutions achieved through the most "efficient" means possible. For multiple technical, social, economic, and political reasons efficiency has come to be equated with lower levels of professional education, quick media-aids to learning, computerized short-cuts to knowledge, quantitative accountability measures—all part of the American imperative to hurry up. One is reminded of the utility of a bridge built in wartime to last just long enough for an army platoon to pass over. Craftsmanship is nonfunctional to that purpose, as it is nonfunctional in many social work programs today.

The mandate to social work to help people cope with their lives and to improve the conditions in which they live is a mandate with many deviations. The bed utilization review policies in hospitals, for example, demand of social workers not craftsmanship but cold hearts and heavy hands as they work to pick up discharge plans to nowhere. The association of social workers with public welfare provides for services to families not because they need them, but because the relief rolls are too high and social services are viewed as the route to self-maintenance. True craftsmanship in social work might indeed lead practitioners to encourage clients to use service agencies more fully, while administrative mandates strongly suggest that success in case management should be equated with lessened use of these services.

The present anti-social service posture of our government would seem to call not for better prepared social workers but for practitioners who will think less independently, who will follow routines rather than develop innovative programs, and who will not be rewarded for doing "beautiful work." The general anti-intellectualism in American society also appears in an increasing number of young people who have turned "inward" toward the occult and the mystical, or toward simply "doing one's own thing" without reference to history, scholarship, or even the full engagement with life in the real world. Perhaps they are suffering from a deep sense of powerlessness and alienation and are searching for purely personal solutions as a way of surviving the technological and impersonal world that is their reality. The effect of this kind of world is a diminishment of a sense of community, an atomization of society that is the antithesis of Richard Titmuss's argument for the "Gift Relationship."

The Search for Excellence

Social work must make its professional stand somewhere in the confusion of all these changing expectations, mixed messages, and sorry tidings. One cannot extract from Lydia Rapoport's essays a blueprint for present action, but there are some hints and some lines one could pursue. A stance can be taken at every step along the continuum of professional preparation, and excellence should be the goal on every level of relevant education, including staff development.

Establishments such as schools, universities, social agencies, hospitals, have experienced almost a decade of harrowing attack and self-examination. The pendulum swing was rapid, from elitist, nonparticipant education, policy, and practice, to a supposed democratization of decision-making, definition of courses, programs, and services as well as a reduction in accrediting demands. Somewhere in between the pendulum swing, as always, lies a balance. Excellence in professional preparation need not be equated with the old assumption of elitism, that a component of education is excellent because the teacher says so. Conversely, relevance is not always best recognized by the student because he is a student. Unfortunately, some teachers have defended some content as the path to excellence because it was the old path, and some students have called relevance that which makes them feel comfortable at the moment and does not stretch their minds. Excellence in professional preparation should include relevance to the social realities of the day, and if possible to the near future. In educational as well as service programs it should reflect the best critical thinking of representatives of all components in the process itself—that is, in a school the input from faculty, students, and administration. The combination of viewpoints imposes tests of reality and validity upon educational decisions. And in a service agency where other disciplines are involved, results increase in value when the contribution of the consumer-client-patient is sought and considered.

Excellence in professional preparation proceeds from the expectation of accountability. Performance based upon hard knowledge and patterned experiences requires of education and staff development that learning must take place—learning that will not only serve to enhance the student's sense of his own competence and well-being, but that will also affect the work to be done. Excellence is achieved in professional preparation, for example, when a practitioner knows how to work effectively with a client population like the aged, even though he may find his greatest personal gratification in developing self-awareness. Excellence on the high academic levels demands that the practitioner be alert to groupings of ideas so as to test ceaselessly for effectiveness in practice. Open-mindedness and continuing and continuous education through reading or through formal courses and institutes are the characteristics of excellence in all professions.

One might ask how a profession like social work, that is so reactive to social pressures, can assume a commitment to excellence in performance while the general social climate seems to demand a contradictory standard. Rapoport points the answer to this question when she writes that social work, like art, participates in "the act of standing aside from society" and assuming a position of alienation and even opposition. Like art, social work is out of the mainstream and reflects society's ambivalence. Carrying the analogy with art further, we note the increasing professionalization of artists, perhaps for fellowship. Rapopprt saw the professionalization of social work as serving that function, as providing a community, an identity that would sustain its members in the lonesome struggle. And, again as in art, the singular path to effectiveness and the surest guarantee against self-serving professionalism in social service is the reach toward excellence: the evidence of "beautiful work" in craftsmanship.

The Growing Edge of Practice

Lydia Rapoport's view of social work practice changed as the world changed and as the boundaries of social work knowledge expanded and interacted with other kinds of knowledge. She could hardly remain the same after her experiences in the field of public health, the London School of Economics, and the United Nations. While she sought to integrate fresh concepts about society and people, she continued to see herself as a caseworker—although her image for that role changed as well. Many new approaches to practice have been developed in the brief period since her death, but a careful reading of the latest articles in this collection will show that her contributions to a developmental view of practice, an ecological perspective, and a life model were fully articulated when these ideas were still inchoate.

Training social workers in mental health to think "beyond their clinical skills" means that social work practice must turn the older theory of casework, often mistaken for psychotherapy, toward the new goal of social work as an individualizing service. Through her work in crisis intervention, Rapoport explicitly adhered to the idea that it is sufficient for people to be motivated for relief of their suffering, that it should not be a requisite of service that they be motivated for change in behavior and feelings. Of course, the reliance in crisis intervention on the availability of helpers at stress points in variously identified crises opens up totally new questions about service delivery—which have not yet been addressed in the field. This theory also promoted the view of the client's autonomy in exploring and defining mutually agreed upon goals with the social worker. The "life model" is intrinsic to crisis intervention in the effort to prevent regression and to find a state where natural growth can be resumed. As Rapoport sums up: "The patient uses the team to support his inherent capacity for growth and independence . . . for increasing mastery and self-direction in his life."

Such ideas led to the increased use of concepts in ego psychology and diminished efforts to engage clients in intrapsychic conflict resolution. With the ego viewed in transaction with the environment, the internal state with the external milieu, it was at last possible to perceive cases (individuals, families, groups) from a holistic stance. It is no longer necessary to locate the person(s) outside of the significant environment. There is a linkage, a transaction between these physical-psychological-social components that promotes a sharing of events which may be capriciously physical, psychological, or social in their origin, but which result in a combined event or problem in mutual adaptation. The social work practitioner addresses this ecology, the client in his situation, through a mutual definition of tasks, and provides the conditions necessary "to support his inherent capacity for growth and independence."

But Rapoport does not stop there, with the mere components of a modern approach to social work practice, nor can we, as we strive for greater effectiveness. These practice ideas had to be explicated before social work could move on to efforts for social change. From an ecological perspective the client in the "life model" can in a sense be anyone. No longer must he qualify for social work service by being sick, poor, mentally ill, or deviant in any of several ways. Neither, of course, can he be excluded from services due to any of these conditions, and in fact specialized practice must evolve for these and other categories. The important point is that through developing a life model for practice, it is possible to de-clinicalize, de-hospitalize, de-prisonize, de-welfarize social work practice and take the major twentieth-century step from residual to developmental services. As long as social work practice remains solely in the arena of residual problems, social services will develop haltingly in the developmental sphere, and even that degree of development will be reached without individualizing services. In order to advance we needed the revision of the clinical-normative mode.

Toward a Developmental View of Services

In this country there is a great ambivalence about social policy, undoubtedly deriving from our social Darwinian tradition and a government that says, "Ask not what your government can do for you, but what you can do for yourself." The combined pressures of poverty, racial conflict, failing social institutions, inappropriate public priorities, and a kind of popular malaise have resulted in hesitant public social policies, where they are articulated at all. Either ambivalent and begrudging attention or no attention at all is paid to every condition and every problem with which social workers are concerned. This climate makes the task of the social worker either a holding action or a retreat. Some practitioners confront the institutions themselves in search of change and improved services, but the sad truth of this political era is that no one seems to listen; or if they listen, they seem not to care; or if they care, they seem as helpless as social workers to affect the political-economic-social state of this country.

It is important to make these comments because many social

workers are reflecting the mood of the present regressive atmosphere in America. Currently there is a retreat to narrower definitions of service, to choosing the specialized problems that show greater hope of improvement through psychotherapy. Clinical social workers, in selecting particular groups with which to work, have gone back to older definitions of case problems that view the environment as external to the case or not within the unit of attention. Perhaps because it seems that so little can be done to alleviate environmental stress today, the clinically oriented practitioner is frustrated and at times overwhelmed. Despite these difficulties one must attempt to maintain the forward-looking attitude which Lydia Rapoport valued. The time will come for the use and appreciation of a truly modern practice of social work. It has taken almost sixty years for Mary Richmond's casework to find its way into the social work mainstream along with other methodologies. Now that stream of methods is finding its place as it associates itself with social problem areas, age levels, and population groups. The opportunities for specialization in fields of practice are numerous, and if social work as a profession does not regress along with the government but keeps its treasured "alienated status" like the artist, it should be able to participate in the formulation of policies and programs that will enable individualizing social work practice to be genuinely effective.

Using family planning as her exemplar, Rapoport wrote of the social work role in policy: "I see the central responsibility of social work in family planning is to close the gap between the impressive changes in expressed public policy as against prevailing public policy, and to address its energy to modifying the behavior of social institutions and creating new social institutions, *taking into account not only societal but also individual human needs.* It is the commitment to this bifocal view . . . or ecological approach . . . which can be the unique contribution of social work."

Family planning is so new a field to most social workers that it might be clarifying to suggest other possibilities to test the usefulness of Rapoport's conception. One might substitute family policies like those related to day care, foster care, adoption, group care, correctional policies, family services, services to the aged or in mental health and health care. The practice roles in many areas are still to be devised, probably because social work has not yet reached beyond traditional boundaries in many instances. The "ecological approach" that Rapoport saw as unique opens avenues of thought and practice toward which social workers have been moving for a century.

The End Is but a Beginning

This collection selected from the writings of Lydia Rapoport is remarkable in its scope. It conveys her impressive range of competence, but still more significantly it illustrates twenty years of rich theoretical development in social work. Even the casual reader will be struck by the fertility of Rapoport's mind and her uncanny ability to reach out in advance of the field and even of her own knowledge. She was not a prophet and she never represented unanimity. Yet because she was closely attuned to her times, deeply connected with human need, and involved in the world, she perceived not only what was but what might come to be. So many experiences had been packed into her repertoire that she understood and exemplified all the traits required of a social work practitioner, as of any true professional—skill, knowledge with wisdom, and a full commitment to the actual world.

Lydia Rapoport:
A Personal Reminiscence

Sanford N. Katz

I first met Lydia Rapoport at Smith College in Northampton, Massachusetts, in the summer of 1965, while we were both teaching at the School for Social Work. Actually I had heard Lydia lecture on the Berkeley, California campus four summers earlier, though she could never recall that particular lecture and always believed I was mistaken. But I was not, because from that very first contact with her, I was struck by her beauty and grace.

There was a kind of radiance in Lydia, even a glow. Her physical traits may have contributed to this: blonde hair, blue eyes, and a very fair complexion. The color with which she identified was red—a shawl, a pair of shoes, or a purse. Her briefcase was red, and her automobile.

There was a private and a public Lydia Rapoport. Music, art, and literature were a cherished part of her personal life. She was an accomplished pianist and harpsichordist who admired the eighteenth-century period in music almost to the exclusion of later romantic composers. She had begun to collect contemporary Israeli painters. She read omnivorously in many fields, and just before her last illness was fascinated by two biographies: *Florence Nightingale* by Cecil Woodham-Smith and David Kennedy's *Life of Margaret Sanger,* which rounded out Lydia's research in family planning.

To her students and conference audiences, Lydia appeared quietly confident, in complete command of herself and the subject she was discussing. Often these listeners found her aloof and at times impatient because of her own quick mind. She was not outgoing and preferred not to reach out to meet new people. One might have called her passive, perhaps because of her shyness. And yet when she entered a room, people surrounded her. I have had the experience of waiting long (and patiently) while former students encircled her to talk and talk and talk.

Because of the contrast between Lydia's physical incandescence and her public image, there was a certain mystery about her. Those who knew her only from the lectern often wondered about her private life.

Her private world was indeed private. She shared her personal thoughts, her dreams, her aspirations, and her disappointments with very few. I think my wife Joan and I were among the handful of people who were part of Lydia's personal life. This poses a particular problem in writing a biographical sketch, for I feel certain she would not have liked an intimate biography. I want to respect her wishes. My purpose is to establish the chronology of her life, record some thoughts about her without breaching confidences, and share the experiences of some friends and students with her.

Lydia Rapoport was born in 1923 in Vienna to an intellectual Jewish family. Without being religious, she identified herself as a Jew and toward the end of her life became emotionally attached to the state of Israel, an aspect of her life I shall comment on later. Lydia's mother had studied to become a teacher before her marriage but never entered the profession and devoted herself to family duties. Her father was a man of unusual gifts and Lydia was closer to him than to her mother. As he entered his eightieth year, long after Lydia's mother had died and he had remarried, he became blind and ill. Although he lived in New York and Lydia was in California, she was a devoted daughter who helped her stepmother keep careful check on his medical problems and arrange for his nursing care. It cannot have entered her mind that he would outlive her.

Mr. Rapoport studied law in Vienna but was more interested in music. He played the violin well and was the music critic on a Viennese newspaper. His major talents, however, lay in linguistics. He could read and write seventeen languages, including all the Slavic, and this proficiency stood him in good stead later in the United States, where he became a translator.

In 1906, Mr. Rapoport left Vienna for Philadelphia with the idea of settling in America, but he was disenchanted with both the city and the country and returned to Vienna. Fourteen or fifteen years later, however, he sensed a growing nationalism and a resurgence of antisemitism in the European countries where he was traveling. He was convinced that within the next decade war was inevitable. He was, of course, proven right. Putting aside his previous disappointment with the cultural shortcomings of

America, he decided to leave Europe. He returned to the United States alone in 1928.

In 1932, Mrs. Rapoport, with her son Emanuel, aged eighteen, and Lydia, then nine, joined him in New York. The decision for the four-year delay was made to allow Emmanuel to complete his gymnasium course in Vienna. Lydia attended New York public schools, and Emmanuel entered and later graduated from Massachusetts Institute of Technology. I do not know exactly why Lydia chose Hunter for her college education, but I imagine that finances played an important part. She was a brilliant student there and was elected to Phi Beta Kappa.

After graduating from college at the age of nineteen, Lydia enrolled at Smith College School for Social Work and earned her Master's degree in 1944. She was twenty-one, I believe the youngest graduate of the school up to that time.

She extended her training in psychotherapy and psychoanalysis in Chicago, where she continued as a social worker. In 1952 she was awarded a Fulbright Fellowship to the London School of Economics. The late Richard Titmuss was then the head of the Social Work Training Program there and was responsible for assigning tutors and supervisors under the program. Although Mr. Titmuss was not her supervisor, they established a close personal relationship which lasted until her death. In fact, shortly before she entered the hospital because of the illness that was to end her life in three months, she lunched with Mr. Titmuss in London to discuss a research project on family planning with significant social policy implications.

The one-year fellowship in England developed into two when her Fulbright award was extended until 1954. This second year in London allowed her to continue work on British mental health and to become associated with the Tavistock Clinic. By that time Lydia had gained recognition for her effectiveness in strenghtening British social work training, and she was invited to lecture extensively at professional conferences, schools of social work, and the London School of Economics. Just before she left Great Britain, in August of 1954 she presented a lecture in Leicester before the United Nations Exchange Plan Seminar for Advanced Study of Social Casework.

Her next momentous educational experience was in the Harvard School of Public Health in 1960. At Harvard's Laboratory of Community Psychiatry she studied with social workers, psychiatrists, and other mental health specialists. Most importantly, she was connected with the research of the late Dr. Erich Lindemann, and the two became lifelong friends. Out of that participation was to come Lydia's major contribution, perhaps the most creative in social casework during the last decade: crisis intervention and short-term therapy.

Lydia's first full-time faculty appointment was in 1954 at the University of California School of Social Welfare at Berkeley, a position she held until her death. The fifteen-year association with Berkeley culminated in her promotion to full professor with tenure. In the 1970s it is common for women in this country to rise in academic rank quickly and to acquire tenure, but Lydia's promotion was unique in the previous decade, especially at Berkeley. Her rank of full professor of social welfare was a singular honor.

From 1960 to 1970, Lydia taught social casework in the Master's program at Berkeley and established an advanced training program in community mental health at the School of Social Welfare. The program attracted trained social workers from all parts of the world and served as a model for other training programs in community mental health. She lectured widely, at Tulane University and the University of Washington among others, and she was almost a regular faculty member at summer institutes for social workers at the University of Chicago School of Social Service Administration and at the Smith College School for Social Work. Since her seminars on crisis intervention were often oversubscribed, she would have to offer more than one section of the same seminar. Occasionally, also, she taught in the Master's program during the summer term at Smith.

I do not know the circumstances that led Lydia to choose to go to Israel, but in 1963 she accepted an appointment as educational consultant at Hebrew University Paul Baerwald School of Social Work in Jerusalem, where she remained for a year. She returned to Israel often; she loved the country, and the people she met there became part of her international circle of friends. She found the Israel social work community so sympathetic that she began to consider spending a few months of each year in Israel. The crosscultural project on the role of social workers in introducing family planning in health and welfare service programs on which she planned to collaborate with Israelis might have been the impetus for a yearly visit.

Lydia's work in international social welfare did not go unnoticed. She was selected to be the first United Nations Interregional Family Welfare and Family Planning Adviser, and in January of 1971 she took leave from her Berkeley post to go to New York. She was hesitant about leaving California, even on a temporary assignment, and returning to New York City. She cherished her small house at 19 Northampton Street in Berkeley for its warmth and charm. It had been recently enlarged and redesigned so remarkably by a Japanese architect that pictures of it appeared in a design magazine. She would be leaving not only house and friends, but two prized possessions: her piano and her harpsichord. Against these losses she weighed the challenge of the United Nations position with its required travel, especially to Israel, and she accepted. When she locked her house in Berkeley that January she had every hope of returning in a year.

It was not to be. Early in 1971 she became ill. The diagnosis of the New York doctors—its accuracy later questioned—was ileitis and the treatment was cortisone. Her illness did not prevent her from working at the United Nations or from traveling abroad. In the spring of 1971 she felt well enough to visit Israel and Switzerland. In June she was in England, in July back in New York. But in mid-July she became acutely ill. She made an attempt to be admitted to a New York hospital, but her physician was not available and she was refused admission. Her condition deteriorated, and finally she was taken by ambulance to the Lenox Hill Hospital, where she underwent emergency intestinal surgery. The surgery was performed on Lydia when she had been in shock for hours, and while the operation was declared successful, the patient did not respond to postoperative procedures. She lay in the intensive care unit at Lenox Hill Hospital for seven weeks, and on September 6, 1971, she died of acute bacterial endocarditis. She could not speak during those seven weeks of agony because of the extensive machinery which had been attached to her. Someone thought she was trying to pronounce the word "mother" just before she died.

It was as if a bell tolled for Lydia when I read Leonard Woolf's conclusion to the fourth volume of his autobiography:

> If one does not oneself die young, the moment comes in one's life when death begins permanently to loom in the background of life. Parents, brothers, and sisters, who were parts of one's unconscious mind and memories, die; the intimate friends of one's youth die; our

> loves die. Each death as it comes, so inevitable of course, but always so unexpected and so outrageous, is like a blow on the head or the heart. Into each grave goes some tiny portion of oneself.

The heritage Lydia Rapoport left behind is her continuing inspiration to friends and students. To many she represented an ego ideal, and as a social work teacher she had few peers. One of her students wrote me:

> Lydia left tracks in the books she was reading, sometimes with her light touch on the margins; but more likely scraps of three by five inch paper, marking something she would return to. In my own reading in the library stacks, I came across a faded three by five sheet on which some one had bothered to print in a hand resembling hers, a passage from Eugene Debs at his trial in 1918: "Your honor, years ago I recognized my kinship with all living beings, and I made up my mind that I was not one whit better than the meanest on earth. I said then, and I say now, that while there is a lower class I am of it, and while there is a soul in prison I am not free."

The student continued:

> I do not know if Lydia did read Ray Ginger's biography of Debs. But it does catch what survives most strongly about Lydia: her belief in the worth of her students, in being able to provoke their intellectual and emotional growth through learning, and in the imperative of continuing education open to all as a matter of personal and societal survival.

In a field without abundant bases of theory, Lydia Rapoport during her relatively short lifespan was regarded as one of the eminent intellects. She was to usher in a new generation of scholars in casework. It is not surprising to learn that at her death both Columbia and the University of Chicago, each unaware of the other's approach, were discussing her joining their faculties and carrying on the tradition of Florence Hollis and Charlotte Towle. But in this context tradition did not mean clinging to the past. What distinguished Lydia Rapoport was her belief that while institutions and theories must not remain static, they should not and need not be recklessly abandoned if at the moment they did not seem responsive to immediate needs. In her paper on reaffirming social casework she wrote:

> We know that an organism or a social institution has a high survival potential when it intrinsically possesses a capacity for flexible and renewed adaptation to changing circumstances. Social casework has such a capacity because basically it is an open and open-ended system of thought that can bend and stretch in a variety of directions and

still maintain its core of identity and its core social purpose. Its having done just that ever since its inception has contributed to its endurance and has endowed it with an open, dynamic, and exciting quality.

Death took Lydia when she was forty-seven, at the prime of her professional life. I thought of that life while I was reading the last line of Lillian Hellman's candid autobiography, *An Unfinished Woman*: "I left too much of me unfinished because I wasted too much time." Lydia Rapoport did not waste time. Her life was not long, but it was full and rich. What does remain unfinished is the success of her efforts to ensure that social work, and particularly social casework, is not destroyed in the current attack upon its institutions, but that it survives, grows, becomes wiser and more effective.

To Lydia Rapoport social casework represented a distinct view of man. For the conclusion of my reminiscence nothing will serve better than her own words:

> The values embedded in social casework are fundamental and enduring and grew out of our Judeo-Christian heritage. Man is the essential unit of concern, the person, who is valuable and to be valued by society. He needs for survival many things, among them a sense of worth and dignity, a sense of self and an identity, and an opportunity to make choices regarding the direction of his life in order to achieve a sense of self-realization. Social casework is the instrumentality in social work through which such value commitments can be exercised and through which personal growth and fulfillment can be realized.

I

The Creative Mind at Work

1 *Creativity in Social Work*

Introduction

Social work traditionally has been defined as both science and art. This dual nature is an attribute of all helping professions. Such dualities, however, create problems for us. For one thing, they lead to an additive approach to defining practice and thereby do violence to the sense of wholeness and process. For another, in the evolution of a profession or discipline, at certain points in time there tends to be an imbalance as to which attribute is more heavily stressed or valued. Thus, Swithun Bowers points out that, before 1930, most definitions of social casework classified it as an art.[1] The last twenty-five years have seen a strong emphasis on making social work increasingly scientific: in its knowledge base, in its methods of study of psychological and social problems, and in its technology of problem solving. The high values attached to scientific methods of inquiry and procedure are not surprising since the yield in certain aspects of understanding and control of our universe has been spectacular. Such values are also in harmony with our generally prevailing materialistic and pragmatic cultural values.

In social work, the high valuation of the scientific is related largely to our urgent sense of commitment to better fulfill our social purpose in the amelioration and prevention of social ills. It is also related to our professional strivings for status and recognition within the value framework of our society.

In contrast, the creative and artistic domain of life in our society, despite recent artificial and sterile attempts at recognition and elevation, remains outside the pale and is regarded at large with some degree of suspicion, if not outright contempt. In the literature of the social work profession as well, the conception of

Source: Reprinted, with minor changes, from *Smith College Studies in Social Work*, XXXVIII (June 1968), 139–61. Used by permission.

artistry is only given a nod.[2] It has not been made the subject of serious inquiry, nor has it been endowed with values, dignity, and institutional supports which a genuine commitment would demand.

It is the purpose, then, of this essay to attempt to redress the balance: to discuss the common links between art and social work as to both their institutional and instrumental nature; and to elucidate some notions of the creative components that are embedded in professional practice.

Clarification of Basic Terms

We begin by anchoring ourselves in Ralph Tyler's classic definition of a profession: "For an occupation to be a profession, it should involve complex tasks which are performed by artistic application of major principles and concepts rather than by routine operations or skills.The application of these principles necessitates an analysis of the particular problem to see what are its unique aspects which will require adaptation of the principle. This adaptation is an artistic task; that is, it involves individual judgment and imagination as well as skill."[3] The merit of this formulation is that it points to where the scientific and the artistic may be located in a practice profession: science refers to how basic knowledge is arrived at; art refers to how it is adapted and applied.

As I understand it, scientific method, in essence, involves systematic observation, classification, and controlled generalization. Some levels of scientific endeavor also call for experimentation for testing and verification of hypotheses. The purpose of the scientific method is to generate laws or principles which have the power of prediction in regard to the behavior of phenomena and hence may lead to the possibility of manipulation and control. It is not my purpose here to defend against those who seriously question whether the profession of social work can legitimately claim to be scientific; nor is it my purpose to elucidate where in the profession's operations the claims of scientific requirements may be met. Suffice it to say that social work is committed to an increasing use of the scientific method. And if, as it is said, the essence of science is an attitude—an attitude of disciplined curiosity—then in that sense at least, social work can be said to be rooted in the scientific approach.[4]

To delineate the essential characteristics of art is a much more complex matter. Philosophers, aestheticians, artists, and critics have explored its dimensions at length. For our purposes we might say that art involves the communication of meaning. Its special attribute is that it communicates meaning directly, enlarging awareness by penetrating directly to mood as well as mind. Since it is a perceptual rather than conceptual medium, art provides for a quality of experience. It achieves this through a process involving transformation of perception by a novel ordering of ideas and feelings or, as in the case of plastic or graphic arts, by transformation of materials which reflect the ideas and feelings. The artistic process involves consciously controlled and purposeful activity which is guided by various aesthetic laws and principles. The end result of this process is the artistic product. In social work, we can speak meaningfully only of process and not of product, although we can state that the process should lead to some satisfying result.

A distinction has been made between fine arts and scientific arts. The fine arts are generally thought to serve a private purpose and may be used as an outlet for personal emotions. The scientific arts may be expressive of some large social purpose and are generally directed at problem solving.

Distinctions have also been made between artistry and craftmanship. Artistry requires creative thought, whereas craftsmanship essentially requires ingenuity in execution. A craftsman is said to be proficient in the mechanics of his art. Herbert Read tells us that in Greek and Roman culture, no distinction existed between art and craftsmanship. The ancient usage of the term "art" is equivalent to our modern terms "skill" and "techniques."[5] The arts were conceived essentially as a "method of imposing human will on matter," or, put more mundanely, a preconceived result was sought through consciously controlled and directed action.[6]

In social work literature, we rarely speak of artistry or craftsmanship, but tend to use the word "skills." Thus, we hear repeatedly that we teach students knowledge and skills, that we have to sharpen our skills, and so forth. We tend to use the word "skills" as a collective noun to mean techniques. It might be preferable to use the term "skillful" as an adjective and as a quantitative concept referring to the degree of competence in the execution of an activity.

It would seem that in social work we could appropriately use the terms creative, artistic, and craftsmanlike (or skillful). By "creative," I mean thought and action which is innovative, which leads to the forging of something new. This may apply to the development of a theory, or to the development of new therapeutic approaches or techniques, or to the novel organization and delivery of services. By "artistic," I mean the ingenious, imaginative, and proficient application of what is already known. "Craftsmanship" involves skillful execution of activities, consciously controlled and directed, in order to achieve a preconceived result. There are many social work activities and procedures that are essentially preconceived, or even routinized, that nevertheless require skill in execution. Creativeness, artistry, and craftsmanship, it should be emphasized, all have a place in each of the social work methods: in casework, group work, community organization, as well as in research, supervision, administration, collaboration, and consultation.

We shall next examine the social purposes, functions, and institutionalized aspects of art and the social work profession.

Social Purpose and Function

The existence of social work as a profession rests on its social purpose and the sanction it receives from society. Art, often thought of as the most private and individualistic vehicle for expression, also has a social purpose. Marion Milner, a psychoanalyst and artist, reminds us that "the artist wishes to cast his private experiences in such a form that they will be incorporated in the social world of art."[7]

One of the functions of social work is social control. This function has only recently been better understood as our knowledge of disordered behavior and social disorganization has increased and as we have come to accept the responsibility inherent in authority. Thus, social work is evaluative and judgmental in its operations and seeks to exert influences that are normative and regulative.[8] The concept of the nonjudgmental attitude which, when operationalized, leads to certain technical considerations is not to be confused with the need to make judgments as an aspect of social control.

Art also has regulatory functions. Perhaps this was clearer in homogeneous or primitive societies with little or no separation of the creative artist from the rest of society. Ernest Kris reminds us that in primitive society everyone dances, or carves, although there may be a master of such arts. There, "art serves purposes of social control, through ritual, religion, or politics."[9]

Contemporary art is also regulatory, although not through social or institutionalized means such as morality or religion. Contemporary art regulates behavior only indirectly by organizing sensory knowledge and experiences into some communicable form and by advocacy. The artist is at once judgmental and nonjudgmental. He does not refuse to judge yet achieves neutrality by taking the position of man as the frame of reference for judging all events.

Both social work and art can be conceived of as instruments of social change. Social work has developed mainly out of the necessity with human problems that result from social disorganization and from cultural and social lags. It has assumed the responsibility of "caretaking" in regard to our failures in social living. This has been referred to as the residual function of social work.[10] At the same time, social work is expected to be instrumental in modifying some of our basic social institutions and to become a potent force in social change. The social change function in social work has always been central but was most visible when social work was mainly concerned with social reform. This concern with "cause" has been revitalized to the point where some view the main role of social workers to be as agents of social change.

Art also may be conceived of as an instrument of social change. Robert MacIver reminds us that "art is immersed in the world, seeking to change something in it, to add something to it, even to remake it."[11] Art is not concerned directly with changing social institutions but with delineating aesthetic and human values. Its stance has been iconoclastic and challenging as it has influenced man's conception of his relationship to nature, to self, and to society. Such changing conceptions also lead to changes in the institutional process.

The social worker, like the artist, acts as spokesman or advocate. Alex Comfort, himself the embodiment of the extraordinary human capacity to achieve outstandingly in both scientific and artistic endeavors, states that "all creative work speaks on behalf of somebody who would otherwise be voiceless."[12] Moreover, the unit of concern for the artist is the individual human being viewed as both product and victim of the environment. He sees a parallel in this stance between artist and physician (and we might add social worker), concerned both with organic process and with intervention. In his view "the artist is under an obligation to concern himself with the entire environment of the times, both by interpreting it and by modifying it."[13] He is talking of the Romantic tradition in art with its emphasis on the universal and humanistic. He is not talking of the Marxist concept which distorts the artist's environmental concern by requiring him to fulfill an ideological or propagandistic function.

In social work, too, the role of spokesman or advocate is being increasingly articulated. Most recently, as part of the war on poverty, the lawyer is also being asked to take on the role of spokesman for the poor. This kind of role has been institutionalized in the Scandinavian countries and in New Zealand in the person of the ombudsman, who is outside the institutional framework of government, law, or social work, but who interprets and intercedes in behalf of the rights of the individual.

Institutionalized Aspects

One common conception of the artist is that he is an isolated man. The very nature and act of creation is a lonely and isolating process. There is also the fact of the artist's social isolation or, more precisely, his societal alienation. Alex Comfort tells us that "art is the act of standing aside from society."[14] The position of spokesman or social critic on the most fundamental level requires a position of alienation or even opposition.

Social work, its social roots and social commitments notwithstanding, also stands partly in opposition to society and assumes a position of alienation. This is true despite the fact that it has been given sanction and support to express society's concern for the welfare of its members. In this respect, social work is said to embody the conscience of society and thereby to reflect society's most highly developed ideals and striving in regard to ethics and values.[15] Nevertheless, social work is also the recipient or target of society's ambivalence. Daily newspaper accounts corroborate this, despite the respectability the recent war on poverty has conferred on human needs. This ambivalence stems from at least two sources. As embodiment of society's conscience, social work serves often as an unwelcome reminder of society's failure as well as of its restitutive impulses. Ambivalence is also generated by the fact that social work avowedly is one of the articulate forces that strives toward planned social change. Forces pulling for change generate resistance and opposition from forces attempting to preserve existing social patterns and conditions. The position of social work vis à vis society has been described as being akin to that of a minority group.[16] The marginality of the profession is due not only to its late arrival on the scene, in contrast to other helping professions, but also to its unique sanction and purpose and society's mixed attitudes to its purposes and functions. From this point of view, it may be said that social work, like art, occupies in some respects a position of alienation from the mainstream of society's values and purposes.

Social work and art also have some similar ways of dealing with society's ambivalence toward them and of coping with the factors of alienation and isolation. The artist, who cherishes his uniqueness, can view his isolation and rejection by society as an affirmation of his role which contains its own reward. Nevertheless, knowing and accepting that one is at "outs" with society and that the price of creation is isolation is not sufficient reward for the artist. His need for fellowship has been expressed through the increasing professionalization of the arts as well as by participation in a special community based on commonly held ideal sentiments and values, which Lionel Trilling calls "Bohemia."[17] Ernst Kris describes Bohemia somewhat differently, namely as "a phenomenon of urbanized civilization where [artists] and art lovers tend to form elite circles distinct in social status, mores, and even language."[18]

Social work, too, has long been preoccupied with establishing its unique role and function. This is part of a complex process in which the profession seeks to establish its identity. It develops symbols, special language, and brotherhoods of professional organization. It has its initiation process and through the means of professional education, for example, inducts its members into the professional subculture. All these devices contribute to the profession's sense of worth and purpose and tend to serve as one bulwark against isolation and societal alienation. They also are a means of exacting recognition from society that social work functions and contributions are understood and valued. Parallel with the need to emphasize uniqueness and thereby exact recognition is a need to establish a collective and common identity. Growing professionalization brings with it an urge to discover and embrace common identity, common core knowledge, and even common social purposes with the social sciences and with other helping professions.

Attributes of the Creative Personality

There has been increasing interest in the nature of creativity and curiosity about the creative personality. A growing literature approaches the problem from different vantage points—biographical, analytical, empirical, and experimental, through studies of creative individuals in both scientific and artistic fields. These diverse works are beginning to yield themes on which there seems to be some consensus. The ideas presented in the following discussion reflect this concensus.

The attributes of personality to be described are qualities of mind and attitude that serve as a framework for the creative act. It should be pointed out that these attributes may be necessary but not sufficient to explain the presence or absence of creativity. Furthermore, the personality studies of creative people that dwell on psychodynamics only as a way of understanding causal relations are also insufficient as a way of explaining creativity. They tend to reduce the most complex phenomena to some singular or simple formula that is devitalized of meaning and becomes indistinguishable from mere description of pathology.[19]

The creative person is often described as being a nonconformist. Conformity destroys creative thinking since it involves yielding one's private opinion and judgment to prevailing opinion or other pressures. Nonconformity has also been contrasted with "counterformity," a term used by Richard Crutchfield to characterize the person who is not truly independent but is motivated by a need to defend his personal identity, his emancipation from a group, and by hostile or aggressive needs. It is the counterformist who is often rewarded by society in his role of social dissident and is, in the end, re-enveloped by the group.[20]

Another attribute of the creative person is that of high motivation and persistence in a task. Such a person is often driven out of curiosity or devotion to a problem which may, in a sense take possession of him. Yet, there is a curious paradox here. Although there is need for a deep commitment, there is, at the same time, requirement for a certain detachment. The commitment is related to the need to understand and master; the detachment has to do with need to remove oneself from the more obvious solutions and to be receptive to other, more novel, possibilities.

Several intellectual attributes seem important. Degree of intelligence in and of itself seems negligible, beyond a certain level. In fact, concepts of intelligence and talent are rather elusive ones and, as such, will not be discussed. More germane is the intellectual quality of openness and general receptivity to new information and ideas as well as a liking for complexity. A psychological need for simplistic reduction and an intolerance for uncertainty work against the creative process. That is not to say that the creative solution may not be the one that is most simple. But simplicity here refers to the solution or product while complexity refers to the nature of the problem to be solved. The creative person has a high tolerance for ambiguities. He does not seek premature closure but can maintain an openness toward the seemingly contradictory or obscure. A tolerance for conflict is also required, with recognition that conflict has generative powers whicy may lead to new solutions.

Intellectual openness and receptivity suggest a state of intellectual freedom that emables the person to detach himself from old conceptual systems or keeps him from making too deep a commitment to certain theoretical positions or explanatory systems of thought. Freedom also refers to a state in which the creative person can allow himself to be dominated by the object or problem with which he is grappling. Perhaps immersion in the problem is another way of stating it. Immersion also implies a state of intellectual preparedness that involves thorough familiarity with and knowledge about all aspects of the problem. Peter McKellar uses the concept of "over-learning"—that is, learning beyond the point necessary to achieve perfect performance or recall.[21] However, this has a built-in hazard insofar as too much knowledge, or the state of being too bound to the known, may work against creative thinking. Thus, Theodore Reik talks of the "courage not to understand,"[22] a refusal to let one's curiosity be satisfied by ready explanation.[23]

Jerome Bruner tells us that the creative act leads to a state of effective surprise. A creative thought or solution has about it a quality of obviousness that produces a shock of recognition. He says that "surprise is the privilege only of prepared minds—minds with structured expectations and interests."[24] This notion of surprise is dealt with in a little-known book by Theodore Reik called *Surprise and the Psychoanalyst,*[25] wherein we learn that effective psychoanalytic interpretation brings with it a surprise response, presumably because of the patient's psychological preparedness and the shock of recognizing the deep truth of the observation.

Another necessary condition for the creative impulse and act is the presence of a special relationship between the conscious and preconscious aspects of mind—one in which the two may be said to be more closely in touch with each other. Many aspects of creation actually are thought to take place within that facet of mind that we call the preconscious. Lawrence Kubie maintains that all learning and thinking are preconscious rather than conscious processes. The input of fragmentary perceptual data from the world around us is overwhelmingly preconscious; the conscious intake is only a fragment of the simultaneous preconscious intake. The conscious mind obviously has important functions to perform in mentation: it relates samples from the preconscious stream of reality; it engages in steps of sampling, checking, correcting, and communicating about them.[26]

Closely related to the free interplay between conscious and preconscious processes is the capacity for limited and controlled regression. As Frank Barron expresses it: "The ability to permit oneself to become disorganized is quite crucial to the development of a high level of integration. One must permit a certain amount of discord and disorder into the perceptual system in order to achieve integration at a more complex level."[27] The capacity for this kind of transitory regression seems to be related to confidence in one's equally strong capacity to return to a high degree of rationality. Thus, the ego can allow regression because it knows it can correct itself.[28] Limited and controlled regression in the creative process is similar to the phenomenon described by Kris in his concept of "regression in the service of the ego" with which we are familar in the clinical context.[29]

These two factors, the role of the preconscious process and limited and partial regression are phenomena sometimes noted in the whole question of the role of neurosis in art. Many references to art and neurosis fail to distinguish their essential differences. In both art and neurosis, the unconscious as well as the preconscious may serve as a source for the content from which the artistic product is fashioned. Neurotic or psychotic art, however, is strictly a private expression reflecting isolation and suffering. In contrast, art becomes valid communication only by conscious elaboration involving criticism, judgment, selection, discrimination, control via form, all of which cast it into a social reality.

Creative and Artistic Elements in Social Work Practice

Social work, like art, is engaged in problem solving, be it the problem of expression, communication, transformation, or change. Both deal with human materials or human themes and both require an intimate "knowing and contact." Both call for creative and imaginative use of self. Both require a special kind of distance and objectivity. Thus, in social work, we are accustomed to thinking about the need for objective appraisal as well as the compassionate response.[30] We shall now discuss the common elements—creative impulse, imagination, intuition, and style.

The drive for creation and artistic expression[31] is considered to be a biologically based human impulse, an innate drive through which consciousness can be acquired and refined.[32] I would hazard the view that the creative impulse is linked not only to innate drives but also to ego functions, particularly to the ego drive toward mastery. In the human being there is a ubiquitous need to bring order out of chaos. This is linked both with the necessity for survival that calls for understanding and predictability, and with the need for creation of pleasure which is achieved essentially by the creation of harmonies. In adult years the basic or more primitive urge can be expressed derivatively in myriad ways: in highly organized fashion via the fine arts, or via the so-called "scientific arts" which are directed at problem solving.

The creative impulse has a bearing on motivation for social work. It is sometimes derisively stated that people enter the profession to solve their own problems. In a sense all human activity is expressive of this need. The relevant question for the profession is to what extent the need to solve one's own problem is expressed directly or derivatively, and with what degree of autonomy or sublimination. The expressed motivation that brings people into social work is "the wish to help people," a statement found on every application to schools of social work. I believe this is the surface and socially acceptable expression of a deeper need and impulse, namely, the creative urge to bring order out of chaos and the striving for harmony and control. The person who seeks out social work as a career wishes above all to work with human material and views the profession as giving sanction and opportunity for this kind of creative thought and action.[33]

Imagination plays an important role in the creative process. Imagination is thought content that is divorced from its perceptual origins. It consists of mental images or ideas which have not been experienced in or derived from reality. According to Beres, imagination belongs to secondary process thinking and is an active, creative force.[34]

Imagination plays an important role in professional practice. We know it best as it operates in the clinical context, where we engage the imagination heavily to bring out the emphatic response without which no movement or growth can take place. Charlotte Towle describes this process as "imaginative projection of one's own consciousness onto another being."[35] It calls for a capacity to put oneself in the place of the other's affective realm without losing one's sense of identity and purpose.[36] In art, empathic response is communicated directly by penetrating mood with symbolic or nonverbal communication. Although social workers rely heavily on verbal communication, effective empathic response is also largely nonverbal and paralingual, transmitted via facial expression, bodily gesture, and expressive tone.

Imagination is also vital in other areas of professional problem solving, insofar as it is a first step in generating a new idea or a fresh insight.[37] It involves visualizing a desired goal as it might be achieved through alternative possibilities, new combinations, or altogether novel pathways. It involves departure from traditional theoretical systems and from previously prescribed practice patterns.

Intuition figures prominently in the creative process and in professional practice since it also leads to new insights. Intuition is knowledge, perceptual rather than conceptual in nature, based on stimuli previously received by the preconscious perceptual system, which are momentarily not available to conscious recall or to conceptualization. Intuition enables us to make judgments without knowing consciously how we arrived at them.[38] Frieda Fromm-Reichman maintains that the intuitive process is essentially the same as all other thinking processes. The difference is in the rapidity of connection and the availability of channels of communication. She describes intuition as "erupting into the conscious mind rather than entering it."[39]

Intuitive knowledge is not mystical or undisciplined. However, like all knowledge, it requires testing and validation. Rather than being suspect, intuition should be highly valued, for it is a capacity for a type of thought which is sorely needed for rapid, economical, or even accurate transactions. Intuition is a great asset in problem solving: it facilitates the rapid penetration of a problem and the grasping of its essential structure and dimensions.

Intuitive thinking is constantly involved in the on-going thought process which we call diagnosis. This is central to all social work methods and underpins all our interventions. Diagnosis is a complex process, similar to the creative process in general.[40] It has been noted that creation is not without its counterpart in destruction.[41] Thus, diagnosis also involves both breaking down and building up. First, there is conscious and preconscious perception of innumerable cues. Then, in order to make rapid connections between seemingly disparate bits of data, there needs to be a "destruction" or dissolution of the total context of information into its abstraction.[42] Finally, to achieve a new synthesis, there needs to be a filtering of data most germane to the problem and a drawing of inferences which can lead to relevant insights.

The end product, then, of both imagination and intuition is insight.[43] Insights, derived from such sources, are frequently devalued as capricious or scientifically unreliable; nevertheless, they often further scientific inquiry.[44]

Creative impulse, imaginative response, and intuitive wisdom must be elaborated and transformed into some kind of communication capable of being externalized and universalized. Here, the more conscious and cognitive processes take over.[45] Here, too, the social work practitioner develops his style, a characteristic manner of expression and execution. While the practitioner may not be guided by aesthetic laws, it is possible to apply some principles of aesthetics to a given piece of social work practice. All of us, I am sure, have responded with a sense of deep pleasure upon hearing about or reading a particular case which we readily label as beautiful. What properties characterize the beautiful case, or any given piece of work in any realm of social work activity?

The satisfaction we derive is based on more than the happy or fortuitous outcome. Many cases may improve without our getting a deep sense of satisfaction. In fact, often an improved situation is apt to take us somewhat by surprise. This is because the outcome had no *specific* relationship to our intentions and activities. Certainly we were helpful, instrumental, or enabling in a general, professional sense. But such work is characterized by much random activity and reveals only the loosest connection between intention and consequence, action and result, or cause and effect. Perhaps, then, the primary property of beautiful work is in its visible and articulated sense of purpose.

This can only be achieved by the choosing of limits which all artistic activity requires. There is a design based on the penetration of the structure of the problem, the choice of limits, and the formulation of a series of ordered goals. Just as a frame in a painting marks off a different kind of reality within from that which is without, so a frame in the helping process serves a similar purpose. It, too, defines its particular kind of reality by marking off the special nature of the relationship, the specific tasks to be mastered, and the ground rules that govern the mutual obligations and expectations of this procedure. The process unfolds within a definite structure which provides, among other things, a beginning, middle, and end.[46]

Within its own frame of reference, the functional school of casework has incorporated some of these notions into its methodology. Without debating the merits or limitations of the Rankian theory of personality on which its method is based, it is still possible to study some of its operating principles and to adopt, within the diagnostic framework, those which seem to have particular utility. The functional school has developed a good deal of sophistication about such concepts as choice, limits, structure, creative use of time, as well as a psychology and methodology of ending. In contrast, on this latter point particularly, the diagnostic school has no literature on termination and seems to ignore in its conceptualizations the dynamic forces that are lodged in that phase of the process. There is much to be debated here, but it may well be that such concepts give the social worker a greater sense of certainty and, at best, an opportunity for more artful application of principles.

We can also speak of elegance in scientific and professional work as well as in art. Elegance includes the principle of economy which can refer to a concept, theory,[47] art product, or professional intervention. Economy in a concept or theory refers to the explanatory power of a particular formulation. Economy in a work of art refers to its expressive meaning and evocative power. Economy in professional intervention refers to growth and change that has been induced with the most limited or economical means. This can only be achieved when clearly specified goals are reached by the application of relevant techniques, within the most propitious time dimensions.

Some Deterrents to Creativity in Social Work

Our last theme for consideration deals with some of the circumstances that interfere with creative practice in social work. Two factors will be examined: the context in which social work is practiced, and the state of knowledge and theory.

Social work is practiced within a specific organizational context—the social agency. The agency can be viewed as enabler to both worker and client: it provides the practitioner with opportunity to carry out certain explicit functions; it enables the client to receive the service he needs. At the same time, the agency also impedes the fulfillment of the helping role by interposing itself between practitioner and client through the structure and specific functions it has developed. We have become increasingly alert to the problems created in bureaucratic organization which are compounded in direct proportion to factors of size and uncreative administrative leadership. Such bureaucratic organization can seriously interfere with both creative innovation and artful practice. It tends to diminish the span of control and the range of decision-making power in the individual practitioner. It also tends to reward conformity and to discourage initiative and innovation. At its worst, bureaucratization and rigidity of structure can interfere with the artful application of principles. Procedures are reduced to rule of thumb operations, and routines replace professional judgment and choice.

The organization and structure of the agency may also interfere with the artful application of method. For example, agency purpose and goal give rise to a specific patterning of both function and method. Thus, an agency with a separate intake department or distinct intake procedure already determines the method by which the initial phase of diagnosis and treatment is to take place. The procedures instituted may not be an intrinsic or necessary aspect of method as such. Indeed, we often confuse certain procedural steps which stem from the specifics of agency structure and function with fundamental aspects of method. Thus, there is nothing intrinsic to the process of diagnosis that calls for the traditional interdisciplinary intake structure in a child guidance clinic. This structure, which at one time could be rationally defended, has been regarded by many as being inimical to the client's receiving more prompt and efficient service. We are stuck in the procrustean bed when we regard structural procedures as the essentials of the helping method. Such an approach prevents us from considering imaginatively how our helping method might be applied in a fresh or novel context.

The problem of bureaucracy as it interferes with creativity has been given a good deal of attention in both industry and scientific organization. There have been many creative innovations to break through the inherent limitations of conventional, hierarchical structure, to open up new channels of communication, and to release as well as reward creativity.[48] It seems to me that in social work we need to think more deeply about this problem in order to maximize the real contribution that a professionally qualified practitioner can make. Some of the experimental innovations regarding supervision and consultation are efforts to circumvent inherent limitations of bureaucratic structure, to mitigate abuses of hierarchical patterns of authority, and to challenge individual responsibility and initiative.[49]

In this connection, one other facet of this problem should be mentioned: the phenomenon of private practice. The arguments pro and con, usually couched in terms of ethical or professional imperatives, need not concern us here. If we are worried about our own problem of the "brain drain," of the most seasoned and able practitioners leaving the public segment of social work practice, we need to pose our inquiries beyond considerations of status and remuneration. It seems to me that a compelling motive that leads people, dedicated and committed to the social work profession, into private practice is the greater opportunity to practice their art. It reflects a deep wish to have a more personal and direct encounter with a client without the complications and often frustrating problems created by intervening structure. In a recent study sympathetic to the development of private practice, Levenstein offers a similar view: "Private practice is seen as the product of socially structured strains in the institution of social work . . . ; it is an innovating response to a situation of converging social pressures."[50] Quite apart from the question of private practice, there is an urgent need to re-examine the structural and bureaucratic context of professional practice, from the point of view of the strains it imposes both on the recipients in need of help and on the practitioner who requires greater freedom and responsibility to develop his professional creativity.[51]

The state of social work knowledge and theory and the way it is taught are also of great significance in enhancing or deterring creativity in social work practice. The long, hard journey from vocation to professionalization, from apprenticeship to professional education, has been achieved largely through efforts of conceptualization and theory building. On this rest any claims to being scientific or professional. Every advance, however, has its price. It is possible that in our anxious strivings we overvalue the conceptual and are too theory bound. Concepts, let us remind ourselves, are abstractions or short cuts that describe reality. But today's workable reality is tomorrow's barrier to exploring different aspects of the same thing.[52] Concepts are useful tools in understanding[53] but they have an intrinsic disadvantage—to some extent they blind us.[54] We also undervalue intuitive thinking. Academic education, while forced to acknowledge its existence, does not pay explicit attention to the development of intuitive thinking, the training of hunches, the courageous leap to tentative conclusions, all those nonrigorous methods of achieving solutions which Jerome Bruner calls heuristic procedures.[55]

A related problem to the danger of overconceptualization is the trend toward overintegration or, more accurately, premature integration of knowledge. We have moved from a state in social work education wherein we latched on to bits and pieces of knowledge in diverse fields and taught them in fragmentary fashion. We cannot afford chaos, nor is this sound education. While intuitive thinking, as well as other forms of thought, needs a base in understanding the connectedness and structural relationships of knowledge, there is a danger in our field of overintegration—of linking knowledge and concepts particularly from different theoretical frames of reference or from different levels of abstraction. We tend to force a premature integration which puts a kind of closure to theory. This prevents the learner from doing his own intellectual work, from identifying theoretical inconsistencies and flaws, and from discovering fresh connections which might lead to better insights and integration.

We must also face the fact, and the implications that follow from it, that the trend toward the conceptual has been achieved at the expense of the experiential. There are educators who would increase classroom learning at the expense of field work, and others who would make the field experience into an extension of the classroom. Those who would reduce and thus undermine learning in the field stand ready to deprive the learner of his laboratory. Such a move would deprive him of the opportunity to translate thought into action and to test for himself the validity and utility of the conceptual. Furthermore, it would diminish the chance to discover his own powers and then to begin, under guidance, the long, arduous, and disciplined nurturance of his creative capacity. It would also delay the hoped for pleasures and rewards that led him into social work in the first place. In sum, if we truly value the quality of creativity in social work, we must more consciously protect and develop this capacity by explicit attention to how we educate the learner[56] and how we organize our practice.

Notes

1. Swithun Bowers, "The Nature and Definition of Social Casework," *Principles and Techniques of Social Casework,* ed. Cora Kasius (New York: Family Service Association of America, 1950), p. 150.

2. Various writers have dealt to some extent with the definitional problem. For example, see Herman Stein, "Social Science in Social Work Practice and Education," *Social Casework,* XXXVI (April 1955), 148–49; Werner Boehm, "Social Work: Science and Art," *Social Service Review,* XXXV (June 1961), 150, and "Social Work and Social Sciences," *Mississippi Quarterly,* Jan. 1956, pp. 46–47; Joseph Eaton, "Science, Art and Uncertainty in Social Work," *Social Work,* III (July 1958), 3–10. These and other attempts to differentiate the artistic and the scientific in social work introduce, however, a variety of ambiguities and definitional fallacies. Thus, Boehm declares that "to juxtapose art and science in social work is to create a false dichotomy," but refers to social work as art and as a profession, and to social work science as distinct from social work practice. Eaton equates "artistic" with the "clinical" and suggests that clinical skill is nonrational and incapable of being conceptualized or communicated, although there is artistry in nonclinical as well as clinical social work methods, and the artistic person in social work is not necessarily unconscious of, or inarticulate regarding, governing theories, concepts, principles, or social purposes.

3. Ralph Tyler, "Distinctive Attributes of Education for the Professions," *Social Work Journal,* XXXIII (April 1952), 56.

4. Robert B. MacLeod, "Retrospect and Prospect," *Contemporary Approaches to Creative Thinking,* ed. Howard Gruber et al. (New York: Atherton, 1962), p. 179.

5. Herbert Read, *The Philosophy of Modern Art* (New York: Meridian, 1957), p. 72.

6. William Schuman, the eminent composer, distinguishes between art and craft in composing music. Music written to describe a certain event or to achieve a predetermined result, such as to "describe" a sunrise or a sea storm in a film, would require no more than craftsmanship. (From personal communication with the author.)

7. Marion Milner, "The Role of Illusion in Symbol Formation," *New Directions in Psychoanalysis,* ed. Melanie Klein et al. (New York: Basic Books, 1955), pp. 17–21.

8. R. K. Taylor, "The Social Control Functions in Casework," *Social Casework,* XXXIX (Jan. 1958), 17–21.

9. E. Kris, *Psychoanalytic Explorations in Art* (London: George Allen and Unwin, 1953), p. 57.

10. H. N. Wilenski and C. N. Lebaux, *Industrialization and Social Welfare* (New York: Russell Sage Foundation, 1955).

11. R. MacIver, *The Contribution of Sociology to Social Work* (New York: Columbia University Press, 1931), p. 11.

12. Alex Comfort, *Art and Social Responsibility* (London: Falcon, 1946), p. 33.

13. *Ibid.,* p. 35.

14. *Ibid.,* p. 32.

15. Charlotte Towle, *The Learner in Education for the Professions* (Chicago: University of Chicago Press, 1954), p. 10.

16. Herbert Bisno, "How Social Will Social Work Be?" *Social Work,* I (April 1956), 15.

17. Lionel Trilling, *A Gathering of Fugitives* (Boston: Beacon, 1956), p. 145.

18. Kris, *Psychoanalytic Explorations,* p. 57.

19. Kris states that psychoanalytic understanding has some contribution to make regarding "vocational choice"—why one artist turns to painting, others to music, dancing, etc. However, we do not at present have the tools to investigate the roots of gift or talent. He states further that the psychology of artists can be approached via patterns of conflict or structural problems and finds the latter more fruitful. See "Contributions and Limitation of Psychoanalysis," *Art and Psychoanalysis,* ed. William Phillips (New York: Meridian, 1963), pp. 278–79, 291.

20. Richard S. Crutchfield, "Conformity and Creative Thinking," *Contemporary Approaches*, ed. Gruber et al., pp. 120–40.

21. Peter McKellar, *Imagination and Thinking: A Psychological Analysis* (London: Cohen and West, 1957), p. 208.

22. Theodore Reik, cited in *ibid*., p. 171.

23. In a similar and ironic vein, Alex Comfort recognizes the binding grip of the closed gestalt when he says, "Once seen and stated, the discovery of a pattern like the recollection of a forgotten name, or a completed sneeze, brings deep satisfaction—which often goes with the creation of a category or the statement of a relationship. There is something about this particular pleasure which generates strong resistance to further analysis of the way in which the pattern was constructed. It produces a disabling sense of enlightenment

which is proof against argument." See *Darwin and the Naked Lady: Discursive Essays on Biology and Art* (London: Routledge and Kegan Paul, 1961), p. 7.

24. Jerome S. Bruner, "Conditions of Creativity," *Contemporary Approaches,* ed. Gruber et al., pp. 1–30.

25. Theodore Reik, *Surprise and the Psychoanalyst* (New York: Dutton, 1937).

26. Lawrence Kubie, "Blocks to Creativity," *International Science and Technology,* XL (June 1965),p. 69.

27. Frank Barron, *Creativity and Psychological Health* (Princeton, N.J.: Van Nostrand, 1963), p. 223.

28. This type of regression is sometimes induced artificially by artists and in various experimental studies through the use of consciousness-expanding drugs. Some clinical observers have noted that there is not always an easy return to rationality and that there may be lingering ill effects from this type of induced regression.

29. Kris, *Psychoanalytic Explorations,* p. 177.

30. The need for objectivity, discipline, and the rigors of scientific method have been overly stressed. Concepts like passion and investment tend to embarrass us. D. H. Malan, *A Study of Brief Psychotherapy* (London: Tavistock, 1963), cites an astute observation of Michael Balint's that the therapist's enthusiasm has a direct bearing on the process and outcome of therapy since it brings with it a corresponding heightened excitement in the patient with the result that repressed feelings come easily to the surface and are experienced with an intensity and completeness so that the further "working through" process may not be necessary. A related phenomenon is the social work students' frequent success with clients beyond the level expected of their knowledge and skill. The factors of enthusiasm, therapeutic optimism, and intensity of commitment and investment have been noted but never examined systematically to see what therapeutic potentials are embedded in them and how they could be used more purposefully and effectively. Roy Grinker comments on this phenomenon but draws a contrary inference: "It has been said that the results from therapy of any type are proportional to the therapist's enthusiasm for this method. This does not insure more than temporary effects. . . . The young therapist's overenthusiastic missionary concept of *self* as a curative agent may become a serious liability." See *Psychiatric Social Work: A Transactional Casebook* (New York: Basic Books, 1963), p. 311.

31. Read, *Philosophy of Modern Art*, pref.

32. Carl Jung, *Modern Man in Search of His Soul* (New York: Harcourt Brace, 1963), p. 169.

33. Richard Crutchfield notes that the creative act is necessarily expressive of the person, but it may not be explicitly directed at *self-expression*. Creativity in the scientific arts requires more task involvement and less ego involvement. See "Conformity and Creative Thinking," pp. 120–40. Charlotte Towle states that "professional education does not prepare for individual self-expression, for individualistic

creativity, for the acting out of one's own urges in the interest of self-gratification or self-realization." See *Learner in Education*, p. 11.

34. David Beres contrasts imagination with "fancy" (Coleridge's term), which he calls imagery or primary process thinking. See "Communication in Psychoanalysis and in the Creative Process: A Parallel," *Journal of American Psychoanalytic Association,* V (July 1957), pp. 408–23.

35. Towle, *Learner in Education*, p. 34.

36. Both Theodore Reik and Robert Katz have elaborated on the process of empathy. Both note that it involves both subjective and logical processes. Reik stresses the therapist's absorption of the unconscious of the patient which is experienced as alien emotions and then is reprojected onto the patient. See *Listening with the Third Ear* (New York: Pyramid, 1964), pp. 19–20. Katz notes four stages in the process: identification or immersion in the patient's feelings; incorporation or the introjection of the patient into the therapist's experience; reverberation or the reflection of the therapist as to how he would react to such an experience; and detachment or the withdrawal from subjective involvement to more objective analysis. See *Empathy: Its Nature and Uses* (Glencoe, Ill.: Free Press, 1963), pp. 41–47. See also Allyn Zanger, "A Study of Factors Related to Clinical Empathy." *Smith College Studies in Social Work*, XXXVIII (Feb. 1968).

37. Ralph Gerard states that imagination produces insight through regrouping sensory material, experience, and knowledge; through recognizing the universal in the particular; and through progressive generalization. See "Biological Basis of Imagination," *The Creative Process*, ed. Brewster Ghiselin (New York: Mentor, 1952), pp. 226–30.

38. Thomas French, "The Art and Science of Psychoanalysis," *Journal of American Psychoanalytic Association*, VI (April 1958), p. 202.

39. Frieda Fromm-Reichman, "Clinical Significance of Intuitive Process of Psychoanalysis," *Journal of American Psychoanalytic Association,* III (Jan. 1955), pp. 7–12.

40. According to Robert MacIver, "Diagnosis is the scientific prologue to practice; it is the place where art and science join hands." See *Contribution of Sociology*, p. 8.

41. Jerome Bruner quotes Picasso: "With me a picture is a sum of destruction. I make a picture and then proceed to destroy it." Presumably this refers to the metamorphosis of an idea and the breaking up of the initial appearance of an image. See "Conditions of Creativity," p. 15.

42. Felix Deutsch, "The Art of Interviewing and Abstract Art," *American Imago*, IX (April 1952), pp. 3–19.

43. Erik Erikson gives a breadth of substance to the concept of insight, stating that insight must be more than the sum of knowledge, theory, and technique which constitutes expertness; it must include them, not abandon or circumvent them. See "Growth and Crisis of the Healthy Personality," *Symposium on the Healthy Personality, Conference on Infancy and Childhood* (New York: Josiah Macy Foundation,

1950), p. 93. Allen Wheelis says insight involves the capacity to organize ego functions for the purpose of mastery. He distinguishes insight from verbal formulations of psychodynamics which, used by the obsessive person, are an aspect of isolation: "Insight consists in the ability to look into obscure aspects of one's personality, to recognize disguised motivations, to integrate what is discovered with various elements of conscious experience, and to utilize one's findings in such a way as to bring about a change in feeling, action, and reaction. It implies a belief that no inner danger is so bad but that knowing about it will be better than not knowing. It presupposes, further, an implicit faith in the adaptive potential of intelligence, and the wish to place at the disposal of intelligence all available information." See "On the Vocational Hazards of Psychoanalysis," *International Journal of Psychoanalysis,* XXXVII, Pts. 2–3 (1956), 1–14.

44. Alex Comfort distinguishes between the hard-centered and the soft-centered approaches to thinking. "Hard-centeredness notes regularity in behavior and assumes it can be explained if we can find out on what the regularity depends. Soft-centeredness states the regularity, calls it a law, truth, or spiritual reality, and treats these names as if they were explanations. Nonetheless, while it takes hard-centered attributes to criticize ideas, it may take soft-centered attributes to see them." See *Darwin and the Naked Lady,* pp. 4, 7.

45. The creative process is often presented schematically as taking place in four stages: (1) conscious preparation; (2) incubation, during which more preconscious thinking occurs; (3) illumination, either as a flash or gradual insight; (4) elaboration, involving verification and exploitation of findings. These stages are not necessarily sequential but rather reciprocal in nature. This description was developed by Graham Wallas and quoted by Philip Abelson in "Relation of Group Activity to Creativity in Science," *Daedalus,* XCIV (summer 1965), 603–4.

46. Mae Irving, in "Communication and Relationship in Social Casework," notes the parallel between the artist who has to give form to his inner experience and the social worker who has to translate the creative force of the relationship into some kind of form through the patterning of experience. See *Social Casework,* XXXVI (Jan. 1955), 13–21.

47. Robert Nisbit, in "Sociology as an Art Form," states that theories should be tested as much by their reach as by their grasp, their importance as their validity, and their elegance as their congruence. See *Sociology on Trial,* ed. Maurice Stein and Arthur Vidich (New York: Prentice Hall, 1963), p. 148.

48. See, for example, *The Creative Organization,* ed. Gary A. Steiner (Chicago: University of Chicago Press, 1965); see also Bruner, "Conditions of Creativity."

49. Lucille Austin suggests that the professional and bureaucratic ideologies may be at variance with each other. See "The Changing Role of the Supervisor," *Ego-Oriented Casework,* ed. Howard J. Parad and Roger R. Miller (New York: Family Service Association of America, 1963), 273–91.

50. Sidney Levenstein, *Private Practice in Social Casework* (New York: Columbia University Press, 1964), p. 17; see also Austin, "Changing Role," p. 278.

51. Sherman Merle, who is opposed to private practice, also recognizes the need for reform: "At this juncture in our professional history, agencies should seriously consider the arguments given by some social workers entering private practice that certain agency routines (recording practice, never-ending supervision, inability to practice creatively, salary scales, and the like) need careful review." "Some Arguments against Private Practice," *Social Work*, VII (Jan. 1962), 17.

52. George Klein, "Cognitive Control and Motivation," *Assessment of Human Motives,* ed. Gardner Lindsey (New York: Holt, Rinehart and Winston, 1958).

53. Allen Wheelis, "The Place of Action in Personality Change," *Psychiatry,* XIII (May 1950), 135–48.

54. Joyce Carey calls the concept the enemy of intuition: "The concept, the label, is perpetually hiding from us all the nature of the real. We have to have conceptual knowledge to organize our societies, to save our lives, to lay down general ends for conduct, to engage in any activity at all. But that knowledge, like the walls we put up to keep out the weather, shuts out the real world and the sky. It is a narrow little house which becomes a prison to those who can't get out of it." See *Art and Reality* (New York: Harper Bros., 1958), pp. 33, 165.

55. Jerome S. Bruner, *The Process of Education* (Cambridge, Mass.: Harvard University Press, 1962), p. 62.

56. There may be a revitalized interest in creativity in social work as there are increasing references to it in the professional literature, if only in passing. The pressing demands on social work to grapple with today's urgent problems call for not only an improved "technology" but creative inventiveness, as well. Eileen Blackey, calling for general excellence in social work education, refers to the teacher as an artist and to education as a medium for creative self-expression. See "Selection and Preparation of Faculty for Schools of Social Work," *Journal of Education for Social Work,* I (spring 1965), 5–12. Esther Clemence demonstrates the creative use of educational processes in "The Dynamic Use of Ego Psychology in Casework Education," *Smith College Studies in Social Work,* vol. XXXV (June 1965).

2 *Social Casework:* An Appraisal and an Affirmation

We are here to celebrate the mid-century point of the Smith College School for Social Work which has been—and has remained—a school justly renowned for its commitment to casework and to psychoanalytic theory of personality as a guide to understanding and working with individuals and families. At mid-century point it is useful to engage in an appraisal of our basic commitments and assumptions. The actual history of social casework, first systematically developed and applied by Mary Richmond, a far-sighted humanist, disciplined thinker, and theoretician, is not much older than the school. We are now in a period in our society of great ferment, marked by the most rapid social and technological changes we have ever experienced, a dizzying speed of communication, a shaking up of values, and a re-examination of larger and enduring questions regarding the nature, rights, and responsibilities of man in society. All of these characteristics serve to generate increasing tensions, doubts, and uncertainties as to future directions. It is an uncomfortable time because doubts are being cast on all facets of our intellectual assumptions, ideological positions, and institutional arrangements; in fact, the doubts have been converted into active challenges and confrontations. Indeed, it is increasingly being said that we are in a period of revolutionary ferment.

The most cogent characteristic of our state of affairs is the increasing polarization of positions—the widening of splits and schisms and the hardening of postures in many aspects of our social and intellectual life—which inevitably leads to distortion of fact and of reality. We are finding it increasingly difficult to encompass a wide range of differences, to tolerate a comfortable eclecticism, or to keep in balance various positions. We are becoming more and more locked into an unfortunate either/or position.

Source: Reprinted, with minor changes, from *Smith College Studies in Social Work,* XXXIX (June 1969), 213–35. Used by permission.

This seems to be the case in our political life and in our social ideologies, as well as our professional ideologies. All these larger struggles and issues are reflected in our profession, which is historically accustomed to do its own soul-searching and in which tensions and changes are being generated by their own dynamics as well as by the great social issues of the times.

One of the significant ways to orient oneself in times of rapid change is to search out meaning by re-examining values, testing out assumptions, and sifting relevant knowledge in order to arrive at a position of reaffirmation of that which is enduring and of value in the present context. We propose here to examine the position and relevance of social casework in the context of today's pressing social problems and requirements. Such a task is particularly appropriate in view of increasingly frequent assertions being made today, coming from many quarters within the profession, that social casework, as a social work approach, is irrelevant to major social problems, is insignificant in its contribution to social change, is ineffective within the context of its claims regarding solutions, and at worst, like God, is dead.

The method of social casework is a remarkable invention of American social work, one which has gained increasing attention and respect not only in Western industrialized societies but also internationally, since it has been found to have cross-cultural relevance. For a long time it was the prestigious method of social work, the best and most clearly developed and articulated, and the method of choice for the overwhelming numbers of students engaging in social work education. Now we are told it is in serious trouble.[1] How has it managed to fall into such disrepute? What is the nature of the disenchantment? And what specifically is the nature of some of the attacks? This paper will examine attacks based on issues of relevance, effectiveness, appropriateness and responsiveness, the medical model, Freudian dynamic psychology, and therapeutic functions.

Relevance of Social Casework

One of the strongest criticisms of social casework is the assertion that it does not solve social problems that press themselves upon us. We are confronted with social problems of an overwhelming magnitude in the nature of poverty, racial tensions, the use of violence for conflict resolution, crime and delinquency, ghetto life, urban decay and housing needs, insufficient medical care and so on. As a society, we are much more conscious of these conditions then we were a decade or two ago. Within recent times, only the socially oriented groups in our society, social workers among them, were conscious of and articulate about these problems. The climate now has changed radically so that there is a heightened demand on the part of a much greater segment of society, particularly among the disenfranchised, the minority groups, the invisible poor, for justice and a more equal share in our country's abundance. The solutions to these enormous social problems lie in a total and widespread attack involving serious and total commitment by all sectors of society. Neither the profession of social work itself, nor any of its methods singly or in combination, has the knowledge or power to deal with these problems. It can and must be an advocate and represent the conscience of society. It can and must be the spokesman in interpreting the consequences of chronic unmet needs, consequences to the sufferers as well as to society as a whole. It can and must work with other professions and segments of society to foster change through the legislative and judicial processes and through planned institutional rearrangements. As to the charge that casework is irrelevant, all that can be affirmed is that casework as a method of social work was never designed to deal with the causes of large-scale social problems. It certainly has a contribution to make in dealing with their effects as these impinge on individual functioning. Alvin Schorr, who is deeply committed to the development of social policy in the social services, offers a balanced point of view. In regard to the attacks on casework he states:

> Yet it would be a great misfortune if we now cantered over to the other extreme, depreciating casework and group work as trivial responses to the needs that surround us or exclusively as techniques for cooling off those who ought to take more drastic action. Casework can be trivial, all right, and it can be made to argue for adjustment to intolerable circumstances, but it can also do other things. Most of all, casework and group work implement the conviction that, when all the studies have been analyzed and our best lobbyists have paused in their labors, something remains that must take place between one person and another. . . . A society that supports significant person-to-person services makes real its devotion to individuality and personality.[2]

In the same vein, but in a different mood, Helen Perlman tests the validity of the individual problem-solving approach in her article, "Casework Is Dead,"[3] by use of a vignette of a troubled and deprived person and the reaction of a non-casework-oriented colleague social worker. The inevitable conclusion was that people need help here and now and always will, while the profession and others fight for more adequate social provisions. We are also told, more as an aside—it is nevertheless a central point—that each "utopia" breeds its own special human needs.

Effectiveness of Social Casework

Another criticism asserts the charge that casework cannot prove its effectiveness and has failed to document its ability to effect change through evaluative research or any kind of scientific appraisal. This is a difficult and troublesome area, one full of rancor and polemics, not to mention the actual difficult methodological problems involved. It is not possible to summarize here the research that has been done both in the psychotherapy field and in social casework on the outcome of treatment. The general consensus seems to be that evaluative studies of various sorts indicate very minimal results for the application of psychotherapeutic or casework methods and that the recovery rate of treated populations is no higher than that obtained through spontaneous remission in untreated groups. Of course, as Elizabeth Herzog points out, "there is no evidence . . . that the treated and untreated groups were comparable in types of problems, severity of problem, or degree of recovery."[4]

The most widely quoted study in the past several years is *Girls at Vocational High,*[5] from which widespread generalizations have been made to show that social work in one or more of its methods is ineffectual. The study itself of a population at risk—predelinquent high school girls at risk of becoming dropouts, unmarried mothers, or delinquents—was an evaluation of objective measures of the effects of casework and group work efforts of prevention. It revealed only minimal differences between an experimental or treated group and a control or untreated group. Most of these differences were in favor of the treated group but were without statistical significance. The caseworkers' modest evaluation of their success exceeded anything that objective measures could show. We cannot conclude that casework or group work will affect the rates of delinquency and indeed these methods are not designed to attack social problems at that level. Alvin Schorr points out: "We can say that casework does indeed help deviant people but mainly in relation to *their* objectives which do not often enough turn out to be society's objectives."[6]

Of the many reviews of the study by various researchers, the most searching was made by Mary E. MacDonald. There are many pitfalls in the study: the lack of clarity of treatment objectives; the change in methodology from casework to group work midstream; the discarding of a piece of the sample of the final group studied; and others which cannot be enumerated here. MacDonald asserts that the authors take the negative results at face value and then generalize the results far beyond their study of a specific program. She agrees that the experimental intervention (which in actuality was the application of traditional approaches characteristic of the mid-fifties, when this work was done) was inadequate to the task. There is agreement that evaluative research requires, among other things, the formulation of testable treatment goals—explicating goals beyond imponderable abstractions such as "improving social functioning" into a series of simpler and more precise concepts. This step has to be taken by the practitioners and researchers conjointly. MacDonald concludes:

> The effectiveness of social work in general is poorly documented: we do not have good scientific proof of effectiveness. On the other hand, we also lack good sceintific proof of ineffectiveness. The situation of social casework and group work in this respect is like that of all psychotherapy—the shallow and the deep, the brief and the protracted.[7]

We can only conclude that the real work in evaluating effectiveness of social work methods is yet to be done. And it needs to be done in a spirit of truly open inquiry. The manner of usage of findings to date suggests that the various consumers of research in the field are primarily interested in seizing on results to vindicate or negate a prior held position to substantiate their bias.

Appropriateness of the Casework Method

A third issue pertains to the supposed inappropriateness of the casework method when used with what is indeed a large segment of our clientele, namely the poor and the near-poor. Casework has been declared to be unresponsive and/or inappropriate to the needs of lowerclass people. We have been told that caseworkers, who are of course middle-class, cannot understand the needs, aspirations, values, and life styles of the lower-class. The term "middle-class" has become an invective. Sociological studies of class origins of social workers show that they, more than other professions, tend to come from lower-class origins;[8] indeed, social work as a profession has been readily available for upward mobility. It could be argued that former lower-class status is all the more a barrier because of the need to deny one's origins. But soon we drive outselves into a corner of absurdities. The fact of the matter is that caseworkers can understand cultural and class variables, that they know deeply the nature of misery, suffering, and troubled feelings that are part of the human condition and that cut across class and ethnic lines. If we insist that the casework method is inappropriate to the needs of the poor, we then must conclude with a caveat uttered by a community organization specialist colleague of mine when he said, "The middle-class gets casework; the poor get community organization." This is, of course, a rank form of discrimination, as is the situation we are likely to confront wherein the middle-class will be dealt with by trained caseworkers, while the poor will be given services by untrained indigenous workers who ostensibly have no communication barriers or problems of professional or social distance. If we are not careful to temper our enthusiasm in using indigenous personnel without discrimination, or in romanticizing the potentialities of people who have been suppressed, deprived, and sometimes seriously emotionally damaged, we will end up with a two-track system whereby the impoverished once again get the short end of the service stick.

The real trouble here, as I comprehend it, is the confusion of elements of the casework method with methods of service delivery. Unfortunately, these two distinct methodologies get intertwined. I do not believe the casework method per se, or any theory intrinsic to it, makes it unresponsive to certain segments of the population. In fact, the chief characteristic of casework, with its grounding in differential diagnosis and differential approaches, is its capacity for differential responses to a wide variety of human situations and needs. Now, it is possible to assert that many kinds of agencies have been unresponsive to certain kinds of populations. The agencies have acquired and maintained numerous constraints, through tradition or inertia or dysfunctional bureaucratic structures, which prevent a flexible use of their potential services. Numerous types of agencies in both the public and private sectors have been guilty of the latter. Some examples might be cited. The child guidance clinic is traditionally thought to be the most selective and limiting as to the patients and problem situations it admits for service. One can say that it had for a time almost barricaded itself behind its own doors. It had a well-developed methodology, thought inappropriate to a good many clients, most of whom never got there, while the few that did soon fled. Now in one community of my acquaintance, the child guidance clinic moved into the ghetto (years before it became fashionable) and reached out to multiproblem families. The service was delivered via a different structure; the method of interpersonal approach and problem-solving remained the same and proved to be relevant, appropriate, and sometimes effective. We do tend to confuse agency structure and casework method theory. For example, again in child guidance clinics, the lengthy diagnostic approach or interdisciplinary overlap in diagnosis is attributed to method theory. Actually it is not intrinsic to theory but is rooted in historical precedent and patterning, now often obsolete or dysfunctional.

Another ironic example might be cited to sharpen the notion of the unresponsiveness of the agency. In one community the family agency, with its tradition of serving families in need, consolidated its district offices in one main office located in the central commercial area of town inaccessible to all but the middle-class or most highly motivated. This family agency increasingly seemed to pattern itself on the model of the psychiatric clinic. At the same time, however, the psychiatric clinic moved into the ghetto neighborhoods with store-front offices and an open door. Here, clearly, the method of service delivery is the crucial variable as to who can be reached, whereas the casework method remains adaptable and relevant. This switch of family agency and psychiatric clinic recalls to mind an analogy David Reisman used in his *Constraint and Variety in American Education* in identifying fashions and fads in education as a long snake wherein the head of the snake is already off to something else by the time the tail catches up with it.

The Use of the Medical Model

A fourth source of attack and confusion is the widespread and cavalier comment that casework is wedded to the medical model and that this linkage has caused it to be obsolete. Nothing that I have read explicates what is meant by a medical model and why it is therefore inappropriate—but the invective stands and is bandied about. I have made an effort to pursue this issue since it baffles me. I have concluded that there is no single medical model. Do critics mean the centrality and inviolateness of the doctor-patient relationship? This relationship refers, of course, among other things, to a method of service delivery although at some point, even in group or clinic practice, or in a national health service or whatever, what goes on between doctor and patient is fundamental. But we might as well call that the pastoral model—because what is more central than the confidential and accepting relationship of religious and spiritual advisor and parishioner? There is another model under the rubric of medical model—the public health model with its priority commitment to serve the health needs of the total community. The ultimate beneficiary is the individual although the means are beamed at the total community. The relevance of this model to social work has been spelled out by numerous writers including myself and will not be belabored here.[9]

Then we have a different area of concern in regard to the medical model which has to do with the concept of causation. Here we have concepts pertaining to acute infectious diseases versus chronic diseases. As to acute infectious disorders, a good deal of medical science and practice (and this is the area where medicine has been most outstandingly successful) consists of tracking down and isolating a specific etiological agent which then can be treated or controlled. The model here is of the well person, who has attained a certain level of adequate health and social functioning and who may then be overcome by an acute and infectious state. This state can be treated but usually it is self-limiting in its acute phase, and may or may not leave residuals in its wake. This model as translated back into social casework is one source of the theoretical underpinning for brief crisis intervention and was incisively delineated by David Kaplan.[10]

But in much of disease we deal with multiple etiological factors where specific cures are not available or are ineffective. Yet, some control is possible and treatment is available on the secondary or tertiary level, that is to say on the level of limitation and control of disability. In social work, too, we deal constantly with a multicausation system. We pick up those factors in the multifactorial chain that are subject to influence, control, and change with the means we have at hand. Thus, we hope to have a salutary influence on the state of well-being and mental health of an individual or family. We do not have a cure, and never will, but we do have the means of interrupting and altering noxious processes that are deleterious to our clients. And we have learned from the public health model of intervention that one can be effective in intervening at any or various points along the chain of linked factors of causality depending on today's state of knowledge, technology, and resources. This intervention can be carried out on a variety of system levels and can be effected by all the social work methods. Casework, of course, would intervene on the individual and family level, primarily. Thus, I conclude that far from having outgrown the so-called medical model, we can profitably search out a variety of models operating within the medical framework to explore and test out their relevance to social work and to social casework in particular.

Freudian Dynamic Psychology

Our next issue concerns the use of Freudian dynamic psychology as a base for understanding human nature and its use in social casework. There is extraordinary hostility currently within and outside of social work to psychoanalytic theory. Some hold it responsible for a number of society's present ills because, in their view, it has created a climate of permissiveness attributable to Freud's impact on child-rearing and education. Another popular charge in this age of scientific supremacy is that psychoanalytic theory and therapy are not scientific, cannot be proven (and by that token cannot be disproven), and have no predictive power so that they cannot be instruments of control and change. It is dubious that we can have an overall science of human behavior that is holistic in its view. Aspects of behavior can be studied scientifically, and translating insights derived therefrom into a therapeutic approach remains basically an art, as it does in any applied field. Freud's contributions to social work and to our culture at large were adequately reviewed in many quarters in 1957 at the time of the centennial of his birth.[11] They cannot be summarized here. Instead, some of the issues and distortions that have developed will be delineated and clarified.

Freud was not only an extraordinary genius who opened up a whole frontier of knowledge, but he was also a very wise man with a gift of prophecy based on his deep insights into human behavior and his interest and knowledge of history. He was mistrustful of the relative ease with which the United States embraced psychoanalytic theory both professionally and culturally. He predicted not only a watering-down and distortion of his basic concepts but also a revulsion and rejection at some point in time and, to quote Robert Coles, "a wounding confrontation with behaviorism." Thus, for example, we now have a rejection of the concept and actuality of the unconscious and a rejection, in some quarters, of the power of unconscious motivation. We also have a rejection of the biological base of human behavior, a negation of instinctual processes, and a stripping down of complex processes to flat and simplistic explanations.

Freud's theories were not addressed merely to the problems of late nineteenth-century Victorian Vienna. They have universality and contemporaneity notwithstanding the arguments as to whether or not the Oedipus complex is to be found universally, such as in matriarchal and matrilineal societies. His contributions were not designed to meet our contemporary social problems, although they offer important insights as to the nature of man which are highly relevant to many current conflicts, including those of racial tensions, violence, and war.

Freud himself valued psychoanalysis primarily as a scientific tool of investigation. He knew the central importance of his theory of human behavior and the impact it would have on society. Lastly, he recognized that psychoanalysis as a therapeutic procedure had powerful but limited application. Psychoanalysis in its classical sense as a form of therapy is relevant to a middle range of patients—those with neurotic conflicts sufficiently intense and pervasive, yet with good ego capacities and healthy enough to stand the process[12] and, we might add, rich enough to afford private fees.

What is psychoanalytic theory is enduring and useful to our current needs? Psychoanalytic theory offers first of all a view of man which perhaps is profoundly pessimistic. It offers also some hope insofar as rationality in human affairs is a goal and can be achieved but only through a difficult historical and individual evolutionary process which we call maturation. Freud has often been quoted, "Where id is, ego shall be." So much of today's malaise and actions, particularly on the part of our youth, is an effort, so to speak, to bypass the ego. This is also true in some of the newer forms of therapy which emphasize only the unbridled expression of emotions.

Secondly, psychoanalytic theory represents a powerful explanatory system of personality development and of maladaptation. There is no other theory extant that offers the same potency as an explanatory system insofar as it deals with and accounts for such a wide range of otherwise puzzling, complex, human behavioral phenomena. Despite assertions to the contrary, it is and remains an open explanatory system which is capable of expansion and absorption of new knowledge and formulations as they emerge. The most obvious developments that can be cited, which it could and did readily incorporate into its explanatory system, have been the concepts of ego psychology, the epigenetic concepts of Erik Erickson with their stages and tasks of maturation and development, and aspects of learning theory. However, there seems to be a restiveness with the complexity of psychoanalytic theory. Most of the theoretical innovations in regard to personality development and in therapy represent attempts to simplify, to find short cuts, and to rest content with unidimensional explanations.

Third, psychoanalytic concepts have a particular usefulness to any field applying knowledge of man for helping purposes because they lead to guiding principles or contain within them a prescription for action. Not all theories have this attribute. For example, role theory speaks to the patterned and reciprocal and interpersonal behavior of man but does not contain within it any guidelines for intervention or remedial work. Some mediating principles for action are needed. Psychoanalytic theory had a great utility which could be apprehended. Interestingly enough, the first profession to grasp the great potential of this then new psychology was social work and not the psychiatric profession. There were a handful of psychiatric pioneers who worked with social workers on this new dynamic knowledge. Social workers were also the first to incorporate this knowledge in their training schools; and the Smith College School for Social Work became the first to offer such knowledge in a systematic way. It took psychiatric training institutions several more decades to bring dynamic psychiatry under their purview. Social workers were receptive to these new formulations because they had struggled at length with recalcitrant, difficult, and puzzling aspects of human behavior, some of which defied rational, common sense, and good will approaches. psychoanalytic insights were welcomed, then, because they enabled social workers to see the psychodynamics beneath surface symptoms and behavior and because they could grapple with issues of cause rather than effect.

They also opened up new levels of communication that could relate themselves to preconscious as well as conscious expressions of feelings and meaning. To quote Helen Perlman: "These insights affected social workers deeply. Moralistic self-righteousness cannot be sustained under their searching light. As a result, social workers came to feel more humble, more self-aware, and thus more self-disciplined and more deeply compassionate in the presence of human frailty and pain."[13]

The utility of psychoanalytic concepts and their inclusion of prescription for action has also posed a hazard for social casework that has led to serious misunderstanding, distortion, and abuse. Essentially, the distortion has been not separating out sufficiently and clearly the usefulness of psychoanalytic insights into human behavior from the methodology of psychoanalysis proper. Of course there have been a whole host of developments of psychoanalytically oriented psychotherapies, of which casework is one, with much effort over the years to delineate the difference in goals and techniques among the various approaches. Yet psychoanalysis as a therapy has remained a basic model, if not an ideal model, in what became a hierarchical system. It also became equated with depth, which specifically in psychoanalysis means the systematic exploration of the unconscious. Other methods, of course, are also deep—deep in the sense of being able to make a profound impact and bring about considerable change in behavior. This change, however, can be brought about not only through techniques of exploration of unconscious factors and the development of insight into unconscious motivation, but also through clarification and supportive measures and through processes of unconscious identification with new parental figures or role models and so on. However, in the value system that developed, the more closely a therapy could approximate the attributes of the ideal approach of psychoanalysis, the better. This, rather than the use of psychoanalytic insights per se in the problem-solving process, is what led social caseworkers astray and called for the invective of "junior psychiatrist." It led to an era in which the exclusive use of office interviews was de rigueur; maximum premium was put on factors of motivation toward attitudinal and personality changes; there was an overevaluation on the efficacy of insight as an instrument of change; there was a tendency toward passivity in interviews on the part of caseworkers and an overemphasis on self-scrutiny on the part of clients;

and so on. All these excesses have largely been corrected by a profession that subjects inself as continuously to self-criticism as does social work. They have also been corrected as new modalities of approach have developed which represent considerable departures from the model of psychoanalysis as therapy.

Therapeutic Functions

The last area of criticism to be identified, which is related to the prior discussion, is directed at casework in its therapeutic or clinical functions. Somehow, social casework had come to be equated with psychotherapy. The psychotherapeutic functions of casework are also equated with long-term treatment. It is ironic when one looks at casework practice in agencies across the board. In actuality, the bulk of cases being seen in the most middle-class–oriented setting, i.e., psychiatric clinics and family agencies, are seen either once or for an extensive period of about five interviews. Somehow the mental image of the model does not fit the reality. In any event, casework can be a form of psychotherapy but it can certainly be and do more. Whatever it does, whatever functions are performed as part of social casework, it can have a therapeutic effect insofar as the goal is always the enhancement of better interpersonal and social functioning, regardless of the means used to achieve this goal.

It is true, for some years, the main thrust of the casework literature had been on explicating the direct therapeutic functions with examination of differential diagnosis and treatment considerations. The nonclinical functions were lumped together under environmental manipulation, which fell somewhat into disrepute in contrast to supportive or expressive measures. I have always maintained that imaginative and resourceful environmental modification (the word "manipulation" is emotionally overladen) takes just as high a degree of skill as any other helping procedure and should involve the same processes of understanding, differentiation, and planning as do the more psychologically oriented measures. It is wrong to maintain that casework treatment requires the application of diagnostic and treatment skills and that environmental manipulation takes action. The beauty of social casework as an instrument for individual and family change, in contrast to other therapies, is its blending of psychological understanding and management with social provision, thus giving us a wide and rich range of choice in the instrumentation of the change process.

We are told by critics of social casework that the clinical or therapeutic functions are overly used, overrated, and inappropriate to non-middle-class clients. Other functions are proposed, sometimes referred to as models, or roles, such as the advocacy role, the social brokerage role, and so forth. These roles essentially are designed to help the client assert his rights vis-à-vis capricious or unjust social welfare bureaucracies, and to help him maneuver through the mazes of the health and welfare systems. In some countries such a role has been established outside the network of professionals in the form of the ombudsman, whose function it is to see that justice is done by championing a client's cause. These activities and functions need to be performed, and perhaps ought to be attended to more often. There is nothing in casework theory that prevents such functions from being performed. It is very limiting, however, to see these roles as the whole of social casework or as its central core. They are at best a part of the total process. If well and sensitively done, they require the use of judgments as to differential diagnosis and overall treatment planning and thus become part of the total process. I can well imagine the day, for instance, when social caseworkers, having elevated the advocacy role to a central position, will be called "junior lawyers." I no more welcome that than their being called "junior psychiatrists."

Adaptability of Casework

I would now like to affirm that casework is here to stay and build a case for such an assertion. Casework has shown itself over the decades to have a high survival value. We know that an organism or a social institution has a high survival potential when it intrinsically possesses a capacity for flexible and renewed adaptation to changing circumstances. Social casework has such a capacity because basically it is an open and open-ended system of thought that can bend and stretch in a variety of directions and still maintain its core of identity and its core social purpose. Its having done just that ever since its inception has contributed to its endurance and has endowed it with an open, dynamic, and exciting quality.

The last fifteen years, for example, have been a real period of ferment and growth, with many changes effected by incorporating new ideas, discarding some, rediscovering some old ones, and reaching out experimentally for new persons to serve with new modes of approaches. For instance, social casework has certainly reached out and incorporated the formulations and insights of ego psychology, which are very compatible with casework goals and objectives. It has also absorbed concepts of Sullivan's theory of interpersonal relationships as well as concepts of social role and of learning theory. In regard to all these theories, it has been selective and eclectic, although one can find on the part of some writers and practitioners greater emphasis on one or the other.

During the 1950s casework took a self-conscious look at itself in relation to its former neglect of clients characterized as the "hard-to-reach." Experimentally and theoretically, it found ways of reformulating its understanding and techniques so that they could be used with so-called multiproblem families and with people who suffered from ego deficiencies or from character disorders. At that time, too, there developed a family-centered approach which moved the attention from the individual client to the familiar context as it impaired or enhanced social functioning. From this approach there developed more radically different procedures which were beamed at families as a unit in a variety of combinations, from conjoint treatment to family group therapy, with single or multiple therapists. Crisis-oriented brief casework treatment has been another development which took its impetus from public health work and crisis theory. Reflected on the short contacts that characterized the majority of our clientele, it reoriented practitioners to doing goal-focused and goal-limited intervention, for maximum effect, with refined attention to healthy functioning as well as to psychopathology. Such a development has great relevance to practice in many, but not all, settings and builds on the knowledge and practice wisdom that has accrued to date.

These several developments are cited as examples of the adaptability of the casework method and demonstrate the evolutionary change process. The changes were not brought about without some pain, since all change is anxiety-provoking and painful, but they did not cause an upheaval or present a fundamental break with so-called traditional practice.

The question needs to be posed as to whether the elasticity of the casework method is infinite or whether there are some boundaries to be observed if we wish to preserve the essential character of casework. For those who have become dissatisfied with what is referred to as traditional methods—and let us assert that our traditions are very short-lived indeed—there is an opportunity to cast about within our own and neighboring fields to come up with something more radical and new. Our problem is not the paucity but the superabundance of ideas and approaches, although many are poorly developed, poorly tested and of questionable value. But because they are "over there," the grass may appear very green indeed. We have available for choice a broad spectrum of therapies and approaches, some developed within the clinical casework field, some developed within clinical or social psychiatry, and some within psychology or elsewhere. Some approaches are psychoanalytically based, some are unanalytic, and some are frankly antianalytic. Let us list a few: there is family therapy, crisis intervention, reality therapy, behavioral therapy, rational therapy, existential therapy, transactional therapy and, of older vintage, Sullivanian therapy, Jungian therapy, Rankian therapy, Horneyan therapy, and many others. These can be examined along many dimensions, but essentially they range from therapies that stress deep personal encounters to the point of mysticism while emphasizing personal growth, to largely manipulative and mechanistic transactions that emphasize control.

Behavioral Therapy

We will now examine one of these therapies which belongs to the so-called action therapies to pinpoint the issues of elasticity and boundaries more sharply. Behavioral therapy or behavioral modification therapy today has great appeal in many quarters among some social workers and psychiatarists, but mostly among psychologists. It is practiced in various settings, mainly in state mental hospitals, where individualization of patients and patient management have always been a problem. It is also used with a wide variety of clients—the mentally ill, the mentally retarded, autistic children and a variety of neurotic disturbances. In its theory it reaches back into the work of Watson and more recently Skinner. Its view of man is a limited one, essentially conceiving of the human organism as a machine, albeit a complex machine, which is fed by stimuli resulting in a behavior response or output. The chief approach is the modification of behavior and the elimination of symptoms through various techniques such as operant conditioning, selective reinforcement through punishment and reward, extinction, and shaping. It achieves the modification of behavior as a central goal without reference to considerations of self-determination and choice, notions of motivation, striving and self-realization, reference to unconscious factors, or considerations of the whole person.

The current literature of behavioral therapy, some of it a bit strident in tone, is vociferous in claiming impressive results. It has been successful in altering behavior with the grossly deviant where basic socialization or retraining are foremost needs. It is a method that is more akin to, and therefore suitable to, earlier developmental levels since many of its techniques are part of the natural child-bearing process although not usually so systematically applied. There is serious question as to how much of its technology is appropriate to adults. Even adult schizophrenics, for example, are not children although some of their behavior may be childlike. Nevertheless, most other therapies, including casework, make their approach and appeal to that part of the adult ego that remains intact and try to strengthen it through supportive and sustaining measures.

Behavioral therapy is a radical departure from other approaches since it considers psychotherapy nothing but a form of behavior control in which the therapist is a behavioral engineer or social reinforcement machine. It seeks to exert direct influence on behavior. Here I should like to quote Kenneth Colby, a psychoanalyst, who has experimented with psychotherapy done by computers.

> There should be no objection to viewing a therapist as an influencer. Influence is not necessarily a term of opprobrium. The therapist does attempt to influence a patient, and the patient wants him to; otherwise, he would not be there. The objection is to viewing the therapist as nothing but an influencer and in such a crudely reductionistic way.[14]

Behavioral therapy is classified as an action therapy, and casework, by contrast, would be called a talking method which, critics are quick to point out, makes it unsuitable for clients who are essentially nonverbal or who are action-oriented in their life style. As a matter of fact, there is considerable confusion here. Lower-class clients are not necessarily less verbal, although their style of verbalization and expression may differ from middle-class clients. The real issue is the extent to which *thought*—not speech—itself has become an established problem-solving technique. On this level there may be class differences as well as differences among people within the same class. In any event, this distinction is again an unfortunate polarization because it obscures factors of subtle communication, yes, even of relationship, to be found in behavioral therapy, and negates the important action components in social casework. I doubt if anyone believes in the magical properties of just talk, although the cathartic value from abreaction through talking can be very great and useful. Talk is directed to some end, whether it be insight, which only some can achieve and even fewer can use, or more relevantly some kind of translation into altered states of feeling and behaving—that is to say, behavioral change. Again, we are not lacking in theoretical concepts or underpinnings. Allen Wheelis, a psychoanalyst, in an important paper written in 1950, makes a profound contribution to ego psychology and puts into perspective the dimension of action in regard to personality change. He states that

> therapy can bring about personality change only in so far as it leads a patient to adopt a new mode of behavior. A real change occurring in the absence of action is a practical and theoretical impossibility. The personality changes result necessarily from the repeated actions, and could not come about in the absence of such actions. The new mode of action is a new mode of energy discharge, and the discharge of energy in large quantities leaves its mark . . . . Action usually has definite environmental or interpersonal consequences, some of which are irreversible; thought is largely confined within one's self, and—in and of itself—has no external consequences. By thought one can stage an action in miniature, rehearse it, revise it, change the ending. If it suits one, he may then enact it in reality; if it does not, he may discard it without paying the penalties that an unwise action would entail.[15]

Some of the techniques of behavioral therapy can be found embedded in some of the principles and techniques of casework where, however, they are flexibly and differentially utilized. For example, in casework we have learned to use authority selectively and constructively. We mete out rewards through the use of active approval, an interpersonal force, rather than meting out tokens or candy. We use supportive measures to strengthen and reinforce positive steps taken. We are less cautious, not true in our days of passivity, in offering advice and guidance where needed on the basis of a client's confusion or on the basis of simple lack of knowledge and experience. We engage in a form of action by helping people anticipate and prepare for difficult steps by anticipatory guidance and rehearsal for reality, by role playing when appropriate. We understand and use the concept of partializing and are sensitively aware of the need for timing and dosage in relation to a client's ability and readiness to absorb and to grapple with specific aspects of his problem.

Thus far, we have described some of the forces that have challenged the viability of social casework. We have discussed its elasticity, its ever-widening scope which it could achieve because it is an open-ended system of thought and action. However, some of the newer developments or off-shoots represent a narrowing of focus and an impoverishment of thought and understanding. We now will try to develop a statement that might give perspective to social casework in terms of its essential core and its role in the social welfare complex.

The Essence of Social Casework

The founders of social casework had a vision and a long view. In Mary Richmond's classic definition she spoke of the process which develops personality through adjustments, effected individual by individual, between men and society. She saw the need for a method that was in sharp contrast to wholesaling and the need to slip from under the then domination of the economists because casework has shaped too often by wholesalers. In 1920 she wrote of the potentialities of understanding clients from the viewpoint of small-group psychology, a field that had yet to be developed and which now gives a foundation to family-centered casework, among others. She saw it as only natural that caseworkers should turn more and more to psychiatrists and that they would continue to need their help in the analysis of mental mechanisms of the individual. In 1924 she wrote a statement that is as apt today in its wisdom as it was then. There was a

> great wave of enthusiasm for wholesale measures of reform—a wave which passed over this country between the years 1905 and 1914. That wave brought with it many changes which made better social casework possible, but some of the leading social reformers of the period lost their heads to this extent—they were sure that legislation and propaganda, between them, would render social work with and for individuals quite unnecessary, and they did not hesitate to say so. One of my fellow directors, on the monthly all-day trips that I used to take at that time to the meetings of the board of a large hospital for the insane, was in the habit of declaring with a magnificient air that "prevention was the watchword of the hour." Perhaps this mouth-filling phrase was responsible for the fact that I could not interest him in providing therapeutic occupations for the vacant-eyed and vacant-handed women inmates of the hospital. During all that

period, I know, it was uphill work to interest either the public or the social reformers in any reform that dealt with people one by one instead of in great masses. It was a time of slogans. A professor published a book on the Abolition of Poverty in which war was no more than mentioned, and he published it, of all years, in the year 1914.

Do not misunderstand me. I am as eager to see poverty eradicated as anyone can be, but the verb "to abolish" has for its synonyms "to repeal, to revoke, to rescind, to recall, to abrogate, to annul," and I submit that poverty is not a political or even a social status, to be abolished or rescinded by an amendment to the Constitution of the United States or by a presidential proclamation. You cannot "lay the axe to its root" in those ways because it has a thousand roots. It is like some noxious weed, which can be eradicated in time with patient labor, but only after cultivating and enriching the soil in which it now grows. Prevention is another of those words which, as used in proverb and slogan, has been much abused. Who that is familiar, for instance, with the history of the tuberculosis campaigns in this country can ever place "prevention" and "cure" in antithesis to each other again? The two processes interplay at every turn, and cure, in and of itself, is a form of prevention, for we learn how to prevent by honestly trying to cure. In other words, prevention is one of the end results of a series of processes which include research, individual treatment, public education, legislation, and then (by retraced steps) back to the administrative adaptations which make the intent of legislation real again in the individual case.

The interplay of these wholesale and retail processes is an indispensable factor in any social progress which is to be permanent.[16]

Social casework represents first of all a distinct view of man. The values embedded in social casework are fundamental and enduring and grew out of our Judeo-Christian heritage. Man is the essential unit of concern, the person, who is valuable and to be valued by society. He needs for survival many things, among them a sense of worth and dignity, a sense of self and an identity, and an opportunity to make choices regarding the direction of his life in order to achieve a sense of self-realization. Social casework is the instrumentality in social work through which such value commitments can be exercised and through which personal growth and fulfillment can be realized.

Social casework as it was conceived and as it has developed is primarily a method of individualizing human need and individualizing social services. There has never been and there will never be an era in which this is no longer a basic requirement. Social casework can also be a therapeutic method, central in such an intent, or as a by-product of other actions in behalf of an individual or family. Out of the commitment to individualization grows the technical imperative to engage in a process which came to be called differential diagnosis. There we are committed to a bifocal view of man—to the psychological and social factors that are relevant to his situation. Some aspects of the psychosocial diagnosis have been well developed; the integrative aspects are less well developed since we do not yet understand fully the complex interrelation of personality and social milieu. There can be no by-passing or substitutes for the ongoing diagnostic process without violating the commitment to individualization.

We are equally committed to differential treatment or casework management, or intervention. Here we have an ever-broadening range of modalities to choose from as to dimensions of time, place, frequency, intensity, focus, level of intervention, unit of intervention, use of interpersonal processes exclusively or in conjunction with social provision, and so forth. In all of this, there is the centrality of the helping relationship, a purposeful and consciously directed process involving the use of professional self through which growth and change in the individual can take place. Our goals are the enhancement of better personal and interpersonal functioning, a strengthening of the adaptive capacity, and a greater potentiality for self-direction.

The Unique Contribution of Social Casework

The foregoing capsule statement of the essence of social casework leads us to consider its unique contribution, which is its role as a humanizing force. All of our mighty endeavors in the social welfare enterprise are geared to the enlargement of human welfare. But it is very easy in the heat of battle on the policy, legislative, or administrative fronts to lose touch with what we are about. To quote a recent paper of Henry Maas: "To keep humanistic ends in view we need to keep perspectives on the person in the forefront of our thinking."[17] The social caseworker is the message bearer and the interpreter of basic human needs and is in the enviable, opportune position by commitment, training, and function to keep this perspective of understanding alive and highly visible.

Any field or profession that represents the humanistic point of view of fulfills a humanizing function is sorely needed especially in the world today with its ever-increasing technology, automation, and concomitant impersonality. The chief complaint from many segments of society is the feeling of alienation and dehumanization. We therefore urgently need institutions in society that can counteract this trend. From this point of view, it becomes very worrisome to listen discussions of the widening split between the clinical functions in social work and other social welfare functions, with the suggested solution that indeed this schism should be acknowledged and each should go its own separate way. The splitting of clinical functions from the rest of social welfare would deprive us of a crucial source of understanding and nourishment which we need to feed back into social policy and program development. To quote Alvin Schorr again: "It is precisely in day-to-day practice that we should find what is wrong with yesterday's policy. Practice and policy are—or ought to be—symbiotic."[18]

Social caseworkers need simultaneously two essential attributes: a capacity for righteous indignation and a capacity for compassion. Compassion is the core feeling that underpins the empathic response needed for sensitive, individualized casework. Righteous indignation arises in response to the apprehension of forces that impinge upon, undermine, or destroy individual or family integrity. A lack of either effective state, or a split in roles that emanate from these states, would be tragic for social work and would undermine and weaken the profession.

It is now time to sum up this paper. It can best be done in the words of the late Charlotte Towle, which reflect succinctness and wisdom:

> Among professions social work has had very little stability. It has been continuously in the making and remaking. It has never really had a chance to jell. Its orthodoxies have been relatively weak and its segmentation, as implied in specialization, short-lived. The tempo of its growth, always under necessitous circumstances, disposes it to ready identifications, both as a means to learning and as a defense. . . . It is vulnerable to new integrations; here lies its potential for growth or regression. Therefore it will take the best of us to keep our bearings in these eclectic times in which new integrations will take place. It is to be hoped that in synthesizing we will not become synthetic; that in retaining and sloughing off we will continue to build social work as an organic whole. This implies maintenance of the difference of the parts. Integration is not to be confused with coalescence. There is nothing like fusion to gum up the works. It is time for judicious extensions and discards.[19]

Notes

1. J. Scott Briar, "The Current Crisis in Social Casework," *Social Work Practice* (New York: Columbia University Press, 1967), p. 19.
2. Alvin Schorr, editorial, *Social Work,* XI (July 1966), 2.

3. Helen Perlman, "Casework Is Dead," *Social Casework,* XLVIII (Jan. 1967).

4. Elizabeth Herzog, *Some Guidelines for Evaluative Research* (Washington, D.C.: U.S. Department of Health, Education and Welfare, Children's Bureau, 1959), p. 95.

5. Henry Meyer, Edgar Borgatta, and Wyatt Jones, *Girls at Vocational High: An Experiment in Social Work Intervention* (New York: Russell Sage Foundation, 1965).

6. Alvin Schorr, "Mirror, Mirror on the Wall—," *Social Work,* X (July 1965), 112.

7. Mary MacDonald, "Reunion at Vocational High," *Social Service Review,* XXXX (June 1966), 188.

8. Ruth Goldman, "Patient Concepts and Their Relationship to Therapist Variables" (unpub. doctoral diss., University of California, Berkeley).

9. Lydia Rapoport, "The Concept of Prevention in Social Work," *Social Work,* VI (Jan. 1961), 3–12.

10. David Kaplan, "A Concept of Acute Situational Disorders," *Social Work,* VII (April 1962).

11. See, for example, Helen Perlman, "Freud's Contribution to Social Welfare," *Social Service Review,* XXXI (June 1957); see also Lionel Trilling, *Freud and the Crisis of Our Culture* (Boston: Beacon, 1955).

12. Robert Wallerstein, "The Current State of Psychotherapy: Theory, Practice, Research," *Journal of American Psychoanalytic Association,* XIV (Jan. 1966), 198.

13. Perlman, "Freud's Contribution," p. 197

14. Quoted in Wallerstein, "Current State of Psychotherapy," p. 215.

15. Allen Wheelis, "The Place of Action in Personality Change," *Psychiatry,* XIII (May 1950), 145.

16. Mary Richmond, *The Long View* (New York: Russell Sage Foundation, 1930), pp. 586–87.

17. Henry Maas, "Social Work Knowledge and Social Work Responsibility," *Journal of Education for Social Work,* IV (Spring 1968), 47.

18. Schorr, *Social Work* editorial, p. 2.

19. Charlotte Towle, "Implications of Contemporary Human and Social Values for Selection of Social Work Students," *Social Service Review,* XXXIII (Sept. 1959), 264.

3 *In Defense of Social Work:* An Examination of Stress in the Profession

No other profession is as self-examining and critically self-conscious as social work. There are many reasons for this phenomenon. In part, it relates to the profession's young history, to its ambiguous position in society, and to its multiple purposes and functions. Social work, operating in the vortex of social change, seeks to move, modify, and "mop up" the residue of social change. In more elegant and "scientific" language, social work activities consist of provision of resources, restoration of functioning and prevention of dysfunction, and promotion of social well-being.[1] These are formidable goals and expectations.

Criticism comes from both within and without the profession. Social work, more than older, socially valued, and traditional professions, is on the firing lines.[2] Pot shots, such as Marion Sanders's article in *Harper's Magazine*,[3] may irritate, amuse, or concern. Bigger blasts of censure are often fired by allied and related disciplines. For example, on the theme that social work is expected to be in the nature of "all things to all men," Iago Galdstone, a social psychiatrist, in a friendly remonstrance, chides us that "social work has a champagne pretension and a rootbeer performance."[4]

But the really "big guns" of criticism are fired within the social work profession. There has been much social work literature of a self-diagnosing nature highlighting our inadequacies and lacks. Moreover, much of social work self-criticism and introspection has been in the nature of professional self-castigation. In contrast, there have been very few efforts at self-study of a more objective and self-accepting nature. For example, we have had a plethora of professional papers emphasizing our neglect of the truly "social" dimension in social work. There have been only two

Source: Presented on June 16, 1959, as a lecture at the School of Social Welfare of the University of California, Berkeley. Reprinted, with minor changes, from *Social Service Review,* XXXIV (March 1960), 62–74. Used by permission.

papers in recent years which examine social work as "work" in which a delineation is made of some of the stresses inherent in the profession as it is organized and practiced. Dr. Charlette Babcock and Esther Schour, in their masterful companion articles, made an important contribution to professional self-understanding.[5] More recently, there has been increasing study of the profession as a social institution in society. Sociologists and other workers have added knowledge and insight to our professional "self-portrait."

This paper is in the self-examining tradition of the social work profession. An attempt is made to describe some of the stresses inherent in the social work profession, to consider their nature and source, and to identify some of the dilemmas and paradoxes with which the social work profession is confronted. Hans Selye in his book, *The Stress of Life,* tells us that "knowing what hurts you has an inherent curative value."[6] By identifying the nature of this stress we seek to supplant self-castigation by more compassionate professional self-understanding and thus to reduce the negative impact of inevitable stress.

To this end, stress will be examined as it arises from the ambiguous roles of social work in society; as it emerges out of the nature of social work activities and is contained in the nature of the problems with which social workers deal; as it emanates from limitations of knowledge and professional equipment; and, finally, as it is lodged within the nature and structure of the social work profession.

Stress Related to the Position of Social Work in Society

Social work, in contrast to other professions, is often designated as the only completely socially oriented profession. Such a statement refers to the fact that social work, as its major tasks, renders social services and fosters social change and, in its focus throughout, is deeply concerned with the social functioning of man. At the same time, social work is also concerned with the adequacy of those social institutions which intimately affect the functioning of the individual. Charlotte Towle once characterized social work as the profession which embodies and expresses the social conscience of society.[7] Perhaps this conception endows social work with a kind of loftiness of purpose and marks its direct lineage with organized religion, ethical tradition, and democratic values.

It also puts an immense responsibility and burden on the profession as one whose task is to affirm and implement moral and social values to which society itself may give only contradictory or partial expression and support.

The role of embodying the conscience of society may be a lofty, but thereby isolated and unenviable, role. It requires a commitment to a particular moral and political stance. Thus, social work seeks to embrace and implement some principles and values which may be essentially unpopular and uncongenial to the dominant social order. Hence, in some respects, social work seems to be outside of the mainstream of society. The profession symbolically serves as an ever-present reminder of society's failures and lacks in its social and moral responsibilities. Those so reminded may react with individual or collective guilt which, as we know clinically, often mobilizes anger, distrust, and negation as secondary defenses. This particular role of the profession, as has been observed, gives it the attributes of a minority group in society. A minority group is ambivalently tolerated or feared; it may be isolated or outrightly depreciated or attacked. This factor has also been commented upon by Herbert Bisno, who asserts that the minority status position of social work is an additional insecurity added to the burden of daily professional tensions and frustrations.[8]

The reference to the minority status of social work has also another implication. It has been noted that social workers ideologically tend to identify with the problems and needs of the economically and socially disadvantaged groups which they largely serve. They tend not to identify on matters of social policy with other status-seeking middle-class groups, with other professions, or with the dominant socioeconomic class.[9] Thus, as a profession in society, social work holds a position of marginality. In addition, its social views tend also to alienate social workers as individuals from their own class and intimates.

The ambiguous position of social work in society has been identified by Wilensky and Lebeaux as a dilemma of another kind. They see it as arising from a kind of ideological dualism which characterizes our conception of social welfare. On the one hand, organizations for social welfare are conceived of as a "residual agency, attending primarily to emergency, temporary functions, and are expected to disappear when the regular social structure [family and industry] is again working properly."[10] This conception is consistent with the traditional American ideology of individual responsibility and initiative. On the other hand, there is another conception which views social welfare organization and services as a proper, legitimate, ongoing function of modern industrialized society in which the individual is not expected to provide all his needs for himself within the institutions of family and work. The authors point out the antithetical nature of these views and the attempt, in practice, to combine them and to tread a middle course.

This ambivalence has its effects on public social policy and has its impact on individual social workers charged with interpretation and carrying out of programs which may have contradictory and shifting purposes. Many specific instances can be cited. A most familiar one is the shifting purpose of the Aid to Dependent Children program, in which enhancement and preservation of family life as one goal is undermined in the insistent push to make mothers self-supporting. Here we see the ambivalence in social welfare philosophy as between makeshift and temporary aid versus the acceptance of incomplete families which need sustained support as a fact of modern life. As a result, the social worker is often caught in the cross-purposes of philosophy and program. The stress here is immediate and omnipresent, since this kind of conflict affects the social worker's daily operations in evaluating and meeting family needs.

If social work serves as the expression of the "conscience" of society, it may also carry a greater degree of accountability to the community. Yet the tasks with which it is charged and for which it may be held to account may be unclear or contradictory. For example, social work is charged with playing a decisive role in social change, but the community may not agree with social work as to the direction social change should take.

Within recent years especially, there has been considerable agitation within the social work profession regarding the weakening or abandonment of social work's more traditional role in social reform and social action. Some believe a shift in social work from "cause" to "function" with its concentration on methods and techniques has led to a kind of neutralism in matters of broad social policy. Most of the literature on this point is strongly exhortative in nature, emphasizing the need for the profession to concern itself more actively with larger social problems and their alleviation. Other contributors to this theme have commented on some of the existing social factors that impede or discourage social action, such as the contemporary conservative social climate; the less gross, more subtle, and infinitely more complex nature of social problems; the changing nature of social reform efforts requiring organizational and group methods instead of personal initiative and leadership; the changing culture within the social work profession which may frown on militancy, which is at variance with a more scientific, validated, fact-gathering, and educational approach.[11]

The essential dilemma here is between the role of social work as a molder of culture and the recognition that social work as a social institution is also markedly shaped by prevailing cultural influences. If the prevailing contemporary American culture is one which is striving toward conformity, so, too, will the social work profession reflect such conformity-strivings. Conformity needs may lead to a reluctance to pioneer or to engage in social action. The prevailing and dominant values of conformity will also find expression in the profession's own goals, such as striving toward professional respectability and social acceptance. It could be speculated further that conformity as a value might be more readily assumed by a profession in a minority position as a way of gaining greater status. Another factor operates in the dilemma of conformity versus social change, and this one is lodged within the nature of social work methodology. Both individual and group processes are oriented heavily toward strengthening adaptive capacity. Moreover, social work has taken on some of society's functions of social control. Adaptation and control, therefore, even if dynamically and not statically conceived, become not only a value for the client groups but also a norm for the profession's own behavior.

Stress as Inherent in the Nature of Social Work Activity

The major core of social work activity consists of provision of various basic personal and social resources for those unable to provide for themselves and of restoration of social functioning in individuals and groups whose behavior, through a combination of inner and outer circumstances, has become maladaptive.

Dr. Charlotte Babcock noted some years ago the impact on social workers of being constantly confronted with the problem of human need and misery.[12] This problem is worthy of deeper study. It often goes unrecognized as a source of stress because social workers handle it through adaptive mechanisms which they have developed as individuals and which they have acquired through the process of becoming professionalized. Even when adaptation is "successful," there are hidden consequences which may be costly and which may be yet another source of stress.

In addition to being confronted with the chronicity of known unmet human needs, social work continually strives to identify and address itself to less well-defined and latent human need. This shifting concern is an outgrowth of the ever-changing nature of social problems and needs and the increasing complexity of these problems. Thus, as some need-fulfilling services are recognized and institutionalized by society and the polity, social work surges forward into other areas of social disorder or need. In the current view of social work purpose and activity, it is clear that present-day activity is not finite and, therefore, we shall never "put ourselves out of business."

Thus, far from having adequately solved the core tasks of provision and restoration, we are now in addition being challenged within and outside our profession to assume responsibility for activities defined as prevention of social ills and promotion of social well-being. The push toward preventive and promotional activities may also be related to the dissatisfaction with and inadequacy of our curative and restorative efforts.

There is another hidden source of stress in the shifting nature of need and in the kind of more contemporary distress which many clients bring to social workers. Increasingly, our clients come from the middle class. David Riesman characterizes the prevailing adaptive mode of the middle class as being "other-directed." He sees the middle class as searching for direction, reassurance, and response.[13] Dr. Allen Wheelis, in describing the American social character, stresses the contemporary difficulty in achieving a coherent sense of self, in finding a purpose in life to which firm commitments can be made and around which a sustaining mode of living can be forged.[14] Our middle-class clients, whose needs are often related to internal distress, are exemplary of problems of "anomie," and of "identity crisis.[15] These clients are often in search of norms, values, standards for behavior, and meaning in life. They express feelings of despair, and they press for answers to problems that social workers, coming from the same middle class, may not have solved for themselves. Dealing with such problems arouses anxiety and a feeling of helplessness out of too close an identification. It may present even more of a strain and a challenge than finding resources for unmet physical and material needs.

Social work is a helping profession which demonstrates the helping role in the giving of service to individuals and groups. All professions are concerned with giving service. Social work, however, is deeply committed to the giving of service in a very particular way. In its value system, body of knowledge, and techniques, there is central concern with the psychology of giving and receiving help.[16] This involves understanding and utilizing the helping relationship in a conscious and purposeful manner with the goal of enlarging the individual's capacity for self-management.

The helping relationship is the central dynamic in the helping activity. The social worker is the direct instrument of professional help. His focus must therefore be on the helping relationship: its meaning, its vagaries, its potential for further growth and self-direction. Purposeful use of relationship calls for a high capacity in the social worker for the tolerance and absorption of the onslaught of all kinds of negative feelings, massive anxieties, and needs by clients and groups; it calls for a high degree of self-awareness and self-control. In order to master the controlled, conscious, and imaginative use of self, the social work practitioner must possess a high degree of maturity and a deep sense of personal and social responsibility. The adequacy of social work operations, therefore, rests in large measure on the individual social worker's success in integrating appropriate professional values, attitudes, and knowledge with his private value system and characteristic ways of functioning. In that sense, what we do is what we are. Here the stress lies, first, in the high demands made for professional maturity and, second, in the necessity for harmonizing personal capacity and inclination with professional behavior and values. This type of stress is both mitigated and enhanced in the institutionalized framework of social work education and of agency practice, to be discussed later.

Stress Related to Social Work Knowledge and Tools

Social workers, particularly social work educators, are continually trying to identify the knowledge base on which the profession rests. The primary knowledge of the profession, empirically acquired, is that of the immense range of human problems as they are revealed by the individual in his situation and as they emerge in their cumulative aspects. The specific knowledge needed for the many problem-solving activities of the profession has to be drawn from numerous allied disciplines concerned with the human organism and with society. As the complexity of problems increases and as the profession's problem-solving activities expand, the demand for new and greater knowledge becomes imperative.

Two problems emerge here. Social work understandably has not been primarily concerned with systematic knowledge-seeking or theory-building. We have not yet been able to systematize and conceptualize this rich empirical knowledge, sometimes referred to as "practice wisdom." Instead, social work has relied heavily on knowledge contributed by the behavioral and social sciences. For our purposes such knowledge as we need to use from each science is partial. But, in addition, we are limited in the use of knowledge from other basic sciences because we have not been steeped in the full discipline of that science. This factor also limits the ease and readiness with which the profession can translate knowledge from other fields and adapt it for use in social work practice. Thus, we are constantly confronted by limitations of our own knowledge, by limitations of our knowledge of other sciences, as well as by gaps between what is theoretically known and understood and what has been translated into principles of practice or operational tools.

In addition to the problems presented by the need for new and greater knowledge, the source of this knowledge and its translation for use, there is the problem of the changing nature of knowledge and its advancement. Helen Perlman recognizes this potential stress when she states, "Knowledge, no sooner grasped, leaps forward again to excite new pursuit, and this is both the gratification and the frustration of trying to work on problems-in-change."[17]

There is a lag not only in needed knowledge for the tasks at hand but also in the techniques at our disposal. Social work functions call for a wide area of competence in even a larger area of problem-solving activities. This is an ever-expanding horizon, not only in the scope of our activities, but also in the shift in viewing and approaching the problem. For example, social work has always assessed the problems in its purview from a psychosocial point of view. The knowledge regarding individual behavior and that regarding social institutions and processes have been very differently conceptualized, particularly as to principles which guide action. In addition, there is no conceptualized knowledge, operationally useful, which adequately explains the interrelatedness of these two fields. This is a particular hardship to social work since this is the precise area which it needs to understand and with which it needs to deal professionally. We have paid closer attention alternately to one aspect or to the other. As our focus shifts from thinking about the individual in his adjustment to a broader dimensional view of the individual as a participant in an interactional field of psychological and social forces, we need differently conceptualized knowledge and a different approach and techniques. Therefore, as the scope of our interests and problem-solving activities increases, both knowledge and technique lag. Tension arises from the recognition of what needs to be done and from the realization that our knowledge and methods are inadequate to the demand.

Stress Lodged in the Institutional Nature and Structure of the Social Work Profession

One of the deep struggles of the social work profession has been its search for a professional identity. This struggle has taken various forms. One task has been to establish the role and position of social work in our society. Another has been the struggle to define the boundaries of its operations. A third has been the task of differentiating itself clearly from other, older, and more traditional helping professions. This search for identity has led to a preoccupation with defining the profession of social work and emphasizing its uniqueness.

The problem of achieving identity is always a major task for the young, whether it be for an individual or for a young profession. It is doubly difficult for a profession that moves toward maturation in a period of marked social change. The social work profession is trying to find its boundaries in a period of cultural change while it simultaneously is charged by society to contribute to the furtherance of profound social changes.

Thus, the profession strives after stability and definition of role and function and, concurrently, and of necessity, strives toward the enlargement of the field of its operations. The search for professional identity may be a means to achieve professional maturity.[18] However, it may also be an expression of a cultural response to anxiety engendered by the phenomenon of rapid and basic social change.

While we are concerned with differentiating ourselves from other helping professions, there is at the same time a great pressure or surge toward interdisciplinary functioning, both in multidiscipline settings in which social work operates and on the community level. This close and common activity again frustrates and blurs the continuing need for the maintenance of differentiation. There is also the additional factor of the increasing "socialization" of the other professions. They, too, are becoming concerned with the "whole" of man and with man as a social being. They, too, share in a common fund of knowledge about society and individual behavior which social work considers basic to its operations.

Thus, the definition of uniqueness becomes a more difficult and, in some respects, a spurious endeavor. While attempting to refine such a definition, social work is simultaneously forced to become increasingly concerned with the recognition and identification of its commonness with other helping professions.

One of the characteristics of social work as it strives toward professional maturation is its increased "professionalization," which involves the increasing application of systematic and scientific procedures to its techniques of operation. "Professionalization" is achieved through professional education, continued in-service training, research, and theory-building. This process is unquestionably valuable and important, but in some quarters there is concern about what possible losses might ensue. For example, during my stay in England I was continually challenged by thoughtful English social workers who expressed anxiety about the "overprofessionalism" of the American social worker. Not all such expressions were examples of resistance to matters American or a fear of American "exports." Some of this anxiety was a response to American social work literature and American social work scholars and practitioners working abroad, simultaneously welcomed and feared. To many English social workers, Americans appear overly immersed in and narrowly preoccupied with technical concerns and refinements. This is seen as resulting in a weakening of humanistic philosophy, social concern, and identification with broad social problems.

From an entirely different vantage point comes a similar concern. Dr. Gerald Caplan suggests that "professionalization increases the distance between the professional person and the client."[19] Some distance or objectivity is appropriate and necessary. It can become problematic at times when it serves to block the social worker in his emphatic and correct perception of his client. Dr. Caplan discusses this phenomenon in reference to mental health consultation, which has as one of its objectives the reduction of the distance between the helping person and the person served.

Increasing professionalization, therefore, on the one hand enhances our status, affirms our identity, and increases our effectiveness in large measure. At the same time, however, it tends to remove us from the impact and sense of urgency and need of those whom we are charged to serve. A kind of immunization takes place which enables the social worker to deal more objectively and effectively with a particular problem, but this immunization or insulation may also somewhat dilute our social concern and feelings of social responsibility.

Within the social work profession there exists a rather explicit demand that its practitioners be both generalists and specialists. The argument over generic versus specific in both education and practice is like a tired horse, beaten nearly to death. Often, when the question is discussed, the specific referent is obscure. *What* should be generic and *what* must be specific are not always clearly stated. The fact is, the profession is moving simultaneously in both directions, and perhaps this movement is inevitable. The movement toward a generic social work profession is taking place most clearly in professional education with its emphasis on teaching generic concepts and principles, and in professional organization with the amalgamation of formerly specialized membership organizations. Thus, the two major unifying forces—education and professional organization—move toward a broad base and a generic conception of social work.

At the same time, social work practice is becoming increasingly specialized, particularly as it moves into newer areas and newer secondary settings, such, for example, as rehabilitation. It is axiomatic that advancement in any technical sense can come only through increasing specialization. It is only increased specialization, bringing with it depth and knowledge and precision of skill, that will develop and improve social work practice. Despite the acceptance of the urgent necessity to move in this manner (and such is the inevitable movement of all scientific endeavor), there prevails some mistrust and suspicion of this development. Social workers are continually reminded that they must have expert knowledge and competence in all areas of problem-solving activities. There may be some valid component in such exhortations. However, such unrealistic expectations may reflect anxiety which pushes toward conformity, sameness, "togetherness," and a leveling that can result in premature standardization and mediocrity.

These divergent views and tendencies, whatever their merits, do need to be harmonized and reconciled in any given situation. This obvious fact of professional life is presented here only to emphasize the existence of contradictory and conflicting demands.

Social work is practice undertaken in a social agency. This classic definition puts professional practice within an institutional framework and specific setting. Other professional persons may function as individual or private practitioners, or within institutions. They achieve additional professional status and security through licensing or registration from a legally constituted authority. For social workers, it is the agency which makes practice possible and which is the source of sanction or censure. Social workers, therefore, have to maintain a dual identification and loyalty, both to the agency and to the professional body, with the primary tie being to the agency.

All institutions have both supportive and tension-producing features. In social work, one of the sources of tension is the lack of consistent professional attitudes and values within social work agencies and institutions. The lack of professionalism is most often noted on the practitioner level. However, much of social work administration and social-policy determination, as well as elaboration of procedures, is done by laymen. These laymen may function on high administrative levels or may exert their influence as members of agency boards. What may be laid down as desirable program goals and procedures may be at variance with professional values and professional conceptions regarding the nature of and the needs of human beings. Professional staff members may not always be able to make their conceptions strongly explicit or to influence policy and administration. The practitioner then must work within a framework which in part may be incompatible with professional values, ethics, and standards.

Another source of stress is the often-discussed problem of the social worker's independent and responsible functioning, held as a value but often impeded by agency hierarchical structure and tradition. The most prominent feature of this area of stress is the system of prolonged supervision. The problem, which is receiving more adequate attention and study now will not be elaborated here. Since the Babcock article on "Social Work as Work," in which supervision is identified as a source of stress for many workers, much more material has appeared on this topic. The chief area of concern is the prolonged dependency on supervision, which is viewed as a detriment to self-dependence and full professional maturation.

Another facet of this problem has to do with career advancement in social work. As part of the sociologist's portrait of the profession, referred to earlier, there is a growing body of information about social workers. Thus, we are learning about how the social work profession is regarded by segments of the public, what kinds of career patterns social workers follow, and a host of other data. However, the motivation for becoming a social worker has never been studied in depth. The explicit motivation for entering the field seems to stem from an impulse related to a wish to help people or to be involved in solving social problems. One may speculate that the impulse, however expressed, is a derivative manifestation of a creative urge which finds fulfilment in creating order and harmony. We sometimes emphasize, but not often enough, the creative components in social work practice and, indeed, often define social work as being both science and art.

All creation takes place within a framework, within a controlling medium, and within some structure and laws, whether they be aesthetic laws or laws governing social relationships or job definition. The question is whether the institutional framework in which social work is practiced allows for maximum expression of the creative urge and potential in the individual or whether it hampers and frustrates the basic urge.

On a less abstract and more concrete level, this problem may find expression in a variety of ways. It seems that the most creative and satisfying professional role for many social workers is the direct-service role to individual clients and groups. This role allows for personal relationships and intimacy of contact, however limited and purposefully directed; a direct connection and perception of the sequence of problem-intervention-solution;

and a direct and total creative use of professional self. Many social workers do not and cannot remain in the direct-service role. As they move up the professiona ladder, other important but less direct helping roles are taken on. One is repeatedly struck by the profound yearning expressed by the older, more advanced social worker for this basic and professionally more satisfying role. Thus view finds support in the study of social work career patterns by Ernest Greenwood. His findings are summarized as follows:

> Most social workers began their social work careers engaging in the giving of direct service to clients. But at the peak of the career the subject who practices at the direct service level is the exception. This phenomenon conforms to facts in other bureaucratically organized professions where career progress raises the practitioner into supervision and administration, and alienates him from practicing the skills for which he was originally trained. The data show that the apex is not ipso facto the most gratifying stage of the professional career.[20]

Professional advancement as provided through agency structure requires profound shifts in role. The shift may be characterized as being from "professional man" to "organizational man," or from the direct-service role to the indirect role and symbol manipulation. This fact is an important source of stress. The conflict therein lies between the demand and need for professional advancement and the yearning for what appears to be a personally and professionally more satisfying endeavor.

There is one more area to which brief attention must be given, and that is professional education in its institutionalized context. Professional education has been exhaustively scrutinized in terms of curriculum development and the psychology of learning.[21] A growing interest is developing in the sociology of learning, which considers the educational institution as a social and cultural environment which can either facilitate or hamper professional objectives and learning.

Professional education can be defined as a socialization process in which adult individuals are inducted into the culture of the profession. This takes place through didactic teaching and direct learning, and through indirect or attendant learning in which appropriate professional attitudes and values are absorbed, largely by identification. Schools of social work exert both pressures and supports. For example, there is the problem of maintaining and reinforcing motivation in relation to the generation of anxiety, and of keeping motivation and anxiety in balance through the social arrangements and patterns of the educational process. The stresses and supports in professional education have been studied from this point of view by Robert Merton and others in relation to medical education. Many observations and inferences in their book[22] have direct relevance to social work education.

One of the major tasks for the student, and a key stress point, is the necessity for blending incompatible or potentially incompatible values and norms into a consistent and stable pattern of professional behavior. There are innumerable such contradictory demands in social work education which cannot be adequately identified here. Two that are of central importance will be considered.

The first is a stress that springs from a unique requirement in professional education for social workers. The student is required to master, both intellectually and emotionally, knowledge regarding the nature of the individual, including the structure and forces of his most intimate, hidden emotional life. Intellectual mastery in this area requires objectivity and the opportunity for creation of distance between learner and subject. However, in social work education there is a contradictory demand, namely, that the student simultaneously maintain an emotionally open, empathic attitude toward clients whom he is learning to serve and that he continually and systematically develop his capacity for self-knowledge and self-awareness. The stress is lodged in the opposing demands for the maintenance of nearness and distance, of involvement and detachment, of rapport and objectivity. This demand is not made to the same degree of students in other professions such as medicine and psychology, which require a more rigorous intellectual effort. Moreover, they offer the student a kind of moratorium in which learning and use of professional self take place in more distinct and sequential stages. Greater distance and objectivity can be maintained because professional service and use of self are delayed. Therefore, the student can more readily protect his own integrity while he is free to learn emotionally stressful material. This delay or moratorium, not available to the social work student, creates other problems for the beginning practitioner in those disciplines. He must later develop the professional attitudes and the elements in use of relationship which require an openness and receptivity in the emotional system, after having learned sometimes too successfully to close this off.

The second problem is the requirement of tolerance for uncertainty. Reference has already been made to lacks in knowledge and technique in social work practice and the stress these lacks impose on the practitioner. To the student, uncertainty poses an additional strain. A student undertakes professional education with the anticipation of acquiring knowledge and techniques which he expects are definitive and established. He soon becomes aware that the uncertainties in knowledge and point of view are very great and that his pressing need for answers will not be met. He must learn to bear a double uncertainty—that of the limits of his own capacity and present knowledge and that of the limitation of the entire field. At the same time, he has to act, make choices and decisions, and implement them in problem-solving which requires, at any given moment, a sense of certainty and sureness. Thus, tolerance for uncertainty has to be developed and cultivated as a necessary part of professional education and practice, without, however, weakening the capacity to act decisively and constructively in behalf of people in need.

Summary

This paper has been concerned with stresses in social work, some of them hidden, remote, and indirect, others, overt, obvious, and immediate. The stresses identified are of varying orders and genesis. Some are lodged in values and philosophy, some, in our culture; others are lodged in the profession's ideology and framework, while others are lodged in the institutional structure in which social work is developed and in which it operates. Some of the stress is inevitable and unalterable. Some is modifiable and remediable. There has been no attempt to order these factors into some kind of diagnosis or to suggest a remedy. Neither diagnosis nor cure is readily available. Professional self-understanding, clarity regarding pressures and forces, with the possibility of increased comfort in professional functioning, must be the goal.

Notes

1. Werner Boehm, "The Nature of Social Work," *Social Work,* II (April 1958), 10–18.

2. The late Albert Deutch, a friend of social work and a militant social reformer, stated that "few professional groups in our population have been subjected to so much unwarranted abuse as the

social workers." See "The Social Worker's Contribution to American Culture"(unpub. paper).

3. Marion Sanders, "Social Work: A Profession Chasing Its Tail," *Harper's Magazine,* CCXIV (March 1957), 56–62.

4. Iago Gladstone, "How Social Is Social Work?" (address delivered at the Alumni Conference, New York School of Social Work of Columbia University, March 26, 1955).

5. Charlotte Babcock, M.D., "Social Work as Work," *Social Casework,* XXXIV (Dec. 1953), 415–22; Esther Schour, "Helping Social Workers Handle Work Stresses," *Social Casework,* XXXIV (Dec. 1953), 423–27.

6. Hans Selye, *The Stress of Life* (New York: McGraw-Hill, 1956), p. 260.

7. Charlotte Towle, *The Learner in Education for the Professions* (Chicago: University of Chicago Press, 1954).

8. Herbert Bisno, "How Social Will Social Work Be?" *Social Work,* I (April 1956), 15.

9. *Ibid.,* p. 14.

10. H. L. Wilensky and C. N. Lebeaux, *Industrialization and Social Welfare* (New York: Russell Sage Foundation, 1955), pp. 98–99.

11. Harry Lurie, "The Responsibilities of a Socially Oriented Profession," and Donald S. Howard, "Social Work and Social Reform," in *New Directions in Social Work,* ed. Cora Kasius (New York: Harper, 1954).

12. Babcock, "Social Work as Work."

13. David Riesman, *The Lonely Crowd* (New Haven: Yale University Press, 1950).

14. Allen Wheelis, *In Quest For Identity* (New York: Norton, 1958).

15. Jose Ortega y Gasset describes crisis as a "condition in which man holds only negative convictions. It prevents him from deciding with any precision, energy, confidence, or sincere enthusiasm what he is going to do. He cannot fit his life into anything; he cannot lodge it within a specific destiny." See *Man and Crisis* (New York: Norton, 1958), p. 87. See also Nathan Ackerman, M.D., *The Psychodynamics of Family Life* (New York: Basic Books, 1958), pp. 11–12, and Erik Erikson, "The Problem of Ego Identity," *Journal of the American Psychoanalytic Association,* IV (Jan. 1956), 56–121.

16. Commission on Social Work Practice, National Association of Social Workers, *Statement on the Definition of Social Work Practice* (New York: The National Association of Social Work, Dec. 1956).

17. Helen Harris Perlman, *Social Casework: A Problem-Solving Process* (Chicago: University of Chicago Press, 1957), p. 27.

18. Charlotte Towle states that social work's concern with professional identity is a reality-based, rather than phobic, concern and is, moreover, indicative of good ego functioning. See "Implications of Contemporary Human and Social Values for Selection of Social Work Students," *Social Service Review,* XXXIII (Sept. 1959), 260–73.

19. Gerald Caplan, *Mental Health Aspects of Social Work in Public Health* (Berkeley: University of California Press, 1956), p. 154.

20. Ernest Greenwood, "Social Work as a Profession: Research in Progress" (unpub. paper presented May 1, 1957, to the faculty of the School of Social Welfare of the University of California, Berkeley).
21. Towle, *Learner in Education.*
22. Robert K. Merton, ed., *The Student Physician* (Cambridge, Mass.: Harvard University Press, 1957).

4 *Teamwork in a Rehabilitation Setting:* A Case Illustration

A rehabilitation program for physically disabled persons invariably requires the participation of many helping professions and the imaginative use of numerous resources both within the rehabilitation setting and in the community. All aspects of a person's life—being, doing, and feeling—are affected by a serious handicap. Restoration, therefore, involves equal considerations of medical, social, and psychological factors.

An effective rehabilitative program demands a "total push" effort. Such an effort requires close and purposeful collaboration of multidiscipline personnel in both the intramural setting and in the community. The recent advances in knowledge in all the helping disciplines, as well as the development of a high degree of specialization, have greatly enhanced the possibility of restoring the patient's health and his ability to function. These technical advances, however, have resulted in an increasing fragmentation of knowledge and a tendency on the part of various disciplines toward separateness, distance, and isolation. Teamwork is an instrument to counteract fragmentation, to reduce distance, and to mobilize appropriate resources for effective care of patients.

Teamwork involves both a philosophy and a process. Leonard Mayo has said, "In essence a team is the outward sign of an inner conviction and philosophy concerning the whole person and how his needs can be best defined and met."[1] Effective teamwork requires a climate characterized by mutual confidence, knowledge of and respect for one's own as well as other disciplines, and the conviction that effective diagnosis, planning, and implementation can be achieved only through joint endeavors. Much has been written regarding the importance of teamwork, its rationale and principles. In this paper, we shall undertake to illustrate

Source: Written with Kate S. Dorst. Reprinted, with minor changes, from *Social Casework,* XLI (June 1960), 291–397. Used by permission.

some of the principles of teamwork by presenting a case illustration.

Background of Patient

William, age 21, was severely handicapped from birth by spasticity due to cerebral palsy. Almost quadruplegic, he was confined to a wheelchair and had only limited use of his hands. His assets were intellectual capacities of at least high-average level and unimpaired speech.

His entire life history was characterized by severe frustration and open rejection by his family. His parents were first-generation immigrants of low socioeconomic position and minimal education. Physically abusive to his wife and son, William's father told him repeatedly that he was worthless, subhuman, a burden to his parents, and predicted that he would never achieve anything. The father regularly threatened the boy with placement in an institution for mental defectives. William's mother, a physically fragile woman, was less hostile, but equally pessimistic about his future. She pitied him and tried to protect him from his father. She had a firm, openly expressed conviction that William could not exist without her and that, in the event of her death, he would "have to go with her."

At age 8, and again at 14, he underwent major surgery, each procedure designed to make ambulation possible. Both attempts (followed by long periods of hospitilization and physical therapy) were ultimately unsuccessful, partly because of the father's active sabotage of the outpatient, physical therapy program. Soon after the second attempt, the boy's mother suffered a severe stroke and became a resident of a custodial ward in the county hospital. There she remained for nine years, deteriorating physically and mentally. William's father paid no attention to her, and the boy concluded that his father had power to dispose of burdensome dependents by way of institutional placement.

Despite continued physical neglect and deprivation, William managed to complete high school. He then attempted door-to-door selling from his wheelchair and also tried to run a newsstand. Neither effort resulted in a reasonable hope of economic independence. When he learned about the rehabilitation ward in the county hospital (then a special demonstration program), he decided to make one more attempt toward physical restoration. Although he was desperately eager for another chance, he was fearful that his admission to the hospital might lead his father to incarcerate him permanently. He timed his application so that admission occurred just after his twenty-first birthday so that he would be able to sign himself into, as well as out of, the hospital.

The major events during the three and a half years following his admission will be described and discussed. The total time span will not be covered. Instead, four periods of varying length will be presented. Each period had significance for the patient as well as for the team.

First Period: Admission plus Six Months

At the first ward conference, William was considered a good candidate for the rehabilitation goals he had outlined in his application, which were self-care (dressing, bathing, and using the lavatory) and relearning to walk. Three months after admission he had mastered many of the self-care techniques; his ambulation, though far from being really functional, had returned almost to the level achieved at the end of his hospitalization seven years previously. This progress, as well as the improvement in his mental attitude, was mentioned in an evaluation conference. It was decided to intensify the self-care training but to discontinue ambulation training, since it appeared certain that the patient could never achieve a useful level of walking. The vocational counselor—provided especially to this ward by the state vocational rehabilitation office—had already had contact with William and had accepted him for vocational rehabilitation. The goal was placement, rather than training. He had started a search for a small retail store which could be operated from a wheelchair.

The decision to discontinue ambulation training was a severe blow to William; he nevertheless continued to work hard at his self-care training. Three months later the vocational counselor began arrangements for the purchase of an apparently suitable store. Concurrently, the social worker helped William apply to the public welfare agency for sufficient funds to live in a boarding home. The ward physician wrote a letter supporting this request.

Thus, William found himself—six months after admission to the hospital which he feared would be the "end of the road"—eagerly anticipating a pleasant living situation, a business of his own, and the beginning of economic independence.

On the day before confirmation of purchase of the store, the counselor discovered factors that precluded its successful operation by a severely handicapped person. William was extremely upset; he discontinued all activities for several days, staying in bed and weeping. He then sought out the psychologist, telling him tearfully that his life seemed shattered; he said he had tried every other kind of therapy and now wanted to try psychotherapy.

After several initial exploratory sessions, the psychologist told William that she thought psychotherapy might be helpful. She explained that her knowledge of his rehabilitation program and goals was not too clear and she, therefore, proposed a meeting at which all staff members concerned, as well as the patient, would be present. He agreed to the plan. Participating in this conference were the patient, the psychologist, the physical therapist, the occupational therapist, the social worker, the vocational counselor, and the physician in charge of the patient's medical rehabilitation program. At the conference, the team worked out a new program. The vocational counselor would continue his search for a suitable small business. Self-care training would continue until the maximum benefit was reached. Physical therapy would continue the program of stretching which had replaced the earlier ambulation program. The patient could stay in the hospital until suitable vocational and living situations were found. Two hours per week of psychotherapy were to be provided.

Discussion. During the first period, initial goals were formulated with the patient by the medical team. These goals were changed in a subsequent evaluation by the team. The shift in goals, with the elimination of functional walking, led to an emphasis on social factors; the vocational counselor and social worker therefore were added to the team. Community resources were enlisted and the team was thus expanded beyond the intramural setting. The authority of the ward physician was used to support social goals, that is, to enlist the cooperation of the public welfare agency. A new goal of psychological growth and rehabilitation was introduced by the "self-determination" of the patient; his participation in the conference made him an active member of the team. The team conference clarified for each member the goals, the next steps, and the function and role of each. It had major significance for the patient in two respects: (1) it provided opportunity for reality testing and orientation which would have value if the patient later became suspicious toward professional personnel; (2) it created a therapeutic milieu, that is, the team evolved in the patient's mind as a kind of "therapeutic family" that planned with him in his behalf. When psychotherapy was added to the patient's program and his emotional rehabilitation became a vital goal, the team leadership shifted to the psychologist, who assumed responsibility for coordination.

Second Period: Fifteenth to Eighteenth Month

William's physical and medical status remained constant during these months. He could dress, shave, and wash himself unaided in two hours. This represented his maximum achievement. Maintenance physical therapy was continued. The vocational counselor pursued his search for a small business. William worked steadily in his psychotherapy, now scheduled three hours weekly.

This period was an eventful one. At the beginning of it, William's mother died. He was agitated and grief-stricken; also he was frantic about his mother's lifelong prediction that he, too, would die when she died. During this crisis he received sympathy and support from patients and staff to whom he freely expressed his anguish.

Soon afterward, the psychologist went on vacation. Arrangements were made for another psychologist to see William on an "as needed" basis. The substitute psychologist learned that, because of shortage of beds in the rehabilitation ward, plans were under way to transfer him to a custodial ward in another building. She knew about his intense, unresolved fear of being "put away" and understood that the transfer at this time would have a devastating effect on him, since his mother had been "put away" and had died in a chronic ward of the same hospital. She was successful in delaying the transfer until the regular psychologist returned. Through informal consultation with the nursing staff, who quickly grasped the problem, she protected William from learning about the proposed transfer.

Upon her return, the regular psychologist interpreted to the administration personnel the destructive effect that the transfer would have upon William. Transfer to a less controlled ward which, in the opinion of the psychologist, would be tolerable to the patient was arranged. Also, permission was given to allow time to prepare him for the transfer; it was agreed that the psychologist would notify the physician in charge about the transfer date. After three weeks of psychotherapy focused on his feelings about the transfer, William himself notified the physician that he was ready for the transfer and he made the change with relative ease. Soon thereafter, his case was reviewed in a progress evaluation conference. At his own request William participated in the conference and ably summarized his achievements. With feeling and eloquence he expressed his gratitude to the staff for "having given me a chance to live." His expression of gratitude at this conference was in striking contrast to his usual responses. Although he had a somewhat jovial manner, he was a profoundly hostile, suspicious, overly dependent, and emotionally labile young man.

The psychologist also requested a change in ward policy for William. Previously, he had not been assisted with self-care. Self-care took four hours daily and it seemed unrealistic to expect him to devote so much time to it. Although the skills required were valuable tools, it seemed desirable to let him judge when to use them. It was considered urgent for him to begin to experience independence in making decisions. Thus, the psychologist recommended that he be permitted to use his self-care skills when he saw fit but to be given such help as he requested. This recommendation was accepted by the nursing staff.

Toward the end of this period, the psychologist made a slight reduction in the patient's therapy time. William reacted with strong feeling, since the change reactivated his long-standing conviction that all professional people are basically insincere and consider handicapped people as worthless. He was intensely bitter and angry, felt rejected and deprived, and turned to patients and other staff members, particularly his social worker, to air these feelings. He also attempted to have the social worker intercede for him with the psychologist who, he felt, was punishing him for some unknown sin. The psychologist and social worker recognized that such "acting out" was inappropriate and that his attempt to use the social worker as an intermediary was unrealistic. The social worker, therefore, gently but firmly refused to intercede. She deflected his attempt to exploit her by redirecting him to the psychologist for discussion of his grievances. He soon became calmer; the wisdom of reducing the therapy time was subsequently confirmed.

Discussion. During this period, a temporary team member was introduced at the time of a crisis in the patient's life when he was coping with strong feelings of loss. Since it seemed desirable to provide "something extra," the substitute psychologist as well as the other staff members gave the patient the emotional support he needed while reacting to his mother's death and the fears her death aroused.

Because the psychologist understood the special meaning to the patient of placement in the custodial ward, she took steps to modify the environmental situation, thus averting additional stress for the patient during this critical period. The nursing staff responded positively to the interpretation of the trauma involved in the pending transfer and kept this knowledge from the patient. The intervention by both psychologists, afforded necessary protection for the patient. The administrative need for bed space was related to the patient's needs and a plan was evoked that permitted time to prepare the patient for the change. By giving the patient some degree of independence in determining his readiness for the transfer, his capacity for self-mastery was enhanced. Meeting with the therapeutic "hospital family" increased the patient's positive feelings toward professional personnel and the experience of encountering unity of purpose among the team members furthered his capacity to trust others.

When the patient's behavior was infantile and unrealistic, the team members were united in their refusal to accept or abet it, agreeing to set limits and to direct him to the proper staff member, who would hear his complaints and help him work through his feelings. Such consistency was therapeutic since it served as an "emotionally corrective experience" for the patient; his hospital family, in contrast to his natural family, presented him with a strong, united, consistent attitude which had the value of enhancing his emotional maturation.

Third Period: Nineteenth to Twenty-sixth Month

Another change in vocational goals became necessary as prospects for securing a store diminished. A plan for the patient to engage in variety selling from an electrically powered car to be supplied by the rehabilitation agency, was proposed. He used his psychotherapist to discuss the new vocational situation.

The social worker helped William to apply to the county welfare department for funds for boarding-home placement and also to secure a home; one was agreed upon after several meetings between the patient and proprietor. After discharge from the hospital, William continued to see the vocational counselor and the psychologist.

An interagency conference was then held, attended by county welfare personnel as well as the hospital social worker, psychiatrist, psychologist, and vocational counselor. The welfare department reported that an evaluation had been made of the home of William's father and that it had been found unsuitable; the father was still openly rejecting of his son. The application for general relief has therefore been granted with provision for the father to contribute financially. The rehabilitation progress of the patient was reviewed and current psychotherapeutic and vocational goals were discussed. The welfare officials agreed to assign the case to a special division so that the agency, rather than William, would be responsible for collecting money from the father.

Soon after William's discharge, the psychologist went on vacation and the substitute psychologist again became available on request. During this time, William's relations with the boarding-home owners deteriorated and he was asked to leave. The only placement that was available was a rest home for the aged and chronically ill. Largely through his own efforts, William located another boarding home and arranged with the proprietors and the welfare agency to move there.

During this crisis, William was upset and anxious but was able to use the substitute psychologist to vent his feelings and to use his hospital social worker to help him work out arrangements for moving. The social worker, the substitute psychologist, and welfare officials maintained close contact with each other, endeavoring to support William through the crisis and to encourage his efforts to be maximally active and independent in making new living arrangements.

Discussion. Events during this period required increasing flexibility on the part of the patient and team members. Another shift in vocational goals was necessary. The patient was faced with another loss, that of the possibility of becoming an independent entrepreneur. Active and intense psychotherapy was provided to help him make the necessary shifts.

Once he had accepted another type of vocational goal, he was understandably eager to begin. He exhibited initiative and capacity for planning by undertaking to do selling on weekends, even prior to discharge from the hospital. At this point, the patient was leading the team.

The interagency conference, which was focused on long-range planning, served an important purpose. The patient's financial and emotional needs were interpreted to the welfare department, which acted judiciously in assuming responsibility for dealing with his father regarding finances. Money had always been an extremely tense area in their relationship. Action to remove such tension provided the possibility of a better future relationship between the patient and his father. In addition, the patient was protected from unnecessary stress during a period when he was realistically coping with many new adjustments to the world outside the hospital.

The patient also showed remarkable initiative and energy in planning for boarding arrangements after the failure of his first placement. The public officials were rather sanguine about the use of the rest home for the aged and chronically ill. Such a placement, however, was psychologically unsuitable and would doubtless have resulted in regression and despair in the patient. His energetic fight to maintain himself in a noninstitutional setting was an expression of his growing strength.

Fourth Period: Twenty-seventh to Forty-eighth Month

The events during this long time-span can only be briefly described. Psychotherapy continued on a supportive rather than intensive basis. Appointments varied from once a month to once a week.

There were periodic crises in William's living arrangements; one home closed and others proved inadequate. The welfare department had no suitable placements available. William kept close contact with the welfare department as he endeavored through his own contacts to find a suitable place to live. Finally, the rest home seemed to the the only available resource. With the support of the psychologist, William accepted placement there as a temporary solution. He was now able to recognize that all persons endeavoring to help him were motivated by a desire to provide for his physical welfare and were not motivated—as his father had been—by a wish to destroy him through incarceration.

Another factor that enabled William to accept temporary placement in the rest home was his growing desire to continue his education. He had had this wish for some time and he now became more serious about it as he found that his variety business was yielding only a minimal income, despite his best efforts. He was seeking more intellectual stimulation than his daily contacts provided. He realized that living in the home, which temporarily met his physical needs, enabled him to focus attention and energy on his further education.

Another, and more radical, change in his vocational goals was therefore indicated. He used psychotherapy to strengthen his decision to pursue and to implement his educational plans. Before making a firm commitment, he wanted to assess his intellectual abilities and his level of academic achievement. Independently, he financed evaluations by a reliable private testing agency to which his psychologist had referred him. Concurrently, he kept his vocational counselor informed of his plans. His decision became firm when test results indicated that college training was appropriate after some junior college preparation.

The rehabilitation agency was apprised of this plan and the staff's cooperation and approval were enlisted. William carried the entire responsibility for planning, suggesting, scheduling, and presiding at an interagency conference which was attended by the vocational counselor and supervisory personnel from the rehabilitation agency, his welfare department worker, and the psychologist who had done the testing. Before the meeting, William arranged for a report of the intelligence and achievement tests to be available.

At the conference, discussion was candid and lively. The following plans emerged: William was to register for a part-time program in a junior college and retain his car and a nominal interest in his variety business; the rehabilitation agency was to provide tuition, books, transportation to school, and the mechanical appliances necessary to aid in written work; and the welfare department was to continue to provide funds for maintenance. It was agreed that if, after a semester, William's academic performance proved adequate, the long-term educational plan would be approved.

The initial school experience presented many complex problems for William; mostly these related to physical management of the environment. His tentative educational goal is counseling work; his severe handicaps would not be a prohibitive factor in this field. William has a long and difficult program ahead, but he is strongly determined to become an economically self-sufficient and socially responsible community member. From his efforts thus far, and the evidence of his impressive maturation, it would seem that the prognosis is favorable.

Discussion. A marked change in team functioning took place during this period. In contrast to the earlier team, this one became almost entirely extramural. With the exception of the psychologist (who represented continuity of relationship[2] to the patient, which was a crucial factor in his progress) its composition changed completely. The hospital social worker was replaced by the social worker from the welfare department; the vocational counseling services continued but were carried by four different individuals; medical and paramedical personnel no longer were active; and the patient emerged as the leader of the team. The patient now mobilized the team in his own behalf, as is exemplified by his activities in presenting his vocational and educational goals at the joint conference. In preparation for the conference, he had fortified himself with documentation of his intellectual capacities and had used the psychologist who had done the vocational testing as "consultant" to the team.

An anology may be drawn between the changing functions of the team and the shifting nurturing and protective functions of the family. The initial hospital team provided physical care and protection for the patient. As his growth and maturation warranted, the team's functions changed to promoting self-direction and initiative. An effective team eventually eliminates the need for its own existence. In this case, the necessary long-term nature of team activity was determined by the severity and permanence of the patient's handicap and the unfavorable nature of the patient's social and economic life circumstances. Nevertheless, he utilized the team to support his inherent capacities for growth and independence.

Conclusions

An impressive array of personnel and agency resources was utilized in the rehabilitation of this patient. Seven distinct professional disciplines, and numerous specialists within the disciples, were involved in his care. The medical personnel included a psychiatrist, an internist, a physiatrist, and a dentist. The nursing profession was represented by registered nurses, vocational nurses, aides, and orderlies. Social work was represented by a medical social worker, a public welfare social worker, and the group worker (the recreational therapist). Other disciplines included physical and occupational therapy. Psychology was represented by clinical psychologists, the vocational counselor, and the psychometrist.

Community agencies were represented as follows: the county medical institutions; the rehabilitation unit; the state vocational rehabilitation office; the county public welfare department. In addition, services were provided by other community resources, such as boarding homes, service clubs, and municipal departments granting peddling licenses. Interested friends, hospital personnel, and patients not only gave general support but became William's customers. Thus we see a wide network of professional personnel, other specialists, health and welfare services, and other community facilities and resources brought to bear on the rehabilitation of one person.

This massive effort, which ensured the achievement of a purposeful and unified rehabilitation program was guided by several principles which may be briefly summarized. A team is a fluid and changing system, both structurally and functionally: to maintain its dynamic energy it needs to be flexible and permit change in the composition, function, and roles of its members. A team creates the climate and the opportunities for a patient's rehabilitation. It also operates as a dynamic force through which a patient's needs are met. It serves as the channel through which needs and services, perceived in a fragmented and partial context, can be related to the total needs of the patient. Coordination of team activities is vital. The greater the number of team members and disciplines, the more cumbersome the process, and the greater the strain on communication, consensus, and implementation. Coordination comes about through team leadership. The specific leadership may change over a period of time; in the case presented, it shifted from the medical personnel to psychological personnel and then to the patient himself. Leadership provides clarity of purpose and goal, and it fosters energetic mobilization of effort and resources. The team leader serves as a catalytic force (or devil's advocate if necessary) in order to create those conditions and services essential to the realization of the rehabilitation goals.

The satisfactory outcome in this case is a tribute to the felicitous combination of the patient's motivation, the enhancement of his capacity through consistent and sensitive management, and the team leaders' provision of appropriate opportunities from which the patient gathered strength for increasing mastery and self-direction of his life.

Notes

1. Leonard W. Mayo, "Rehabilitation and Social Work," *Journal of Rehabilitation,* XXIV, no. 1 (1958), 5.

2. In this connection, Miss Haselkorn has stated: "Handicapped people need the security and continuity provided by a single personality. This person can be any member of the rehabilitation team, but frequently it is the social worker . . . because of [his] psychosocial focus." See Florence Haselkorn, "Some Dynamic Aspects of Interprofessional Practice in Rehabilitation," *Social Casework,* XXXIX (July 1958), 400.

In this case, it was the psychologist who assumed this role and who, in addition, shifted focus from intrapsychic concerns to external reality and community concerns, as this became appropriate. For discussion of the role of the psychologist in the field of rehabilitation, see B. A. Wright, ed., *Psychology and Rehabilitation: Institute on the Roles of Psychology and Psychologists in Rehabilitation* (Washington, D.C.: American Psychological Association, 1958).

II

Crisis Theory and Preventive Intervention

5 Crisis Intervention as a Mode of Brief Treatment

Characteristics of the Theory

Crisis theory, and its application in brief casework treatment, has rapidly gained sizable attention and interest in the last decade. Crisis theory is not as yet a well-formulated or holistic theory which has systematically validated propositions. It probably is premature to dignify it with the term "theory." At best, and pragmatically, it exists as a framework for viewing individuals and families in situations of urgency and stress, and as an approach it leads to the generation of useful practice principles applicable to both clinical work and modes of primary prevention in mental health work. There is no one articulated school of thought with its own disciples, although sizable recognition is given to the seminal work, both research and applied, of Erich Lindemann and Gerald Caplan and their colleagues at Harvard and the Wellesley Human Relations Service. There are increasing numbers of workers in both social work practice and the mental health field who make use of some central notions that are general guidelines to action. The parameters of crisis theory have not been spelled out, and thus the theoretical framework needs to remain open-ended. There is a growing body of literature in social work and in allied fields of social and clinical psychiatry, social and clinical psychology, and psysiological research. Unfortunately, as is characteristic of social work theory, we do not consistently build on the available contribution of our own and allied fields.

Crisis theory as it is emerging is not radically new. It is essentially eclectic in nature, and has come to represent a new synthesis. This feature may be one factor in its general attractiveness

Source: Reprinted, with minor changes, from Robert W. Roberts and Robert H. Nee, eds., *Comparative Theories in Social Casework* (Chicago: University of Chicago Press, 1971), pp. 267–311. Used by permission.

and acceptability among practitioners. it incorporates a good deal of familiar and accepted knowledge and clinical notions as well as relevant principles and techniques geared toward behavioral and personality change. The theoretical framework thus far developed perhaps brings so-called conventional casework theory more into line with the actualities of much of casework practice. For many practitioners who have familiarized themselves with crisis theory, it has provided a rationale, an underpinning, and a conceptual frame of reference which has been useful in structuring and guiding a sizable portion of their practice. For some workers, integration of crisis theory in practice has required considerable philosophical and theoretical reorientation. For others, less firmly or consciously grounded in other theoretical perspectives, it has filled a theoretical vacuum.

Because of the propensity of social workers to latch on enthusiastically to new ideas and even fads, probably out of a sense of frustration and need for approaches that work with better "payoff," there is the danger of uncritical and undifferentiated usage and application as a new panacea. We need more and better systematic and experimental applications if this approach in order to achieve a better developed model. At this point in time, the intellectual work required to specify answers as to when, where, and with whom this approach is a method of choice has not been done. These and other issues are discussed in the last section of this chapter.

Origins of the Approach

Crisis-oriented brief treatment had an interesting beginning from the point of view of the development and convergence of different ideas and separate endeavors over both time and space. The convergence of different concerns was aided by certain catalytic forces centered largely in the burgeoning community mental health movement. The two major areas of convergence were in the fusion of concepts of crisis and concepts of brief treatment.

Concepts of crisis have been developing mainly in studies of population groups or communities confronted with states of disaster or extreme situations. Most of these studies by social scientists gave a description and analysis of the event and its impact from a social-psychological perspective. Some of these studies focused on people confronted by natural disasters such as floods and tornadoes and on extreme situations such as war and concentration camps. There have also been field observations and clinical studies of individuals under stress ranging from extreme life threatening experiences to less catastrophic stresses such as threats of surgery, polio epidemics, or reactions to burns. The prototypical research that generated many new developments was the often cited study of the disaster of the Cocoanut Grove fire in Boston by Lindemann.[1] This study investigated the impact of death and loss on individuals and families and examined the experience of bereavement. The leads in this classic study lay fallow and were not picked up until some years later when the field of social psychiatry developed. Social psychiatrists, with other researchers, then brought a perspective to these studies that elicited some bridging concepts from the more macroscopic events and their meaning in individual and family functioning or breakdown. This perspective generated principles applicable to modes of intervention and prevention. For example, Caplan's early work in crisis intervention in Israel grew out of the experience of mental health work with large population groups of immigrant children in institutions during the postwar period. This work sharpened the recognition of the impact of a crisis on a child's life and on the caretakers and institutional setting. It also discovered a potential for remedial action within the crisis situation.[2] This early work also gave rise to subsequent technical developments which led to the formulation of mental health consultation as a distinct methodology and as an indirect method of intervention in the mental health field.

Concepts of, and references to, brief treatment or brief services have been available in the literature for many decades. In casework, "brief" was linked with service that was understood to be concrete or specific in nature, such as providing resources or referral elsewhere. It was distinctive from psychological approaches, which were traditionally conceptualized as needing to be long term. This dichotomy, and the high prestige and value attached to the long-term psychotherapeutic model, prevented the field from examining the potentialities of brief intervention. However, there were cues in the literature all along and other trends awaited to be exploited. Contributions of early theoreticians such as Bertha Reynolds,[3] the theories of the functional school, and later Helen Perlman's concept of "focus" in problem-solving,[4] highly developed brief service practices by such specialized agencies as Travelers Aid,[5] numerous studies on the vicissitudes of both the waiting list[6] and the actual length of contacts with clients—even highly motivated clients in voluntary counseling agencies—all raised serious questions regarding the model of the ideal casework client and the ideal casework procedure. Further investigation of casework "dropouts" in follow-up studies revealed the astonishing information that numerous clients felt helped by the brief contact and claimed improved personal and social circumstances. Nevertheless, many professionals remained skeptical about such reports, since they conceptualized "dropouts" as indicating a failure to engage clients in long-term casework and because the brief contact had not been purposeful or by plan.

Outside the social casework field, in psychoanalysis and psychoanalytic psychotherapy, there were attempts to reexamine the classical model. Alexander and French's book *Psychoanalytic Therapy* was an early landmark in departing from the psychoanalytic model.[7] Their concept of brief treatment, however, was seen in relation to a long-term classical psychoanalysis, and brief treatment as they described it would be considered long term by present-day practice. Worthy of note in this context was the observation made by Malan in *A Study of Brief Psychotherapy* that in psychoanalysis "the most easily identified tendency, manifested repeatedly as each new advance was made, has been towards an increase in the length of therapy. Thus anyone who tries to develop a technique of brief psychotherapy is trying to reverse an evolutionary process impelled by powerful forces." He noted further that early analyses were achieving therapeutic results with much briefer time, by being more active and ignoring manifestations of both resistence and transference. This, of course, was labeled later as primitive.[8]

Many pressures and forces operated as catalysts in the reexamination of our social work practice and theoretical models: the impelling commitment to serve greater numbers and more population groups, more diverse as to social class, ethnicity, and personality structure; the hopeless and widening gap between needs and manpower resources; research studies which questioned the efficacy of results of conventional treatment modes; pressures for new service structures, service delivery systems and modalities of intervention; expectations that the profession realign the proportion of effort in remedial work to a greater effort in basic provision and modes of prevention. Similar exigencies and pressures have also characterized the mental health field. Therefore it was propitious that there was reactivation of interest in brief methods of casework treatment at a time when a conceptual orientation was available that could put brief treatment efforts into the context of crisis theory. The blending of these two frameworks opened up new perspectives and possibilities in brief treatment work, which, although widely practiced previously, had been used not by conscious intent but largely by default.

Behavioral Science Foundations

As implied earlier, crisis theory represents a synthesis of a wide spectrum of concepts, empirical observations, and clinical insights drawn from the behavioral and social sciences as well as from several practice fields. Rather than listing each concept and identifying its origins and original usage and specific adaptation, this section identifies the range of sources from which crisis theory is drawn and describes, in essence, the central concepts and core notions of crisis theory as it has developed.

Crisis theory, insofar as it requires an understanding of the individual, needs to be anchored in personality theory. Psychoanalytic theory, first as it developed as a theory of the neuroses and in its later evolution into a theory of personality with its explication of personality structure and development of psychopathology, seems still to serve as a most useful base because of the comprehensiveness of the phenomena described. Of particular relevance is the developmental psychology of Erikson with its explication of biopsychosocial maturational stages and potential for crises and the relevant psychosocial tasks required for subsequent maturation and growth.[9] All developments in ego psychology are of great significance in crisis theory. Ego psychology has moved from an explication of the dynamics of defense mechanisms[10] to questions of synthesis, adaptation, and coping.[11] The ego, viewed as either endowed with neutralized energy or endowed with intrinsic energies of its own as an autonomous force, and its complex functions of exploration, manipulation, motility, language, perceptual and cognitive functions, and reality appraisal and testing directed to adaptation, coping, and mastery, becomes a pivotal concept in dealing with the important issue of effectiveness.[12]

Stress theory contributes fundamental concepts to crisis theory, and indeed, the terms are often used interchangeably in some of the literature.[13] The term "stress" is used to denote three different sets of phenomena: (1) it is equated with the noxious stimulating condition, the stressful event or situation, sometimes referred to as "stressor"; (2) it is used to refer to the state of the individual who responds to the stressful event, and thus we talk of the client who responds with feelings or symptoms of stress; (3) more often, stress refers to the relation of the stressful stimulus, the individual's reaction to it, and the events to which it leads.[14]

Stress conditions can be disruptive and cause serious disturbances in biological, psychological, and social functioning with disturbed affects, motor and behavioral reactions, changes in cognitive functioning, and physiological changes. Stress is generally conceived of as a powerful pressure which greatly taxes the adaptive resources of the biological or psychological system. It is considered to be a noxious stimulating condition, one which has pathogenic potential. The term "stress" has its origins in engineering, where its consequences are conceptualized as "strain." The concept has been adapted in physiological research, where the homeostatic model is a central concept.[15] It has been further adapted for use in the psychological realm, where a "steady-state condition" is posited but can be less readily specified.

A vocal critic of the use of the concept of stress in mental health states:

> Of all the metaphors the human behavioral sciences have borrowed from their sister sciences and from literature, none has been more in the need of habitation and name than the concept of stress. Yet in the past its metaphorical habitation has mostly been in the house of hardship, retardation, insult, and affliction, and its name has been synonymous with noxiousness. . . . Stress as the grand metaphor of life and living has found little if any place in a philosophy or psychology of normal development and health.[16]

In the homeostatic model, the potentiality for change, either maladaptive or adaptive and progressive, is thought to reside in the energy that becomes available for change in the fluid personality state which ensues as a result of the disequilibrium. This concept is somewhat at variance with some thinking in ego psychology. One view is that ego functions which are neurosis free *themselves direct and facilitate the adaptational shift* rather than that the energy itself shifts. It has been pointed out that conceptualizations are needed to account for the dramatic shifts that are regularly observed to occur in life . . . spontaneous shifts in personality style during the growth process, particularly during adolescence, sudden improvements in psychotherapeutic patients, transference itself, and the formation and disappearance of symptoms. Stage theories, such as Piaget's or Erikson's, are based upon the assumption that clear shifts such as restructuring or reorganization do occur.[17]

Other relevant and enriching sources for crisis theory are learning theories concerned with cognitive processes and functioning.[18] The sources here are widely diverse and reach back into both clinical and academic psychology from child psychology, the developmental work of Piaget, to the work of ethologists. Motivation, competence, and modeling in social learning theory all seem to deal with more complex formulations, and are therefore more readily useful to the clinician than earlier work of academic learning theorists. The renewed interest in operant or instrumental conditioning is also of interest. It should also be noted that the interpersonal process in psychotherapy is being reconceptualized by some as a form of modification which takes place through learning. Alexander dealt with the psychotherapeutic transactional process in terms of learning theory, emphasizing the role of cognitive insights as a means of breaking up neurotic patterns, the concepts of reward and punishment, and the influence of repetitive experiences.[19]

Crisis theory concepts are applicable not only to the individual but also to the family matrix and probably, with some modification, to larger social systems as well. Many studies have examined the vicissitudes of family life under the impact of crisis.[20] The research in, and concepts of, family structure, interaction, and functioning are of immediate relevance in dealing with the family unit in crisis. Social role theory has an important place in the analysis of family roles,[21] since impairment of social role functioning is usually one consequence of the state of crisis. Furthermore, the concept of role transition and the vicissitudes of role changes throughout the life cycle are considered to be one dimension of stress that may precipitate a state of crisis in an individual or in a family unit.

Another important frame of reference in crisis theory and its application is derived from the public health model of practice. The concept of prevention is central and is conceived of as a continuum of action classified as (1) health promotion; (2) specific protection; (3) case finding, early diagnosis, and treatment; (4) disability limitation; and (5) rehabilitation.[22] The first two categories are in the nature of primary prevention, early diagnosis and treatment are secondary prevention, and disability limitation and rehabilitation are tertiary. In general, most public health activities are directed at designated groups in the community which are considered, on the basis of epidemiological study, to be populations-at-risk. The public health framework can, therefore, be applied for crisis intervention on a primary preventive level for those crises that can be identified and anticipated for a designated, vulnerable population, and the secondary prevention level can be used for brief clinical intervention of crises that are identified through early case finding.

The public health approach represents a modification of what is usually referred to as the medical model. There is a good deal of current criticism of the medical model insofar as it has been co-opted in social work, but there is little clarity as to what is meant. There is no one medical model, but there are various patternings and constructs, some of which are more appropriate to social work formulations than others. For example, David Kaplan developed the concept of the "acute situational disorder.[23] This represents one type of medical model in which crises are conceptualized as akin to acute infectious disease states which are usually self-limiting and which may occur in a healthy person or may be superimposed on long-term chronic disease states. Crisis intervention would be limited to the alleviation of the acute, reactive state without attempting to deal with the underlying, chronic pathology.

Some of the basic concepts in crisis theory will now be delineated briefly. A crisis may be defined as "an upset in a steady state." This definition rests on the postulate that an individual strives to maintain a state of equilibrium through a constant series of adaptive maneuvers and characteristic problem-solving activities through which basic need fulfillment takes place. Throughout the life span many situations occur which lead to sudden discontinuities by which the homeostatic state is disturbed and which result in a state of disequilibrium. The individual may possess adequate adaptive or equilibrating mechanisms. However, in a state of crisis, by definition, it is postulated that the habitual problem-solving activities are not adequate to the task for a rapid reestablishment of equilibrium. The hazardous events or stress factors that precipitate the crisis require a solution that is novel to the individual in relation to his previous life experience and usual and normal repertoire of problem-solving mechanisms.

The hazardous events pose a problem in the current life situation. Because they also may contain a threat to current instinctual needs, they are likely to be linked with old threats to instinctual needs and may reactivate and trigger off unresolved or partially resolved unconscious conflicts. This linkage may serve as an additional burden in the present crisis and may contribute to the overloading of affect. It has been observed in crisis work that old problems which are linked symbolically to the present may be stimulated and may emerge into consciousness spontaneously or can be uncovered and dealt with relatively easily in brief therapeutic work. Thus the crisis with its mobilization of energy may operate as a "second chance" in correcting earlier distortions and maladaptations.

Three interrelated factors produce a state of crisis: (1) one or a series of hazardous events which pose some threat; (2) a threat to current or past instinctual needs which are symbolically linked to earlier threats that result in vulnerability or conflict; and (3) an inability to respond with adequate coping mechanisms.

A hazardous event can be experienced by the individual as either a threat, a loss, or a challenge. A threat may be directed to instinctual needs or to an individual's sense of integrity or autonomy. A loss may be that of a person or an experience of acute deprivation. A challenge may be to survival, growth, mastery, or self-expression. Each of these states has a major characteristic affect. Threat carries with it high anxiety. Loss is experienced with affect of depression or mourning. Challenge is accompanied by some anxiety but carries with it an important ingredient of hope, release of energy for problem-solving, and expectation of mastery.

Other characteristics of the crisis state, such as the phases of upset during the crisis, phases of problem-solving attempts (both adaptive and maladaptive), and the tasks required for mastery are discussed in the section on diagnosis. Here the state of crisis is conceptualized as a time-limited phenomenon. The individual or family does manage in due time to achieve some solution to the crisis. It may be resolved and a state of equilibrium is once again achieved. The outcome, however, may be variable. Thus, from a mental health point of view, the new state of equilibrium may be the same as or worse or better than that achieved before the crisis. The outcome itself is dependent on numerous variables. Current adaptive capacities and favorable environmental factors are of key importance. Less important in influencing outcome is the nature of the prior personality structure or psychopathology. Most important of all is the need to accomplish certain specific psychological tasks and certain related problem-solving activities. This is discussed in more detail subsequently.

Assessment of the Client in His Situation

Crisis intervention work requires some important modifications in both the concept and the method of diagnosis as developed in conventional casework. Traditionally, diagnosis in casework consists of a psychosocial description which may be blended with a clinical diagnosis based on psychiatric nosology. There is a further blending of both a dynamic and a genetic formulation. The genetic orientation is concerned with origins and causes and is less relevant in crisis-oriented brief treatment. It may be hard to relinquish this view if one is schooled in a developmental psychology of personality structure and functioning. Traditionally, we have been taught to formulate explanations of causal phenomena by way of reference to origins. "Why" is answered by "how one got that way." This kind of diagnosis is an incomplete formulation. According to one psychiatrist, "genetic accounts can be enlightening but all too frequently they 'explain away' without really explaining."[24] In a similar vein, Bandler states that "everything genetic in the client's personality is not operative in his current dysfunction. The past is not only silent, much of it may also be quiescent. What is genetically determined in the formation of the personality is not necessarily dynamically relevant."[25]

What is most relevant in crisis-oriented brief treatment is a way of diagnosing acute situational stress and a way of classifying hazardous events and people's reactions to them. We also need understanding of the process of personality functioning; that is, how ego processes function in transaction with the external milieu and the internal state. Our usual attempt to appraise ego functioning often is no more than an inventory of ego strengths and the specification of the existence and the strength of certain traits without accounting for the person's appraisal of his situation and the restructuring and adaptations he is making. Here we lack the necessary conceptualizations to formulate the interaction of these factors.

It is my belief that some appraisal of basic personality structure and identification of basic defenses as well as habitual adaptive patterns is relevant and important in crisis intervention in order to be able to designate more sharply both the appropriate goals and the techniques for intervention. It does make a difference whether one is dealing with a person in crisis for whom the crisis has laid bare an underlying psychotic personality or whether the current state of disorganization occurs in a person whose habitual capacity for coping and mastery are adequate to his life goals. The goals in either situation may be largely restorative, but such differential knowledge leads to differential thinking and management in regard to reality possibilities. Such a clinical appraisal is not necessary for crisis intervention which may be developed by community caretakers as part of primary prevention efforts beamed at a designated population-at-risk.

The ability to identify personality structure, defenses, and adaptive patterns has usually been based on a systematic investigation—history taking with its vertical and horizontal exploration—with a chronological scanning of development, emotional and social functioning, manifestations of psychopathology, and consideration of both genetic and dynamic factors. Crisis-oriented brief treatment does not lend itself to such a systematic inventory and may not even lend itself to the task of selected history taking, largely because of the crucial factors of time and the need to intervene quickly. Some of the literature on brief treatment still stresses the need for a social and psychological history.[26] These brief treatment methods, however, are not conceptualized as being part of a crisis-oriented approach.

If insights into personality structure, defense, and adaptation are important in addition to understanding the state of acute upset, and if the appropriateness of history taking is questioned, what then becomes the source of information and data for diagnosis in brief treatment? Here, there is a strong case for the experienced and skilled clinician who can generate and test hypotheses quickly on the basis of clinical experience, knowledge of personality organization, and the ability to appraise the significance of the client's behavior in reference to himself, his problem, and the social worker, and to the beginning interaction that is generated in the interview. In addition to overt and conscious communication as a source of information, the worker is alert to marginal clues that may be revealed, and focuses especially on preconscious communication and patterns of behavior that may yield insight about the subjective meaning of the precipitating stresses and the special areas of vulnerability which led to the state of crisis.[27] A major, initial diagnostic task is to develop quickly some working hypotheses about the nature of the crisis, the relevant precipitating stress or stresses, the general adaptive capacity of the individual and reasons for present impairment or inability to cope, as well as the extent and degree of his dysfunction. The next step is to appraise his potentialities for adaptive responses and the availability of salient internal, intrafamilial, and community resources that can be mobilized quickly in order to restore some sense of equilibrium.

Another source of knowledge and data which is highly relevant in crisis intervention is research findings concerning the typical or modal responses of people in crisis. This knowledge offers short cuts to generalized insights and understanding of how people behave and try to cope in a crisis situation, and provides a map or an inventory of likely behaviors and responses. A clinician armed with such knowledge is enabled to explore such clinical data for vertification, testing, or discarding where irrelevant.

First, characteristic signs are present when an individual is in a state of crisis. The emotional signs are high anxiety, tension, shame, hostility, guilt, depression, and so on. The state of upset is also characterized by cognitive confusion wherein the individual is bewildered and literally does not know how to grasp and understand what has been happening to him, how to evaluate reality, or how to anticipate, formulate, and evaluate the possible outcome of the crisis and the possibilities for problem solving. In extreme states of anxiety, in addition to cognitive confusion, there may also be perceptual confusion in the spatial, temporal, or interpersonal sphere.

Second, there are typical phases that characterize the period of upset. In the initial phase there is a rise in tension in response to the initial impact of stress which may result in a peak of anxiety with a concomitant feeling of great helplessness. During this phase, habitual problem-solving mechanisms are called forth. If the first effort fails, there will be an increase in the level of tension with an increase in feeling upset and ineffective. This state may then call forth "emergency problem-solving mechanisms."[28]

Three things are likely to happen: (1) the problem may actually be solved; (2) they may be a redefinition of the problem or a reorganization of expectations and goals in order to achieve need-satisfaction in line with reality possibilities; (3) the problem may be avoided through need resignation and relinquishment of goals. If the problem cannot be solved in any of these ways a state of more major disorganization may ensue.

Third, there is general knowledge of patterns of adaptive and maladaptive coping. Maladaptive coping behavior may take the form of disorganized activities which represent attempts to discharge inner tension rather than solving reality problems. An individual may deal with the hazardous events and his feelings about them with magical thinking or excessive fantasy, avoidance, or denial. He may respond with regressive forms of behavior, with somatization or, in extreme situations, with withdrawal from reality. Coping patterns that are essentially adaptive in nature may be described as follows: the activity of the individual or family is task-oriented; the problem is broken down into component parts, and efforts are made to solve each aspect; the "mental work" is directed toward correcting the cognitive perceptions involving the prediction of consequences and the anticipation of outcomes through cognitive restructuring. Mental work may also entail "rehearsal for reality" and preparation for anticipated activity or affect. The individual or family may seek out new models for identification and for the development of new interpersonal skills as part of problem solving, particularly in crises involving role transition. In general, the pattern of responses for an individual or family necessary for healthy crisis resolution may be described as follows: (1) correct cognitive perception of the situation, which is enhanced by seeking new knowledge and by keeping the problem in the forefront of consciousness; (2) management of affect through awareness of feelings and appropriate verbalization leading toward tension discharge and mastery; and (3) development of patterns of seeking and using help with actual tasks and feelings by using interpersonal and institutional resources.[29]

A fourth area of knowledge that is becoming available is most fruitful for developing diagnostic understanding and for defining implications for treatment. It should be made a priority area for further research in crisis intervention. This knowledge is concerned with the identification of the specific problem-solving tasks that need to be accomplished to achieve a healthy resolution of a specific crisis. For instance, in regard to the problem of bereavement, Lindemann notes that the duration of the grief reaction seems to be dependent on the success with which a person does his "grief work." A normal course of grief reaction begins when the bereaved: (1) starts to emancipate himself from the bondage of the deceased; (2) makes a readjustment to the environment in which the deceased is missing; and (3) forms new relationships and patterns of interaction that bring rewards and satisfactions.[30]

In regard to the problem of the birth of a premature baby in a family, the specific psychological tasks and problem-solving activities necessary for positive crisis resolution have been identified by David Kaplan and are cited in detail as follows.[31]

Phase 1. Mother and infant are in the hospital after delivery. During this critical period the mother is faced with the following psychological tasks: She has to acknowledge that the infant's life is threatened and that survival in the early postnatal period may be uncertain. She has to acknowledge a sense of disappointment and even failure at having been unable to carry a baby to full term. In order to accomplish these psychological tasks, she must prepare for possible loss of the baby with some anticipatory grief reaction such as sadness or depression. Denial of the real threat or too early an optimism and cheerfulness are considered risks from a mental health point of view. Since a sense of guilt and self-blame is frequently aroused, the mother must be able to deal actively with such feelings in order to reduce their intensity and possible later negative effects.

Phase 2. The mother is at home; the infant remains in a hospital nursery for premature babies. The psychological tasks require the development of some hope that the infant will survive and will be home soon, and recognition that a premature infant needs special care but that eventually the needs and characteristics of the infant will be those of a normal child in regard to weight and other developmental factors. The problem-solving activities require that the mother take an active interest in the details of the progress of the baby while it is in the nursery and that she prepare for its needs.

Phase 3. The infant is now at home. The chief psychological task is the establishment of a tender and nurturing relationship between mother and infant, which has been prevented from developing by the premature birth and in some instances by long separation. The problem-solving tasks require the assumption of the nurturing role, attention and sensitivity to special needs, and (in some instances) coping realistically with congenital abnormalities frequently found in prematures.

Certain patterns have been identified which are considered maladaptive and which prognosticate a poor outcome to the crisis of prematurity. For example, some mothers deny heavily the threat to life and the implications of maternal failure. Some fail to respond with hope to indications that the infant will survive. Some have no interest in the details of the baby's development and may refuse to visit or be active in securing information about the baby's growth.

Another example of the delineation of problem-solving tasks was developed by Rhona Rapoport in her study of a normal crisis: the status and role transition involved in getting married. She identifies three tasks salient in intrapersonal preparation for marriage: (1) making oneself ready to take over the role of husband or wife; (2) disengaging (or altering the form of engagement of) oneself from especially close relationships that compete or interfere with commitment to the new marital relationship; (3) accommodating patterns of gratification of premarital life to patterns of the newly formed couple (marital) relationship.

The tasks involved in the couple's interpersonal preparation for marriage are: (1) establishing a couple identity; (2) developing a mutually satisfactory sexual adjustment for the engagement period; (3) reaching a mutually satisfactory system of communication between the pair and with relatives and friends; (4) developing a mutually satisfactory pattern of decision-making; and (5) planning specifically for the wedding, honeymoon, and early months of marriage.[32]

Such a detailed specification of tasks both helps in identifying where the individual has failed in appropriate coping and offers a framework for intervention. Emphasis on the need for coping and the successful management of psychological tasks helps to clarify the earlier statement that the outcome of a crisis is not necessarily contingent on the underlying personality structure and psychopathology of the individual. These problem-solving tasks have to be undertaken regardless of the underlying personality structure and patterns. The tasks can be taught and developed, and the capacity to deal with them can be strengthened.

Of course, the ease and readiness with which people respond, achieve, or fail to accomplish them is related to general personality and ego attributes and capacities, but not exclusively. Other important factors are the nature of the interpersonal and institutional supports that undergird and sustain such efforts.

Specification of coping tasks is also useful for predictive purposes in intervention. It is the kind of knowledge that can be taught to professionals who are not clinically trained, such as nurses and clergy who work with people in a variety of crisis situations. Further research is needed to identify the relevant specific psychological tasks in many other kinds of crisis situations such as accident, disability, unwed pregnancy, or mental illness in the family.

Another area of knowledge and conceptualization that is also of help in rapid diagnostic assessment is the beginning of a classification scheme of hazardous events which offers directions for locating sources of stress. At this point the scheme is one-dimensional and is not linked with the possible reaction patterns of people who go into a state of crisis. What we need is a crisis-state typology which combines both factors.

The classification of hazardous events can be conceptualized as follows. The first categorization is along the dimension of whether the hazardous events are largely anticipated or unanticipated. Under *anticipated crises* (which are often overlooked as they are considered to be natural) are the developmental crises identified by Erikson. They have a biological underpinning but also have psychological and social components. Examples are the oedipal period in childhood, identity development in adolescence, beginning parenthood, the climacteric, and senescence. A second category of anticipated crises, related to biological maturation, concerns transition points related to shifts in status and role: school entry, whether at the elementary or college level; entry into the labor market or military services; promotion; engagement and marriage; departure of children from the home; loss of job, demotion, or retirement; moving to a new community; and so forth.

Under *unanticipated crises,* sometimes called accidental or adventitious circumstances, there are three subcategories: (1) loss or threat of loss—such as separation owing to death or hospitalization, desertion, or divorce; or threats to well-being such as illness, accident, or disability; (2) accession or the introduction of an unprepared-for member into the social network, such as a premature child or an infant with congenital defects; return from prison or military service; or an aged parent joining the family; and (3) community disruptions or natural disasters such as floods, tornadoes, or fires; sociopolitical upheavals such as war, displacement of population, or riots; economic disasters such as depressions, bank failures, or factory foreclosures; and ecological changes such as urban renewal or school bussing.[33]

It might be noted that by giving emphasis to anticipated or "natural" crises, of both a biological and a role transition nature, the potential is developed for building in supportive services at various entry points to facilitate the transition and to sensitize caretakers and institutions to the mental health implications of such entries. This would have the character of primary prevention. The popular assumption that an event or experience is natural denies the potential for stress inherent in experiences such as childbirth[34] or entry into military service. The unanticipated crises are generally not subject to prevention and control, so that the clinician and others have the responsibility of dealing with the casualities of such crises. However, some events, such as urban renewal or school bussing, can be prepared for to some extent through explicit attention to the concerns and anxieties of the population to be affected.

The Initial Phase

It is almost impossible to describe the initial phase in crisis-oriented brief treatment, since it cannot readily be isolated from the total process. Some brief treatment consists of only one interview, although four to six interviews are more typical. Some brief services build in opportunities for as many as a dozen interviews. This discussion will confine itself, therefore, to the initial interview, which is of special significance in all treatment approaches. In brief treatment, however, the initial interview assumes extra significance because of the condensed time dimension. There is, so to speak, no margin for correcting error or neglect.

Certain basic assumptions of crisis theory which influence the nature of the initial interview need to be made explicit. A state of crisis is conceptualized as a time-limited process during which there is a peak in the state of upset. There are no clear indications of how long this state persists. No doubt it varies with individual vulnerabilities and patterns of response. Caplan suggests that six weeks is a usual time limit.[35] It is clear that the acute phase of a crisis does not go on indefinitely because the individual or family system pushes toward re-establishing itself and achieving some new kind of equilibrium. This equilibrium, however, may be in the direction of greater pathology. The important point is that the natural history of the crisis, with its built-in time limits, requires that intervention take place during this period if one wishes to influence the outcome briefly or economically. It has also been noted that the person or family in crisis is more susceptible to the influence of "significant others" in the environment. Moreover, the degree of activity of the helping person does not have to be high. A little help, rationally directed and purposefully focused at a strategic time, is more effective than more extensive help given at a period of less emotional accessibility.

The principle that emerges from the foregoing discussion is that in order to help people in a state of crisis, social workers must have rapid access to them; and, more to the point, clients must have rapid and ready access to helping persons. This then requires a structure in agencies and services that can meet requests for help within a few days, or at most a week, from the time of the request. It presupposes open intake and no waiting list. It presupposes further that there will be continuity in contact with a worker, with no separation of application interviews from treatment. It also presupposes that there will not be a formal period of study or diagnosis. In conventional casework theory, emphasis has often been given to the principle that diagnosis and treatment go hand in hand. In crisis-oriented treatment, this principle must be operationalized in fact.

As in all initial interviews, the primary task for the worker is the development of a tentative diagnosis or working hypotheses of the presenting problem. The primary need of the client is to experience in the first interview a considerable reduction in disabling tension and anxiety. One way in which this is achieved, which may be specific to the brief treatment approach, is by the worker's sharing tentative hypotheses and structuring a picture of the operating dynamics in language that makes sense to the client. This enables the client to get a manageable congitive grasp of his situation, and usually leads to a lowering of anxiety, trust in the worker's competence, and a feeling of being understood.

Another need of the client in the initial interview is to acquire some hope of improvement in his situation and of mastering tasks which previously appeared hopeless. This imperative leads to the consideration of two factors: the element of hope and therapeutic enthusiasm. Both are necessary attributes of the climate that needs to be generated in the initial interview as well as throughout the treatment process. The importance of these factors has been identified through empirical observation and some experimental work, but they do not often receive systematic attention because they lack a scientific aura or rigor and thus tend to embarrass us. The absence of hope, or hopelessness, was noted as characterizing individuals and families suffering from chronic deprivation which operated as a barrier to motivation and change.[36] Hope has been observed as an ingredient of therapy or as an attribute of the therapist in experimental studies by Jerome Frank and his colleagues. They state that "there has been a unifying thread to suggest that aspects of the therapeutic situation which arouse and strengthen the patient's hope of relief are positively correlated with short-term improvement in a significant proportion of patients. . . . Although a placebo can have such an effect, the essential ingredient in therapy is the ability to convey the therapist's ability to help."[37]

The factor of therapeutic enthusiasm or optimism was commented on by Malan citing an observation of Balint: "The therapist's enthusiasm has a direct bearing on the process and outcome of therapy since it brings with it a corresponding heightened excitement in the patient with the result that repressed feelings come easily to the surface and are experienced with an intensity and completeness so that the further 'working through' process may not be necessary."[38] Grinker also comments on this phenomenon but expresses a contrary point of view. "It has been said that the results from therapy of any type are proportional to the therapist's enthusiasm for his method. This does not insure more than temporary effect. . . . The young therapist's over enthusiastic missionary concept of *self* as a curative agent may become a serious liability."[39] We are not necessarily talking about partisan enthusiasm for method per se, but quality of intensity and investment in the client. Here we have another relevant observation made by many social work educators in regard to the performance of social work students who are frequently successful with clients beyond the level expected from their knowledge and skill. Factors of enthusiasm, therapeutic optimism, intensity of commitment, and investment have been noted but have not been examined systematically to discover what therapeutic potentials are embedded in them and how they can be used more effectively and purposefully.

Qualities of hope and enthusiasm are cited, therefore, as ingredients of a climate that needs to be developed by the worker to instill a sense of hope and confidence in the client. These observations suggest that the worker needs to play an active role in the encounter both in terms of creating a climate and in being firmly in command of the management of treatment. The need for a more active approach in brief treatment seems to be one of the few areas in which there is considerable consensus in the brief treatment literature.

Notions of investment, commitment, and enthusiasm suggest another concept that is increasingly noted in the literature on psychotherapy of many different schools of thought—the requirement of authenticity in the relationship. It may very well be that the increased concern with authenticity is in part a reaction to the widespread psychoanalytic model of relationship which advocated the neutrality of the therapist and a value-free stance. Such a relationship, although conceived of as being instrumental in purpose, upon examination has been found to be largely a myth.

The whole matter of relationship needs examination in crisis-oriented brief treatment. The concept of relationship in casework is central. We are accustomed to thinking that the positive relationship is the chief tool, if not the dynamic force, in treatment. Implicit in this view is the notion that it takes time to develop "a meaningful relationship" and that one cannot treat without it. Relationship is a rather fuzzy concept since we cannot state with clarity what aspect of relationship, what kind, what symbolic value, what degree of intensity, and so on are essential ingredients of treatment. The pertinent question is whether there are components of relationship that can be identified and can be maximized for use in brief treatment. For example, the worker's authority of competence and expertness may be used more powerfully to capitalize on the client's readiness to trust and relate out of feelings of confusion, helplessness, and anxiety. Such an approach may serve even a deeply suspicious client who, in a crisis, longs for protection. Perhaps the component of "attachment" in relationship is less crucial than the degree of involvement, however brief. Attachment is less necessary, since treatment does not depend on a "corrective emotional experience" (which is the essence of Alexander's earlier concept of brief treatment) or on the "working through" process. Brief treatment depends instead more on cognitive restructuring and unlinking the present context from past concerns.

In regard to the goals of the initial interview the following might be postulated. Engagement of the client is an important objective. This is affirmed in the general literature on casework, but is mostly dealt with in terms of strengthening the client's motivation for longer-range goals or of working on a restructured definition of the problem. In brief treatment, engagement refers to immediate problem solving in relation to mutually defined and agreed upon goals. The determination of goals to be worked on depends on the worker's assessment of what might be called "the useful next step,"[40] a shorthand designation of what in the client's internal or external state can readily be altered which would result in an immediate lowering of anxiety. The most useful or necessary next step may be some form of environmental provision, protection, or modification. Or the useful step may consist of the clarification of the nature and meaning of the precipitating stresses. There have been interesting studies showing that the detailed exploration and understanding of the precipitating stress and its specific meaning is often in itself of such great therapeutic value that no further help may be needed.[41] In this instance, the clarification gives the client a cognitive grasp of the relevant factors in his situation leading to intellectual mastery. This may be a first step in later emotional mastery and may open up a new perspective on appropriate problem-solving steps.

The process of exploration and definition of mutually agreed upon goals in the initial interview should eventuate in what is sometimes referred to as a contract. In the contract there is a spelling out of mutual expectations to avoid confusion or unrealistic expectations which are grounded in fantasy or magical wishes. This step also reduces the proclivity toward a regressive transference. The need for greater clarity in defining mutual expectations and goals has been identified in numerous studies of client dropouts. These studies identify the disparities in both perspective and expectation between worker and client. Social class and cultural factors which produce different styles of problem solving and conceptualization have led to barriers between workers and clients. One source of lack of congruence that has been identified is the worker's reliance on psychodynamic concepts in explaining behavior and lack of attention to cognitive elements, which are also instrumental in affecting behavior.[42] In one experiment on long-term therapy, role induction interviews were conducted to help patients develop appropriate expectations for treatment and therefore behave as "good patients." This procedure significantly improved the results of subsequent treatment.[43] All this points to the importance of the need for clarity of expectations.

Another crucial initial goal which remains a focal point throughout the brief treatment process is the re-establishment in the client of a sense of autonomy. This needs to be started in the initial interview so that the client can experience being able to again take charge of himself in regard to both life circumstances and feelings. The area in which this might take place may have to be minor, or have largely symbolic significance, but nonetheless is vital in the re-establishment of a sense of mastery. One example is the case of a man in his early forties with a known history of instability and periodic active mental illness who again came for clinic treatment at a point of crisis when his work situation, a main stabilizing force in his life, became drastically altered. Symbolically the alteration in the nature of his job represented a threat to his concept of integrity and autonomy. The worker quickly perceived that the main issue was the fear of loss of control. Thus, in the second interview she deliberately came without a watch and put the client in charge of keeping time. This was a beginning step, actual and mostly symbolic, in his reassumption of control and the enlargement of his sense of autonomy.

Thus far, factors such as the mobilization of hope, engagement, reduction of anxiety, re-establishment of a sense of autonomy, and the establishment of a contract as goals pertinent in the initial interview have been discussed. These goals are facilitated by the flexible and appropriate use of both structure and time. Here, as in other aspects of this work, a good deal can be learned from the functional school of casework. Time can be used to provide both the structure which provides a framework and boundaries for problem solving, and limits. This is reassuring to a person whose ego is deteriorating and is in itself ego-restorative. The setting of time limits can operate as leverage and as pressure for both client and worker to get on with the problem-solving task. It can relieve the client of his anxiety about becoming dependent upon the treatment situation and serve as counterforce against the client's self-concept of being emotionally "sick" or incompetent. Time limits can also be used, along with other techniques, to prevent tendencies toward the development of a regressive transference, which is to be avoided at all costs in brief treatment.

The actual manipulation of time lends itself to various approaches and innovations. In many brief treatment services, the length of time available for problem solving may be set arbitrarily for administrative reasons and be made known to clients in advance. This gives the worker some external controls and makes it easier not to slide into long-term relationships. However, it may introduce certain aspects of inflexibility. Another approach, which has not been sufficiently experimented with, is to encourage the client to specify how much time he thinks he needs in order to work on his problems. He should be able to set both the length of time and the frequency of the encounter. I refer to this as a "self-demand schedule." The opportunity to do this is another means of strengthening the sense of autonomy referred to earlier. In order for a worker to be comfortable with this approach he must have enough faith and be sufficiently free of anxiety to be able to accept the client's time schedule. The administrative structure must be flexible enough to permit the scheduling of interviews at other than once-a-week intervals. There is nothing magic about weekly appointments: they may fit our patterns of working but not necessarily the client's immediate needs. The client may need three appointments in a row, or one each day for a week, in certain emergency conditions. The general experience seems to be that when the client is given a choice he tends to commit himself to a series of interviews well within half a dozen. This would seem to be the "staying power," or perhaps working power, of many individuals. When the agreed-upon time limit has been reached and there is both the indication of need and the willingness to continue working on problems, in some services referral then becomes automatic. In others, where there are no administratively set cutoff points, more interviews might be structured. In that case, it is desirable to renegotiate the contract, to spell out the next series of goals and to again set a limit for further work. Such use of time limits also gives a framework to evaluate what has been achieved and to measure growth.

Treatment Principles and Methods

There is as yet no well-developed treatment methodology in crisis-oriented brief treatment, any more than there is in any other casework approach. Many prevailing principles and techniques are relevant and useful but need to be reordered in keeping with a shift in emphasis. New ones have yet to be devised. It is important to emphasize, however, that crisis-oriented brief treatment is not a short version of long-term treatment, although it is apt to be so unless the work is guided by conscious knowledge and application. If the conscious orientation and requisite techniques are absent, most likely the work is a failure and unproductive. This observation has been borne out in a study by Reid, who notes that "short term treatment suggests that this type of service has a distinct methodology of its own—that clients are being given a different kind of treatment from what they receive in continued service, rather than simply less treatment.[44]

The basic treatment model in crisis-oriented brief treatment should be the life model as suggested by Bandler.[45] The trajectory of the life span with its natural processes of growth, development, and eventual decline is the arena for experimentation, learning, and mastery in regard to need satisfaction and problem solving. The natural, progressive tendencies in human development are strong forces and prevail over the regressive tendencies, barring serious obstacles and obstructions. These natural growth tendencies then become our chief therapeutic ally. This concept challenges that aspect of the medical model which frames maladaptation and problems in living in terms of illness. Crisis theory explicitly refrains from defining or equating the state of crisis with an illness. Indeed, the crisis state, in contrast to the concept of stress, is viewed as having a growth-promoting potential if favorable factors are operating.

In keeping with this view, we need to abandon the concept of cure and shift to the concept of restoration and enhancement of functioning. The term cure evokes the surgical model of medicine, with removal or excision as a goal. It is a static concept which does not fit many conditions of physical disease. For example, in states of acute infectious disease there is an acute flare-up in an organism previously in a state of health or some state of relative equilibrium, followed by a diminution of acute symptoms and a return to the previous state of functioning. This model of acute infectious disease, referred to earlier, is more akin to the life model with its fluctuations of stress and adaptation. Jerome Frank supports the notion that the customary medical notion of cure may not be entirely appropriate for psychotherapy:

> It is quite proper to judge the effectiveness of a remedy for leukemia or cancer in terms of five or ten year results. However, this is only appropriate when the patient's state of illness or health does not depend on a continuous interaction process between him and his environment. It would be highly ambitious to hope to achieve a five year cure for the common cold, for example. The virus and bacteria that cause this condition are always present in some kind of balance with the host. Either a temporary increase in the virulence of the bacteria of a reduction of the host's powers of resistance can upset the balance at any time and the patient will get a cold. The discovery of a way of producing permanent immunity to colds would indeed be a medical triumph. In the meanwhile, most of us would be more than content if we had a remedy that reduced the duration of each cold from, let us say, a week to an hour, and we would regard such a remedy as indeed valuable.

He states further that "the chances of finding therapeutic methods that will confer permanent and total immunity to life stresses are remote."[46]

This discussion points to the need in brief treatment for a genuine acceptance of limited goals. This seems to be hard for many practitioners both on the basis of their understanding and recognition that there are indeed many areas of conflict and pathology in the person and on the basis of their therapeutic ambitions, generally framed in terms of impatience with symptom relief and interest in personality trait modification. What facilitates acceptance of the concept of limited goals (in addition to the hard realities of lack of resources and the inappropriateness of a long-term approach for most of our clients) is increasing evidence that even minor modifications in functioning, values, or attitudes may serve as a nucleus for other more profound transformations in the environment, in interpersonal relations, and even in intrapsychic functioning. Improvement can become self-perpetuating, particularly if there are favorable rewards and responses. From the designation of limited goals flows the corollary notion of the application of a focused and segmental approach with conscious and deliberate attention to what will be dealt with and what will be ignored.

The general goal of crisis-oriented brief treatment can be formulated in a way similar to the more global kinds of formulations that usually characterize casework treatment efforts. Basically, crisis-oriented brief treatment is an ego-supportive method. But from one point of view, all forms of therapy are ego-supportive. To cite Bandler again, "We are most obviously supportive [in] those moments of crisis in which the ego is overwhelmed. . . . Every effort is made to maintain the ego and to forestall further disruption."[47] The goals and measures used in this instance are essentially ego-conservative or ego-restitutive, concerned with the maintenance of defenses and repression of instinctual impulse seeking discharge. In other circumstances of crisis, the goal can become ego-progressive, directed toward progressive forces and the growth of the personality. Specifically, this involves attention to new modes of adaptation and strengthening latent coping mechanisms and to developing new ones.

This formulation is consonant with many others, particularly that of Frances Scherz in her paper "An Appraisal of Treatment Objectives in Casework Practice." She differentiates between the objectives of helping people feel better, cure, and problem-solving. She views treatment objectives as involving (1) delineation of coping, (2) understanding the here and now and life stresses, (3) description of developmental tasks, and (4) provision of skills for problem-solving. She concludes, "Whether the specific treatment goal is related only to the immediate task or to removal of obstacles to further development will depend on the specific assessment of what is most economical, what is safe to undertake, and what can be tolerated in treatment."[48]

The dichotomous formulation of conservation or progression, similar to the FSAA framework of maintaining and modifying measures,[49] although it yields a sort of theoretical simplicity and tidiness, does violence to the richness and complexity of clinical experience. In actual practice, modes of intervention do not fall into these categories. In most instances, both modes and the cluster of techniques that largely characterize each mode are used in crisis and noncrisis treatment situations. The inability to work within this framework is noted in the research study of Reid, in which modifying or supportive measures were to be used in accordance with the requirements of the research design. He concludes that the division of casework into dichotomies as "modifying" versus "supportive" artificially splits apart interlocking sets of techniques. "These techniques may be better seen as constituting the core of the casework method rather than as representing different methods of casework."[50]

The goals of crisis-oriented brief treatment can be more narrowly specified as follows: (1) relief of symptoms: (2) restoration to the optimal level of functioning that existed before the present crisis; (3) understanding of the relevant precipitating events that contributed to the state of disequilibrium; (4) identification of remediable measures that can be taken by the client or family or that are available through community resources.

These are the minimum goals that should be achieved as part of crisis resolution. In addition, where the personality and social situation are favorable, and the opportunity presents itself or can be created, work can be done to (1) recognize the current stresses and their origins in past life experiences and conflicts; and (2) initiate new modes of perceiving, thinking, and feeling and develop new adaptive and coping responses that will be useful beyond the immediate crisis resolution.

Crisis brief treatment is primarily present-oriented, with a strong focus on the "here and now." One of the first tasks is to elucidate and identify the precipitating stresses that led to the state of crisis. The specific accompanying affects are accepted and identified as natural and understandable in keeping with the stressful events. Here the purpose is to lower tension, anxiety, and guilt. The purpose of clarifying the precipitating events and subsequent affects is to help the client achieve a cognitive grasp and mastery of his situation by describing, defining, and reordering recent experiences. There is further exploration of adaptive models of coping that have been useful in the past and that can be reaffirmed or may be extended or modified in the present context as ways of handling conflicts or finding solutions. Similarly, there is exploration of defense mechanisms in order to strengthen those with adaptive utility or to develop new ones.

Where the content lends itself to it, and where the opportunity presents itself, there is selective focus on the past insofar as present stressful events reactivate old preconscious or unconscious conflicts or traumas. Without engaging in actual exploration of past events and their ramified meanings, it is possible to unlink the present stressful events from past traumatic events so that they may be perceived and felt as discrete experiences without the added burden of old unresolved needs or feelings. The kind of material which is necessary to make this linkage diagnostically and then to engage in the unlinking process often comes out surprisingly readily when the person is in a state of crisis. At such times the usual defenses are weakened, and the person is less guarded against the revelation of such pertinent information, which ordinarily is represented or suppressed.

A brief clinical vignette may illustrate this important process. A fifteen-year-old Negro boy recently moved into a newly integrated neighborhood and school. He was a poor student and a serious behavior problem, making many supposedly unprovoked attacks on other children. On the occasion of one such aggressive attack, the school felt helpless and frightened and called the police, who put the boy in handcuffs. He became more violent and threatening, at which point they took him to the local psychiatric ward. His disturbances, outbursts, and threats of more violence increased, and there he was put in restraints. He was given a psychiatric diagnosis of schizophrenia, paranoid type. He was subsequently seen for brief outpatient psychiatric treatment. He was handled in a remarkably skillful manner with a rapid lowering of anxiety so that he soon became quite rational. There were no clinical signs that he was psychotic. In about the fourth interview, almost in the nature of a free-associative expression, he called an experience at age six (which he misdated to age nine) when he had been hospitalized. He did not know what had been done to him. As a matter of fact he had gone in for a hernia repair and at the same time had been circumcised and had his tonsils and adenoids removed. The event, for which he had not been prepared and which he had not been helped to digest, had been experienced by him as a major body assault. All his subsequent defensive mechanisms were geared to making himself invulnerable and strong, against basic castration anxiety. He had experienced the recent events as another assault where he was reduced to total helplessness. The worker was able to unlink the present events from the past trauma, to help him digest both experiences, and to affirm his current capacity to handle himself in keeping with his age and role, showing him he was no longer helpless. Through anticipatory guidance and some role rehearsal he was helped to handle the next stressful situation (a court hearing) with minimum stress or distortion.

In addition to the focus on the present and selected past events when relevant, there is also a heavy emphasis on a future orientation in anticipating needs and tasks that require active coping.

The enhancement of coping patterns is achieved by a process that has decided educational components, such as anticipatory guidance, rehearsal for future reality, learning new social and interpersonal skills, and enlarging the capacity for anticipatory thinking and prediction. In some instances, the educational process may be less verbal and be based more on identification. Here, the worker may consciously offer himself actively a model for identification and encourage the rehearsal of behavior and attitudes in regard to new roles.

The role of the worker, as touched on previously, requires an active and directive stance. The relationship is built not over time through elements of attachment and transference, but on elements of authority based on expertness and competence. It is important for the worker to be more of a real person than a neutral reflector or moderator, and to communicate actively both concern and authenticity. The worker takes advantage of the client's readiness to trust out of a feeling of confusion, helplessness, or anxiety. He also takes advantage of the regressive impulse and longing, without, however, permitting any regressive behavior to develop which would be inimical to short-term goals and the specific goals of quickly re-establishing and enhancing self-esteem and a sense of autonomy and self-direction.

The requirement of being active and directive restores the role of advice-giving to an important and useful technique. Giving advice has become almost taboo for both historical and theoretical reasons. Workers have often withheld information and advice on the misguided judgment that the client's problems were based only on unconscious conflicts rather than on a simple lack of information and knowledge. It is true that in unsophisticated hands advice-giving can be abused. However, it can be used in a potent way, especially if its dynamic meaning can be anticipated by taking into account the client's unconscious needs and impulses. Furthermore, in keeping with a more educational approach, it is possible to use the client's greater accessibility and readiness for influence by taking advantage of the "teachable moment."[51] By the same token, crisis casework treatment can take on the character of the life-space interview since it is conducted during a time when the client is still actively experiencing the effects of stress.

In sum then, from a technical point of view, crisis brief treatment makes use of all the principles and techniques which have been developed in casework methodology that are relevant and useful. However, there is a reordering of, and greater emphasis on, some techniques. The approach is more active, directive, and authoritative. Time limits are used for a framework, to push toward problem-solving and to avoid regression. The client's capacity for autonomous action and decision is maximized. Treatment is highly focused and segmental, and problems to be worked are partialized. Emphasis is on the engagement of the perceptual and cognitive functions of the ego, especially on cognitive restructuring and mastery. The initial task is lowering tension and anxiety through reassurance, but more important is the redefinition and delimiting of the problem and the focus on rapid mastery of some segment of the life experience. There is restoration of old defenses that were previously adequate and adaptive. There is prevention of regressive behavior and transference. Clarification and interpretation are geared to present feelings and current conflicts, and the present stress is unlinked from past unresolved conflicts where possible. Self-understanding or insight is not a goal in itself. Often insight is no more than hindsight and remains unintegrated unless supported by action and behavioral change.[52] In brief treatment the goal is foresight—the enhancement of anticipatory awareness to be used in problem-solving. Focus is on adaptive patterns and ways of handling conflicts and finding solutions. There is a strengthening of coping mechanisms and the development of new social and interpersonal skills through imparting knowledge, advice, anticipatory guidance, and rehearsal for reality, as well as providing new models for identification. There is emphasis on the enlargement of the capacity for prediction and control. There is, of course, mobilization of relevant resources not only for meeting basic needs but also for the opportunity to exercise adaptive capabilities.

Termination in crisis-oriented brief treatment is an important function, if not a phase. It is remarkable that there is almost no discussion of termination as a process in the conventional casework literature in comparison with the emphasis given to diagnosis and the early phases of treatment.[53] Only the functional school has given explicit attention to this phase and process and has made it an intrinsic dynamic aspect of the total treatment process. In brief treatment, termination needs to be dealt with explicity. Depending on how the brief treatment is structured to begin with, and in keeping with the model suggested earlier of a "self-demand" schedule for the client, termination is discussed and initiated in the initial interview. In other words, the ending process is anticipated, if not actually predetermined.

Termination obviously is intrinsically linked with the formulation of specific goals. It takes place when a specifically defined goal has been reached. That may or may not be easily determined. One of the impediments to early termination is the tendency to label certain rapid improvements as "flights into health." This label bespeaks the clinician's mistrust of the natural recuperative powers of people. In actual fact, although it is sometimes difficult, it is possible to distinguish flight into health from genuine changes that are supported by alteration in feeling states and behavior. Another concept, perhaps more useful, is that termination can be achieved when the client *begins* to find solutions to his problems. This means that we do not expect him to work through all his problems, or even those parts of the problem that have been identified for focus. When the client begins to perceive new directions for solutions and new modes of coping, even when they have not been firmly or consistently established, termination can be instituted.

"Letting go" is not easy for social workers, particularly if the client's adaptation is still shaky. But the cost of continuing must also be borne in mind. In one of Alexander's last papers he stated, "Psychotherapeutic treatment must aim to bring the patient to the point where his natural growth can be resumed. Treatment beyond this point—or infantilization—interferes with the natural growth potential and tempts the patient's ego to take the easy path of continuing dependency on parental figures. This dependency is exactly what the therapy tries to overcome."[54] In another paper he speaks of the need to trust the natural recuperative powers of the human personality, which are largely underestimated by psychotherapists. There is a tendency toward overtreatment. He speaks of an early approach in analysis—of planned interrupted treatment called "fractioned analysis"—which has gone into oblivion.[55]

It is easier to "let go" if one operates on the assumption that there will be, within the life span of all persons, periods of adaptive and maladaptive functioning associated with life circumstances. Thus, professional intervention may be necessary at various times in the life cycle. In order to respond to such a view of man, agencies must have an "open door" policy that invites clients to return for further work when they need it.[56] Acceptance of a life model of problem-solving and a door that is really open makes it easier for clients to return without a sense of shame or failure. This view also helps workers. At present, many caseworkers feel a sense of guilt and failure if clients return for more help. We tend to view this negatively; we expect that a problem solved should stay solved for all times. Reapplication for service should be viewed positively. Experience has shown that clients who return after a brief period of help need even briefer help the second time. They may return because of similar stress; yet the crisis is often less intense. They may use a second period of help to consolidate previous gains. In other instances, the need for help the second time may be entirely unrelated to the first situation, and should be dealt with in accordance with current need.

The Target Group

The question, For whom is crisis brief treatment the method of choice? is difficult to answer. From one point of view all people can benefit from brief and focused intervention, particularly in times of stress. At such times, brief treatment offers what has been referred to "as the useful next step." But to suggest that brief treatment is useful for everyone, particularly as a beginning step, is begging the question. We should distrust any approach that is offered either as a panacea or as an undifferentiated approach. More important, failure to identify the specificity of a concept or the differential application of an approach leads to an excessive elasticity of a concept and causes both the concept and the application to lose their essential utility.

Thus this question turns us back to the basic definition of a crisis. Despite various attempts at theoretical definition and description, the fact remains that practitioners find it difficult to identify when an individual or family is in a state of crisis. The tendency is to equate a crisis with an obvious, dramatic state of emergency such as a suicide attempt. The inability of practitioners to define a crisis or to identify the relevant precipitating stresses is noted in a study by Parad and Parad.[57]

One approach to the question is to ask, When is a "crisis" not a crisis? The most obvious exceptions are those numerous types of clients who frequent many social agencies—public welfare, corrections, and particularly protective services—and who live in a chronic state of crisis. For them being in a state of crisis is a life style. The overt manifestations of the upset—sense of urgency, disordered affects, disorganized behavior, and ineffective coping—appear to be similar to those of other people in a state of crisis. Nevertheless, deeper examination suggests that for such individuals and families the crises, in addition to the external hazardous events all are heir to, tend to be largely self-generated. Here we deal with people who have severe and chronic ego depletion and ego damage. According to Cumming and Cumming such ego-damaged persons will experience even simple problems as crises.[58] It is very likely that from the psychoeconomic point of view the crisis, accidental or self-generated, and the response to it are not maladaptive but, in fact, are an attempt at adaptation (although admittedly self-defeating and generating more problems) which serves to ward off deep unconscious depression, anxiety, or an underlying psychotic process. We usually characterize such people as suffering from character disorders or borderline states. These clients are generally not the ones we can help significantly with brief crisis intervention as we have defined it. They often do need emergency and first aid help. Workers consistently complain, however, that when the emergency has been weathered these clients are no longer available for any kind of sustained work. They do not stand still long enough to be available for work between "crises," so to speak. For such clients a different model and set of expectations must be developed. Periodic intervention with emergency provisions and ego conservation as a goal may be the treatment of choice. When agency skills and resources warrant it, more long-term approaches and serious commitment of sustained treatment efforts may yield results in the direction of ego growth and adaptation, as Reiner and Kaufman noted in working with character disorders,[59] or through the adult socialization approaches described by McBroom.[60]

The kinds of people for whom crisis-oriented brief treatment is not appropriate are those disordered individuals and families with character disorders or those in borderline states where acting and flight are major mechanisms of adaptation. It is also not the treatment of choice for people with extremely marginal or low functioning of a chronic nature who need some form of constant, though not necessarily intensive, support as a kind of lifeline—such as certain chronic patients discharged from mental hospitals. For the latter, support is conceived of as similar to an orthopedic appliance, but in a psychological sense. A goodly number of social workers' caseloads are made up of such persons. Both goals and techniques have to be formulated differently for them. Institutional supports and contributions by other caretakers may also have to be provided in new ways.

There is no way to categorize people for whom brief treatment is the method of choice. It cannot be done along the lines of symptoms, syndromes, or diagnostic categories. Of greater significance is the person's integrative capacity or ego strengths, which means, among other factors, the availability of a resilient repertoire of coping mechanisms. When brief treatment is placed in the context of crisis formulations, we have a better way of sorting things out, provided we can identify the crisis state. In this context we presume there has been a prior state of adaptive functioning with some degree of satisfaction. Thus, in general people with acute conflictual problems, or neurotic responses that are immediately reactive to the environment, are more amenable to brief intervention. These are people with an essentially good ego who are under considerable external stress. But chronically disordered persons in acute stress can also respond favorably to brief treatment. For example, brief treatment has been surprisingly effective with persons of borderline character who may be on the verge of a psychotic episode with breakthrough of primitive impulses. Here, active intervention can often restore crumbling defenses and return the person to a previous level of functioning. It appears, therefore, that people at widely separated ends of the mental health–mental illness continuum can make good use of brief treatment. For both, the goal is restoration of prior adequate functioning within the limits of present capacities and opportunities. We have also noted that brief treatment has the potency to do more than restore functioning. It can produce profound changes in personality by facilitating some rapid reorganization of psychic structure and energy. This is most likely to happen at times of maturational crises, such as at adolescence, when the personality is in a greater state of flux.

We have not been able to distinguish sharply, except in broad terms, the types of clients for whom crisis brief treatment is a method of choice. As to social problems or fields of practice, the approach cuts across all areas and seems to be relevant in all kinds of settings. Family agencies and out-patient psychiatric services have moved toward this approach. Older and newer types of psychiatric emergency services are very committed to this method. Other emergency services under nonmedical auspices, such as suicide prevention centers, also use this approach. Medical social work settings are very familiar and comfortable with crisis-oriented brief treatment by virtue of the nature of the problems in such settings. However, they have not, by and large, conceptualized their rich clinical experience in terms of crisis theory. Public welfare workers find this approach highly relevant and congenial. Protective services are very sensitive to the concept of crisis and have turned to crisis theory for help. The tendency, however, has been to misconstrue the nature of crisis and the power and limits of brief intervention and to misapply this theory in work with clients for whom life style crises are most frequently operative. Agencies working with unmarried mothers also respond to these ideas and approaches. The agency most comfortable and experienced with the crisis brief treatment approach has been Travelers Aid, which has developed both a descriptive literature and some conceptualization regarding its work.

In essence, we have taken the position that crisis brief treatment has extensive utility with a wide variety of clients and patients, cutting across traditional diagnostic typologies, social problem areas, and a spectrum of agency services.

Unsolved Problems

There are many unsolved and unknown problems to be defined in a newly evolving framework such as crisis-oriented brief treatment. The most glaring problem of all is that as yet there is very little systematic practice that consciously employs the model as it has emerged to date. There are a few services committed to this mode of practice throughout the country, mostly mental health services. Elsewhere the practice is partial, not designated or set apart from other approaches. Thus, crisis brief treatment tends to be hit or miss. Consequently there exists as yet no systematic study of outcome at termination or of long-term effects. There is a need for both practice and study of experimental efforts with attention to variables such as target groups, social problem groups, and use of differential time dimensions.

From a conceptual point of view, we need a definition of crisis that can be more easily operationalized. As was pointed out, practitioners have difficulty identifying a state of crisis as well as the precipitating stress factors. We also need definitions of the concept of "brief", and these can only be achieved by consciously experimenting with time factors. We need greater clarity about the kinds of people for whom this approach is the treatment of choice, since at present there is little consensus. Another area which has not been sufficiently conceptualized is a framework for diagnosing a family unit in crisis. It has been suggested that crisis brief treatment is relevant to individuals and families, but little has been done to conceptualize the nature of the crisis as it manifests itself in a family system or to develop relevant methods and techniques for treatment of the family as a whole.

We also need better understanding of the dynamics that bring about change. In crisis theory, the dynamic force for change is made possible by the disequilibrium of a crisis that produces a fluid ego as well as an altered environmental state. The goal in crisis brief treatment is action and the furtherance of rapid behavioral change with positive reinforcement. This involves complex processes which should be based on an understanding of psychodynamics. In other models, the dynamics of change are conceptualized differently. They may be based on self-understanding or insight, or the freeing of latent energies formerly tied up with defenses of the infantile neurosis. These concepts need re-examination, testing, and some reformulation in the light of new insights developed.

We also need greater clarity regarding the conceptual underpinnings and what is necessary by way of a knowledge base for crisis treatment. For example, what aspects of psychoanalytic theory, learning theory, social role theory, family interaction theory, and ego psychology are relevant and useful in crisis brief treatment? A major task is to blend and integrate these theories with the knowledge of various conditions of stress. As indicated earlier, there is an urgent need for more knowledge of the specific effects of particular crises and the requisite psychological problem-solving tasks necessary for healthy crisis resolution.

In regard to techniques, it has been suggested that new techniques may need to be developed in addition to those with which casework practitioners are familiar. It may be useful to experiment with selected aspects of behavioral modification and with a socialization approach; there may be a need to develop more nonverbal action models, as well as a need to develop more of an ecological approach instead of almost total reliance on the person-to-person approach.

Crisis brief treatment raises questions which require some modifications in conventional casework theory. We have already touched on the relevance of the nature and kind of diagnosis required, and modification in the concept and use of relationship. The concept of self-determination may also need to be re-examined in the light of the client's need for both self-direction and autonomy or guidance and protection in crisis brief treatment work. The concept of motivation needs clarification in regard to defining the level and nature of motivation necessary for change.[61] Motivation for relief of suffering may be a better starting point than motivation for change in behavior or feelings as it is traditionally conceptualized.

From the point of view of education and training, several issues are unanswered. Is this an approach that can be successfully used only by the seasoned and experienced clinician who knows the long-term process and has an understanding of depth phenomena and can therefore find his way more readily to shortcuts? There is observable evidence that some beginners are very skilled in this approach, whereas seasoned clinicians often have great difficulty reorienting themselves if they suffer from "trained incompetence." Can this approach be taught in professional schools of social work? And if so, at what point in the casework sequence can it best be introduced?

Another issue has to do with how the social work profession as a whole conceptualizes its operations and major commitments and subsequent deployment of manpower. In essence, the question is how much of the professional effort and enterprise should be committed to remedial work and how much should be geared to more systematic efforts at prevention. Crisis theory leads to two levels of intervention—the generic and the specific.[62] The specific level is the clinical level of intervention, designated as early diagnosis and treatment of the casualties of crises which can be dealt with through the methods of brief treatment, as described. The generic level of application, which is more in keeping with a primary prevention effort, can be aimed at various target groups, populations designated to be especially vulnerable or at risk. Here, community caretakers, professionals and nonprofessionals, are the primary helping agents, assisted with knowledge and techniques through methods of consultation and education by mental health professionals. The generic knowledge applicable to people in specific crisis states can be utilized in this fashion both for strengthening coping efforts and for screening failures. In addition to work with other professionals and nonprofessionals who deal with specific populations, social workers can also apply generic knowledge of crisis to work with community agencies and basic institutions in order to sensitize such institutions to basic human needs and to special needs of people in times of crisis, and to help bring about greater responsiveness.

In sum then, crisis-oriented brief treatment is a most useful approach for intervention and help to many kinds of people who turn to social and mental health agencies. It is not a radically new effort, but builds on many values and tested components of knowledge and theoretical frames of reference. It is consistent with the major social casework goals of restoration and enhancement of personal and social functioning. It is an approach which takes into account the multidimensional factors of causation and problem solution. It can also contribute to the greater understanding of the complex forces of interrelationship between social environment, stress, and individual response which might eventually lead to a more ecologically oriented effort and the creation of sounder institutions.

Notes

1. Erich Lindemann, "Symptomatology and Management of Acute Grief," *American Journal of Psychiatry,* vol. CI (Sept. 1944). Also in *Crisis Intervention: Selected Readings,* ed. Howard J. Parad (New York: Family Service Association of America, 1965), pp. 7–21.
2. Jona Michael Rosenfeld and Gerald Caplan, "Techniques of Staff Consultation in an Immigrant Children's Organization," *American Journal of Orthopsychiatry,* XXIV (Jan. 1954), 42–62.
3. Bertha Capen Reynolds, "An Experiment in Short-Contact Interviewing," *Smith College Studies in Social Work,* III (Sept. 1932), 1–101.
4. Helen Harris Perlman, *Social Casework: A Problem-Solving Process* (Chicago: University of Chicago Press, 1957).
5. Ruth Chaskel, "Assertive Casework in a Short-Term Situation," in *Casework Papers 1961* (New York: Family Service Association of America, 1961). Also in *Crisis Intervention,* ed. Parad, pp. 237–47.
6. Helen Harris Perlman, "Some Notes on the Waiting List," *Social Casework,* XLV (1963), 200–205. Also in *Crisis Intervention,* ed. Parad, pp. 193–201.

7. Franz Alexander and Thomas M. French, *Psychoanalytic Therapy: Principles and Application* (New York: Ronald, 1946).
8. David H. Malan, *A Study of Brief Psychotherapy* (London: Tavistock; Springfield, Ill.: Charles C. Thomas, 1963), p. 6.
9. Erik Erikson, "Growth and Crisis of the Healthy Personality," *Personality in Nature, Society and Culture,* ed. Clyde Kluckhohn, Henry A. Murray, and David M. Schneider (2d ed. rev.; New York: Knopf, 1953), pp. 185–225.
10. Anna Freud, *The Ego and the Mechanisms of Defense* (New York: International Universities Press, 1946).
11. Heinz Hartman, *Ego Psychology and the Problem of Adaptation* (New York: International Universities Press, 1958).
12. Robert White, *Ego and Reality in Psychoanalytic Theory* (New York: International Universities Press, 1963).
13. Richard Lazarus, *Psychological Stress and the Coping Process* (New York: McGraw-Hill, 1966).
14. Lydia Rapoport, "The State of Crisis: Some Theoretical Considerations," *Social Service Review,* XXXIV (June 1962), 211–17. Also in *Crisis Intervention,* ed. Parad, pp. 22–31.
15. Hans Selye, *The Stress of Life* (New York: McGraw-Hill, 1956).
16. Eli M. Bower, "The Modification, Mediation and Utilization of Stress during the School Years," *American Journal of Orthopsychiatry,* XXXIV (July 1964), 667–68.
17. Norma Haan, "A Tripartite Model of Ego Functioning: Values and Clinical Research Applications," *Journal of Nervous and Mental Disease,* CXLVIII (Jan. 1969), 26.
18. Jerome Bruner, *Studies in Cognitive Growth* (New York: John Wiley and Sons, 1966).
19. Franz Alexander, "Psychoanalytic Contributions to Short-Term Psychotherapy," in *Short-Term Psychotherapy,* ed. Lewis R. Wolberg (New York and London: Grune & Stratton, 1965), pp. 84–126.
20. Reuben Hill, "Generic Features of Families under Stress," *Social Casework,* XXXIX (1958), 139–58. Also in *Crisis Intervention,* ed. Parad, pp. 32–52.
21. John Spiegel, "The Resolution of Role Conflict within the Family," *Psychiatry,* XX (1957), 1–16. Also in *The Family,* ed. Norman W. Bell and Ezra F. Vogel (Glencoe, Ill.: Free Press, 1960), pp. 361–81.
22. Hugh R. Leavell and Edwin G. Clark, *Preventive Medicine for the Doctor and His Community* (New York: McGraw-Hill, 1958).
23. David Kaplan, "A Concept of Acute Situational Disorders," *Social Work,* VII (April 1962), 15–23.
24. John MacLeod, "Some Criteria for the Modification of Treatment Arrangements," in *Ego-Oriented Casework,* ed. Howard J. Parad (New York: Family Service Association of America, 1965), pp. 165–76. The specific statement quoted was from an earlier version of the paper which was presented in the Monday Night Lecture Series, Smith College School for Social Work, Northampton, Mass., July 17, 1961.

25. Bernard Bandler, "The Concept of Ego-Supportive Psychotherapy," in *Ego-Oriented Casework,* ed. Parad, p. 41.

26. See *Short-Term Psychotherapy,* ed. Wolberg.

27. Mary A. Sarvis, Sally Dewees, and Ruth F. Johnson, "A Concept of Ego-Oriented Psychotherapy," *Psychiatry,* XXII (Aug. 1959), 277–87.

28. Gerald Caplan, *Principles of Preventive Psychiatry* (New York: Basic Books, 1964), pp. 26–55.

29. Gerald Caplan, "Patterns of Response to the Crisis of Prematurity: A Preliminary Approach" (unpub. paper).

30. Lindemann, "Symptomatology and Management of Acute Grief."

31. David Kaplan and Edward Mason, "Maternal Reaction to Premature Birth Viewed as an Acute Emotional Disorder," *American Journal of Orthopsychiatry,* XXX (July 1960), 539–52. Also in *Crisis Intervention,* ed. Parad, pp. 118–28.

32. Rhona Rapoport, "Normal Crises, Family Structure and Mental Health," *Family Process,* I (1963), 68–80. Also in *Crisis Intervention,* ed. Parad, pp. 75–87.

33. Naomi Golan, "When Is a Case in Crisis," *Social Casework,* L (July 1969), 389–94.

34. Grete Bibring et al., "A Study of the Psychological Processes in Pregnancy and of the Earliest Mother-Child Relationship," in *Psychoanalytic Study of the Child,* ed. Ruth S. Eissler et al. (New York: International Universities Press, 1961), XIV, 9–72.

35. Gerald Caplan, from discussions at seminars at School of Public Health, Harvard University.

36. Kermit Wiltse, "The Hopeless Family," *Social Work,* III (Oct. 1958), 12–22.

37. Jerome Frank, "The Role of Hope in Psychotherapy," *International Journal of Psychiatry,* V (May 1968), 394.

38. Malan, *Study of Brief Psychotherapy,* p. 13.

39. Roy Grinker, *Psychiatric Social Work: A Transactional Casework* (New York: Basic Books, 1963), p. 311.

40. Sarvis, Dewees, and Johnson, "Concept of Ego-Oriented Psychotherapy," p. 287.

41. Betty L. Kalis et al., "Precipitating Stress as a Focus in Psychotherapy," *Archives of General Psychiatry,* V (Sept. 1961), 219–26.

42. John E. Mayer and Noel Timms, "Clash in Perspective between Worker and Client," *Social Casework,* L (Jan. 1969), 32–40.

43. Rudolf Hoen-Saric et al., "Systematic Preparation of Patients for Psychotherapy: Effects of Therapy Behavior and Outcome," *Journal of Psychiatry,* research vol. II (1964), 267–81.

44. William Reid, "Characteristics of Casework Intervention," *Welfare in Review,* V (Oct. 1967), 18.

45. Bandler, "Concept of Ego-Supportive Psychotherapy."

46. Frank, "Role of Hope in Psychotherapy," p. 386.

47. Bandler, "Concept of Ego-Supportive Psychotherapy," p. 28.

48. Francis Sherz, "An Appraisal of Treatment Objectives in Casework Practice," *Social Work Practice,* 1962, p. 160.

49. Family Service Association of America, *Scope and Methods of the Family Service Agency* (New York: Family Service Association of America, 1953).

50. Reid, "Characteristics of Casework Intervention," p. 18.

51. Helen Harris Perlman, "And Gladly Teach," *Journal of Education for Social Work,* III (spring 1967), 41–50.

52. Allen Wheelis, "The Place of Action in Personality Change," *Psychiatry,* XIII (May 1950), 135–48.

53. C. Knight Aldrich, "Impact of Community Psychiatry on Casework and Psychotherapy," *Smith College Studies in Social Work,* XXXII (Feb. 1968), 102–15.

54. Franz Alexander, "Psychoanalysis and the Human Condition," in *Psychoanalysis and the Human Situation,* ed. Jessie Marmorston and Edward Stainbrook (New York: Vantage, 1964), p. 82.

55. Franz Alexander, in *Short-Term Psychotherapy,* ed. Wolberg, p. 91.

56. Esther Schour and Jennie Zetland, "The Open Door: A Point of View," *Social Service Review,* XXIX (Sept. 1955), 285–92.

57. Howard J. Parad and Libbie Parad, "A Study of Crisis-Oriented Planned Short-Term Treatment," pts. 1–2, *Social Casework,* XLIX (June–July 1968), 346–55, 418–26.

58. John Cumming and Elaine Cumming, *Ego and Milieu* (New York: Atherton, 1963), p. 55.

59. Beatrice Reiner and Irving Kaufman, *Character Disorders in Parents of Delinquents* (New York: Family Service Association of America, 1959).

60. Elizabeth McBroom, *Adult Socialization: A Basis for Public Assistance Practice* (California: State Department of Social Welfare, 1966).

61. Genevieve Oxley, "The Caseworker's Expectations and Client Motivation," *Social Casework,* XLVII (July 1966), 432–37.

62. Gerald Jacobson, Martin Strickler, and Wilbur Morley, "Generic and Individual Approaches to Crisis Intervention," *American Journal of Public Health,* LVIII (Feb. 1968), 338–43.

References

Bellak, Leopold, and Leonard Small. *Emergency Psychotherapy and Brief Psychotherapy.* New York: Grune & Stratton, 1965.

Bloom, Bernard. "Definitional Aspects of the Crisis Concept," *Journal of Consulting Psychology,* XXVII (Dec. 1963), 498–502. Also in *Crisis Intervention: Selected Readings,* ed. Howard J. Parad. New York: Family Service Association of America, 1965.

Caplan, Gerald. *Principles of Preventive Psychiatry.* New York: Basic Books, 1964. Ch. 2.

Cumming, John, and Elaine Cumming. *Ego and Milieu.* New York: Atherton, 1963.

Jacobson, Gerald F. "Crisis Theory and Treatment Strategy: Some Sociocultural and Psychodynamic Considerations," *Journal of Nervous and Mental Disease,* CXLI (Aug. 1965), 209–18.

Kaplan, David M. "A Concept of Acute Situational Disorders," *Social Work,* VII (April 1962), 15–23.

Klein, D., and E. Lindemann. "Preventive Intervention in Individual and Family Crisis Situations." In *Prevention of Mental Disorders in Children,* ed. G. Caplan. New York: Basic Books, 1961. Pp. 283–306.

Lindemann, Erich. "Symptomatology and Management of Acute Grief," *American Journal of Psychiatry,* CI (Sept. 1944), 141–48.

Malan, D. H. *A Study of Brief Psychotherapy.* London: Tavistock; Springfield, Ill.: Charles C. Thomas, 1963. Chs. 1–3.

Parad, Howard J., ed. *Crisis Intervention: Selected Readings.* New York: Family Service Association of America, 1965.

Rapoport, Lydia. "Crisis-Oriented Short-Term Treatment," *Social Service Review,* XLI (March 1967), 31–43.

Sarvis, Mary A., Sally Dewees, and Ruth F. Johnson. "A Concept of Ego-Oriented Psychotherapy," *Psychiatry,* XXII (Aug. 1959), 277–87.

Selby, Lola G. "Social Work and Crisis Theory," *Social Work Papers,* vol. X. Los Angeles: University of Southern California, 1963. Pp. 1–11.

Wolberg, Lewis R., ed. *Short-Term Psychotherapy.* New York and London: Grune & Stratton, 1965.

6 *Working with Families in Crisis:*

An Exploration in Preventive Intervention

This paper describes preventive intervention work done with families considered to be in a state of crisis because of the birth of a premature infant. The work was an exploratory phase of a larger project conducted at the Harvard School of Public Health Family Guidance Center, which studied the reaction patterns and coping mechanisms of families in crisis. Identifications of patterns, both adaptive and maladaptive, could serve as indices for prediction of outcome and also as a guide to caretakers and helping professions for the deployment of resources and for focused intervention.

Two related frames of reference guided this work: that of prevention as formulated and utilized in the public health field, and that of crisis theory as formulated by mental health investigators and social psychiatrists.

Prevention, in the public health field, is conceived of as a continuum of activities to protect the health of the community. These activities are classified as (1) health promotion, (2) specific protection, (3) early diagnosis and treatment, including case finding, (4) disability limitation, and (5) rehabilitation.[1] The first two categories are in the nature of primary prevention—that is to say, intervention before a problem is manifest. Early diagnosis and treatment are considered to be secondary prevention, while the last two categories are classified as tertiary prevention. In general, most public health activities are directed at designated groups in the community which are considered, on the basis of epidemiological study, to be populations at risk. In this study, prematurity was considered to be a hazardous circumstance which poses a threat to family equilibrium and is likely to precipitate a family into a state of crisis. Therefore these families were

Source: Reprinted, with minor changes, from *Social Work,* VII (July 1962), 48–56. Used by permission.

designated as a "population at risk" and became a target for efforts of preventive intervention. The aim was to prevent mentally unhealthy consequences of the crisis which could interfere with the development of a sound mother-child relationship.

Numerous investigators have contributed to concepts of crisis, particularly Dr. Erich Lindemann and Dr. Gerald Caplan, both of Harvard University. In their formulation, crisis refers to the *state of the reacting individual* who finds himself in a hazardous situation.[2] Crisis in its simplest terms is defined as "an upset in a steady state." There are many hazardous events or circumstances in the life cycle of an individual or family which threaten or upset the balance that has been achieved in the system of need-satisfaction and in the performance of social roles. Certain hazardous events, such as loss of a loved person, have an almost universal impact and would precipitate a state of crisis of varying intensity and duration in nearly all individuals.

Underlying Assumptions

It is postulated that in a state of crisis the habitual problem-solving activities are not adequate for a rapid re-establishment of equilibrium. The hazardous event that precipitates the crisis is of such a nature as to require a solution that is new to the individual in relation to his previous life experience. Many individuals are able to develop novel solutions out of their normal range of problem-solving mechanisms and can deal adequately with the hazardous event. Others are unable to respond with appropriate solutions, so that the hazardous event and its sequelae continue to be a source of stress that creates considerable maladaptation.

The hazardous event creates for the individual a problem in his current life situation. The problem can be conceived as a threat, a loss, or a challenge. A threat may be directed to instinctual needs, or to the sense of integrity. A loss may be experienced as a state of acute deprivation. Furthermore, for each of these states there is a characteristic mode by which the ego tends to respond. Thus, a threat to need or integrity is responded to with anxiety. Loss or deprivation is responded to with depression. If the problem is viewed as a challenge it may be met with appropriate anxiety, fortified by hope and expectation of mastery. This, then, is more apt to lead to a mobilization of energy and to purposive problem-solving activities. In summary it may be said that there are three sets of interrelated factors which can produce a state of crisis: (1) a hazardous event which poses some threat; (2) a threat to instinctual need which is linked symbolically to earlier threats that have resulted in vulnerability or conflict in the personality; (3) inability to respond with adequate coping mechanisms.[3]

There are certain characteristics of the state of crisis. First, the period of crisis is time-limited—that is, the individual or family does manage, in due time, to achieve some solution for the problem. The crisis is resolved and a state of equilibrium is once again achieved. However, the outcome varies. Thus the new state of equilibrium may be the same, worse, or even better, from a mental health point of view, than that achieved prior to the crisis.

The second characteristic of the crisis state refers to phases that occur during the period of upset: first, there is a period of heightened tension; second, there is an attempt to solve the problem with habitual problem-solving mechanisms; third, emergency problem-solving mechanisms may be called on. The outcome may once again be variable: the problem may actually be solved, or the goals may be altered in order to achieve need-satisfaction and greater stability, or there may be a renunciation of desired goals.

The third—and for the practitioner the most important—characteristic is the fact that people are more susceptible to influence during a state of crisis. Moreover, the amount of activity on the part of helping persons does not have to be extensive. A little help, rationally directed and purposefully focused at a strategic time, is more effective than more extensive help given at a time of lesser emotional accessibility.

The outcome of a crisis is determined by numerous variables. Favorable environmental factors and current adaptive capacity are important. Less important in influencing outcome is the nature of the prior personality or psychopathology.[4] Most important of all is the accomplishment of, or failure to accomplish, certain specific psychological tasks and certain related problem-solving activities.

The mother who gives birth to a premature baby has to master certain specific psychological tasks and engage in certain problem-solving activities. These have been described as follows.[5]

Phase 1. Mother and infant are in the hospital after delivery. During this critical period the mother is faced with the following psychological tasks: She has to acknowledge that the infant's life is threatened and that survival in the early postnatal period may be uncertain. She has to acknowledge a sense of disappointment and even failure at having been unable to carry a baby to full term. In order to accomplish these psychological tasks, she must engage in some of the following problem-solving activities: She must prepare for possible loss of the baby with some anticipatory grief reaction such as sadness or depression. Denial of the real threat or too early an optimism and cheerfulness are considered risks from a mental health point of view. Since a sense of guilt and self-blame is frequently aroused, the mother must be able to deal actively with such feelings in order to reduce their intensity and possible later negative effects.

Phase 2. The mother is at home; the infant remains in premature nursery. The psychological tasks require the development of some hope that the infant will survive and will be home soon. It requires recognition that a premature infant needs special care, but that eventually the needs and characteristics of the infant will be that of a normal child. The problem-solving activities require that the mother take an active interest in the details of the progress of the baby while it is in the nursery and that she prepare for its needs.

Phase 3. The infant is now at home. The chief psychological task is the establishment of a tender and nurturing relationship between mother and infant, which has been ruptured by the premature birth and in some instances by long separation. The problem-solving tasks require the assumption of the nurturing role, attention and sensitivity to special needs, and (in some instances) coping realistically with congenital abnormalities frequently found in prematures.

On the basis of preliminary study, certain patterns have been identified which are considered maladaptive and which prognosticate a poor outcome to the crisis. For example, some mothers deny heavily both the threat to life and the implications of maternal failure. Some fail to respond with hope to indications that the infant will survive. Some have no interest in the details of the baby's development and may refuse to visit or be active in securing information about the baby's growth.

Description of the Study

The following observations are based on work with eleven families comprising a total of sixty interviews, all held in the home.[6] In addition, there were contacts with health and welfare agencies in behalf of some of the families.

The case-finding aspects of the project were handled as follows: A psychiatrist staff member developed liaison with the city hospital and was notified of all premature births. During the period of case finding for this study, he interviewed mothers on the ward soon after delivery. These interviews were brief and were not traditional psychiatric interviews with intent of probing. Instead the aim was twofold. First, to make a rapid assessment of the mother's (and when available, the family's) reaction to the current stressful event; to note coping mechanisms with which the stress was being handled; and to make predictions at this early stage regarding the outcome, to be verified later. Second, to obtain sanction for a social worker to visit the family in the home in order to follow developments and offer any help that might be needed. It should be noted that because of hospital regulations the social worker, coming from an outside agency, was not permitted to visit and work with the mothers in the hospital. Therefore no work could be done with the mothers during the first important phase of the crisis.[7]

The families were then visited, whenever possible, during the first week following the mother's discharge from the hospital. The frequency, spacing, and duration of contacts were determined flexibly on the basis of assessment of the families' needs and were sustained wherever possible only until the crisis appeared resolved. The following three case examples are cited to illustrate the range of problems encountered and the kinds of intervention offered.

Case One

The Brown family consisted of a young working-class Negro couple and their premature first-born baby. The mother was seventeen, the father twenty-four. The baby was born during the seventh month, weighing four pounds and four ounces. The mother was seen twice by the project psychiatrist, on the second and fifth days after delivery. She was being treated for a kidney infection, which explains her longer hospitalization. She was in a markedly sullen mood on both occasions, but did warm up to the doctor. She indicated to the worker later that this contact meant a great deal to her because she had an opportunity to talk to someone. She was quite worried about the baby's welfare, exasperated at not getting news, but unable to be insistent in making inquiries. She became more anxious on hearing of the death of a smaller premature infant. She tended to blame overwork, not taking vitamins, and the kidney infection as possible causes for the premature delivery. On the basis of her concern, her ability to express normal anxiety, and her wish to have the baby home soon, it was predicted that she would make a good relationship with the baby and would be a competent mother, although somewhat anxious.

There were six home visits, numerous phone calls, and contacts with health agencies regarding the Brown family. The first visit occurred one week after the mother's discharge from the hospital, at the paternal grandparents' home. The mother was able to express disappointment that the baby was not yet home. Despite a characteristic guardedness, abruptness, and sullen, hostile defense displayed at each contact, she soon warmed up and was eager to discuss the baby, and asked very specific questions. The father was acutely uncomfortable, taciturn, and soon fled from the interview. He was not seen again, and the next visits were focused on the mother's needs.

In the first interview the mother was still troubled with feelings of guilt and responsibility for the baby's early arrival, which had caught her unprepared, especially psychologically. She did not get a chance to wear her new maternity suit, which meant she really did not have a long enough period as young wife without motherhood. Nevertheless, she was eager to get the baby home, was defensive about not having visited, and took pride in the layette she was readying. She and her husband visited subsequently until the baby's discharge. She was appropriately anxious, in view of her inexperience, about the care of the baby. It was the worker's initial impression that she would have ample help from extended family and public health nurses. This was an erroneous impression. The female members were not helpful and no public health nurse or well-baby clinic was available in this town. The worker's role therefore became primarily an educational one. The mother was extremely eager to learn and was found to be very responsive and educable. The emphasis was on helping her find ways of getting information she needed as well as on supplying basic knowledge of infant care and development.

The seond visit, a long one, was scheduled the day after the baby came home at the age of four weeks. Gradually the mother's uncertainities unfolded. She was alone with the newborn, had never made a formula, was worried about room temperature and about his weight. She was upset by his diaper rash, blamed the hospital for negligence, and changed his diapers every fifteen minutes, washing them by hand. She gave the baby orange juice and vitamins, and had little idea of quantity; a month later it was learned that she was giving the baby concentrated undiluted orange juice, which explained his diarrhea. This happened despite carefully detailed discussions regarding routines. Her attitude toward the baby was one of great concern and wanting to do right. She did not appear overly warm or maternal, yet was attentive to the baby's communications and needs.

On subsequent visits more concerns were expressed, despite the fact that the baby was progressing well. The hospital discharged the mother with some printed instructions she had not read: they were in small print and hard to understand. The worker presented her with a copy of Spock's baby book. Some of the language was found to be geared to middle-class education and sophistication. Worker and mother studied the book together; the latter was charmed with the pictures, and learned to use the index. She was eager to make use of health facilities but needed precise information as to how to initiate things. When told exactly, she always followed through. With the worker's active intervention and enlistment of the help of medical social workers at a private pediatric hospital, the baby was taken on for care. The mother followed through, although it required a long trip to a strange community. Despite careful preparation, as with the orange juice, communication failed. The mother went to the hospital without the baby to inquire about eligibility. This was misinterpreted by the medical personnel as an expression of her suspiciousness and resistance. The worker's active and rapid clarification once again smoothed the pathway for this family to develop good patterns of health care.

Case Two

The Kellys, an Irish Catholic working-class family, are an example of prediction of a healthy outcome, confirmed by three follow-up visits. The mother delivered a four-pound premature boy and a stillborn male twin of twelve ounces. Her water bag had broken two months previously and she was carefully followed prenatally. A premature birth had been anticipated, but not a stillborn twin. When interviewed briefly by the project psychiatrist three days after delivery, she had already seen the baby three times through the glass of the nursery. She had three children under six at home. She was able to express concern about the needs of the newborn and was eager to get some idea of when he might come home. She was active in "pestering" doctors and nurses to seek out information about the baby, who was jaundiced and edematous. On the basis of the mother's ability to mourn for the dead twin, to express open concern for the surviving infant, to seek medical information aggressively, and to use warmth and support of the extended family and religious institutions, it was predicted that the outcome of the crisis would be excellent and the mother-child relationship satisfactory. There was no need for preventive intervention, but follow-up was initiated for research purposes and to verify the prediction.

The first visit was made five weeks after delivery. An earlier visit failed to locate the family, who had no telephone. The parents were pleased to see the worker, despite the fact that the visit was unscheduled and the mother in bed with flu. Noteworthy were the parents' ease in communication with each other and the worker and their spontaneous ability to recount in detail, with appropriate affect, the painful events of pregnancy, precipitous birth, the death of the twin, and the prolonged hospitalization of the baby. Before her current illness the mother had visited the baby three times. The father visited daily. More remarkable was their active communication with the medical staff. It was against hospital policy to give telephone information even to parents. Nevertheless the pediatrician frequently telephoned the parents at a neighbor's. The baby was in the hospital longer than anticipated because of anemia, necessitating blood tranfusions. During the second visit, five weeks later, the mother was seen alone. The baby was still not at home because of the blood level and need for surgery for umbilical hernia. The striking feature was the mother's active seeking and using medical knowledge as a way of mastering the crisis. She was appropriately concerned, but also optimistic. There was a definite reduction in her level of tension, despite the disappointment of the long hospitalization.

The third visit, one month later, found the family at home, elated and happy. The baby had been home a fortnight. Prior to his actual homecoming they had suffered a needless trauma due to communication failure; they were told to get the baby and went with great anticipation, only to learn it was an error. They came home, again empty-handed, were disappointed and depressed. This reactivated the original disappointment and loss, but gave them a second chance to work out the mourning process. Now they were relieved and less anxious, even coping comfortably with the baby's colic. It may be noted that from the beginning the infant had an identity and place in the family. He was "little Joey" and was talked about easily and freely. In this last contact with the worker the opportunity was created for the family to relive once again the whole experience from beginning to end. The fortuitous outcome in this case, despite long hospitalization and medical complications, was related to the family's close ties, shared goals, communication patterns, and capacity for conscious problem-solving. The mother had a high degree of interpersonal skills and was able to handle medical personnel in order to get needed information. She did this aggressively but with kidding and lightness of touch, managing her own anxiety and thus avoiding stimulating the feelings of guilt of professional personnel, which so often result in their withdrawal and withholding. Despite the mother's experience in raising babies, she welcomed the possibility of visits by the public health nurse and used the social worker constructively for abreaction and mastery.

Case Three

The Minellis, an Italian Catholic working-class family, illustrate the need for long-term intervention dictated by the fact that the current crisis was superimposed on chronic family problems and repeated crises which were the characteristic family life style. On the basis of two brief contacts in the hospital, the first with the husband present, the project psychiatrist in his prediction expressed uneasiness about the family's adjustment to the new baby. There were indications that the family needed to be visited, for there was danger of neglect for the baby. These ominous predictions were based on the following observations: The baby was born at seven months weighing three pounds. The parents insisted that everything was fine and expected the baby to be home in a month. Two important facts stood out: This was the sixth premature child in the family, all of whom had survived. However, this infant had the smallest birth weight.

It might be expected that with this family history confidence and hope might be high.[8] On the other hand, the expectation of the baby's homecoming in a month showed evidence of unrealistic thinking and denial in view of the extensive prior experience with prematurity. There were other indications of denial. The husband, particularly, did not permit his wife or himself to express any feelings of anxiety. He insisted that once the baby began to eat everything would be all right. When the wife was seen alone without the repressive presence of her husband, she was indeed visibly more anxious but still clung to her denial defenses. For example, at the time of delivery she had been ill with a strep throat, but denied its significance. There was indication that the mother has some real conflict about this baby. Prediction therefore was of a dubious outcome and guarded prognosis.

All the early cues of a very troubled family situation and problematic mother-child relationship were unfortunately confirmed. The family was visited five days after delivery, when the mother had been at home two days. During this visit the family presented a solid, united, euphoric front. The father handled his anxiety regarding the newborn by boasting of the good health and strong development of the other children. Later it was found that all the children had numerous health problems, some severe, all of which were being neglected. The mother was taking expensive medicine (antibiotics)—her "Christmas present"—not knowing what it was for. Her husband's fantasy was that it would "heal up her insides." The parents hardly discussed the baby. The nurse in the premature nursery reported that the mother had shown no interest in the baby and had not come down to visit while she was in the hospital.

This family was visited twenty times, with numerous phone contacts and collaborative contacts with health agencies. Every area of their social functioning was problematic and chaotic. They were in severe and chronic financial difficulties despite the husband's fairly steady and well-paid employment. The children were malnourished and chronically hungry. They were periodically threatened with loss of utilities and eviction by the housing project. There were periodic altercations with neighbors and recriminations in court. Two of the school-aged children were slow learners and were threatened with being left back in school. All children had uncared-for health problems; they were in need of eye surgery, tonsillectomies, orthopedic attention, and polio shots.

There were severe problems also in the mother's inability to manage and control the children. The older ones were defiant and attacking. The mother handled discipline by explosive outbursts, ineffectual threats, bribery, and virtual encouragement of the children to lie and steal. There were severe marital problems. The mother was terrified of another pregnancy but could not handle the sexual relationship because of internal conflicts and external religious prohibitions regarding birth control. The husband was depressed and disgruntled with his job and plagued by physical symptoms for which he refused medical attention. The extended family was in proximity but could offer no help.

The baby was very slow in his development both at the hospital and at home, despite the absence of any abnormalities. For example, at six weeks he weighed only three pounds and eleven ounces. At eight weeks he came home weighing five pounds and two ounces. The relief about this was noted by the mother only in terms of the children having quieted down. The mother had visited the baby in hospital only once, and only at the worker's urging. She did not visit at the time of her postnatal check-up. The baby's subsequent slow development was of concern. He was extremely lethargic, apathetic, and unresponsive, making few demands of any kind. He was given very cursory and minimal handling. His bottle rolled around in the crib and whoever passed by might pop it in his mouth. In contrast to many mothers of premature babies who are overly concerned with diet and push feeding, this mother seemed unconcerned and unable to request help with change of formula even after months had elapsed, although her other children's diet at a comparable age had been enriched. The baby received very little handling and stimulation and was picked up and held, briefly at best, only with the worker's encouragement. He did not have a real place in the family, and began to be identified by name only at the age of six months. The mother found very little pleasure in him. She saw him in a positive way only insofar as he provided something for her—that is, he helped her "keep her mind off her worries." There was evidence that her greater attentiveness at night enabled her to use the baby as a way of avoiding sexual contact with her husband. She admitted that she had tried to abort him.

The contacts with this family had a multiple purpose. The primary task, in keeping with the research, was to focus on getting a relationship going between mother and infant—a relationship in this instance ruptured by the baby's prolonged separation while in hospital and further weakened by the fact of his being unwanted. Active intervention via encouragement and demonstration consisted of stimulating visiting, physical contact, and more adequate nurturing. The mother made fleeting efforts, but her responses were not sustained. Active intervention was also offered regarding health needs for the baby and other children, by opening contacts with public health nurses who had become hostile to this family. Rules were modified, fees were waived, and punitive or negative attitudes on the part of other caretaking personnel were modified by consultation and collaboration methods.

The secondary task (but of prime importance in this chronically disordered family) was to break through the family's denial and inactivity and to involve them in beginning problem solving and coping with urgent demands. Active intervention in this respect consisted of securing free school lunches, concrete help with budgeting, meal-planning, and management of debts; some demonstration of child management, since efforts at modifying attitudes and handling failed; pushing the mother out of her fruitless obsessional worrying by activating some beginning of coping with small pieces of problems and tasks; getting her out of the house, where she was characteristically immobilized over coffee and cigarettes and aimless fretting. It was recognized that this family would need long-term intervention for any sustained results. As is true of many chronically needy and dependent families, this one made no demands and did not make use of resources even when the family was eligible and the resources available to them. Most needs were handled by means of magical thinking and wish fulfillment, or frantic worrying leading to rumination and inactivity rather than direct action. The mother enjoyed the "friendly visiting," made no demands, held herself aloof and detached except for rare occasions when some genuine affect broke through and she turned to the worker to unburden.

The husband was seen less frequently. He managed to remove himself physically or refused to participate, encouraged by his wife, who tried to shield him from worries. Among the children, all but the oldest formed strong attachments to the worker, displayed their great hunger for affection and contact, and at times saw the worker as the embodiment of standards and benign controls for which they still yearned despite the prevailing influences of corruption and chaos that ruled their lives.

Summary and Conclusion

These three cases illustrate a range of responses to the crisis of prematurity. In the first case the family's coping mechanisms were not adequate to the task essentially because of lack of knowledge. Intervention therefore was largely educational in purpose. The second case illustrates adequate coping with the crisis. The third case illustrates great inadequacy during the crisis—a cumulative product of chronic inadequacy which even extended preventive intervention failed to modify.

Preventive intervention with the families studied consisted of a range of activities. They can be classified into three broad categories.

1. Keeping an explicit focus on the crisis. Four specific goals may be subsumed in this category:

Help with cognitive mastery: not all families consciously perceive a hazardous event and their reactions to it as a time of family crisis. A major task of preventive intervention is to help the family gain a conscious grasp of the crisis, in order to enhance purposeful problem solving, leading toward mastery. It has been noted by various investigators that clarification of the precipitating stress, or connection of subjective distress with stressful event, is in itself of therapeutic significance.[9]

Help with doubts of feminine adequacy, guilt, and self-blame stimulated by the failure to carry the pregnancy to term.

Help with grief work and mourning in relation to feelings of loss and emptiness stimulated by separation from the infant.

Help with anticipatory worry work and anticipatory guidance. These activities are carried on in the context of supportive and clarifying techniques with which social workers are familiar. Sometimes it is sufficient to work out the crisis on the level of the "here and now." At other times it may be necessary to make more explicit the symbolic link of the present crisis to earlier unresolved conflicts. These links may be difficult to establish within the context of a brief relationship which is not geared to conflict resolution, or clarification leading toward insight. Nevertheless, because of the pressure of the crisis, such conflicts or derivatives may surge nearer to consciousness and may be accessible to direct interpretation.

2. Offering basic information and education regarding child development and child care through a variety of devices, including use of relationship for demonstration and identification.

3. Creating a bridge to community resources, opening pathways of referral, and intervening in communication failures and in problems of stereotyping and misinterpretation of motivation and need.

Notes

1. Hugh R. Leavell and E. G. Clark, *Preventive Medicine for the Doctor in His Community* (New York: McGraw-Hill, 1958), pp. 21–29.
2. Erich Lindemann and Gerald Caplan, "A Conceptual Framework for Preventive Psychiatry" (unpub. paper).
3. Howard J. Parad and Gerald Caplan, "A Framework for Studying Families in Crisis," *Social Work,* V, no. 3 (July 1960), 5.
4. This concept will seem particularly at variance with traditionalist psychiatric views.
5. These concepts were developed by David Kaplan at the Family Guidance Center, Harvard School of Public Health, and are described in "Predicting Outcome from Situational Stress on the Basis of Individual Problem-Solving Patterns" (Ph.D. diss., University of Minnesota, 1961).
6. Five of the eleven families were visited by a graduate student from the Smith College School for Social Work, supervised by the author.
7. It may very well be that the inaccessibility of the mothers to the social worker during the stress impact period brought into focus some emotional tasks and needs during the second phase which might better have been resolved earlier.
8. A finding of the research project revealed that prior experience with prematurity was not a significant factor in the outcome of the crisis. Birth weight as a factor showed surprisingly that the outcome of the family crisis was better with smaller premature infants than larger ones (see Kaplan, "Predicting Outcome," p. 115).
9. B. L. Kalis, M. R. Harris, A. R. Prestwood, and E. H. Freeman, "Precipitating Stress as a Focus in Psychotherapy," *Archives of General Psychiatry,* V, no. 3 (Sept. 1961), 219–26.

III

Consultation, Supervision, and Professional Education

7 *Mental Health Consultation*

General Definition and Scope

Consultation is a professional activity which, in its simplest sense and by common usage, refers to a process by which an expert attempts to help a less knowledgeable consultee solve a problem. Consultation is an inclusive term under which many diverse and often contradictory meanings and practices are subsumed. Even the title of "consultant" is a ubiquitous one under which many roles and functions may be carried out. Furthermore, neither the title nor even the role, suggests the utilization of a specific method.

Although a prototype of mental health consultation, psychiatric case consultation cannot serve as a complete model for the wide range of activities which consultants are now requested to undertake in the expanding mental health field. Traditionally, psychiatric case consultation has served as an important means by which knowledge about individual cases is conveyed by a psychiatric consultant to other psychiatrists or to persons in related clinical disciplines. In some instances the psychiatrist-consultant examines the patient as part of his case consultation procedure. Regardless of the presence or absence of direct patient contact, generally psychiatric case consultation has been patient-centered and not necessarily focused on the consultee's problems in working with the patient. In contrast, mental health consultation always concentrates on the consultee's work problems, and the mental health consultant would not deal directly with clients. Furthermore, the consultee is usually affiliated with some profession other than the clinical mental health disciplines.

In the past decade there has been widespread interest in the use of mental health consultation as a vehicle for the systemic exten-

Source: Written with Clarice H. Haylett, M.D. Reprinted, with minor changes, from *Handbook in Community Psychiatry*, ed. Leopold Bellak (New York: Grune & Stratton, 1963), ch. 17. Used by permission.

sion of mental health principles and practices to other professionals and community service workers, for possible incorporation into their programs and activities. In most instances, the demands for this new type of mental health consultation have come before a reasonable body of knowledge or sufficient collation of experience has become available to indicate precisely how mental health consultation, or some other method such as mental health education, might be most appropriately selected and applied in any given situation.

Towle pioneered in conceptualizing the consultation process,[1] and Babcock was among the first to describe her experiences as a psychiatric case consultant to social agencies and related groups.[2] Leviton in his discussion of her paper developed several themes that presage the evolution of mental health consultation as presently practiced. Extension of mental health consultation to nonclinical professionals has necessitated further modifications of the traditional medical psychiatric case consultation methods and the recruitment of consultants who are able to apply their professional knowledge in new ways. Berlin and Parker in California, and Caplan and his associates in Massachusetts, have begun to define some of the supplementary methods and knowledge areas useful in this newly evolving type of "mental health consultation."[3] As more experience and understanding are acquired, there will doubtless be further modifications and elaborations.

The small but growing literature on mental health consultation reflects the current diversity of opinion and practices. In an evolving specialty, it is understandable that there will be lack of precise agreement as to objectives, definitions, and methods. Foci of practice and investigation have developed independently in a number of diverse geographical areas, influenced, among other factors, by idiosyncratic conditions of local community need and response. Theory and terminology have been borrowed from more than one field and professional discipline. Thus, familiar terms may appear in new contexts, imbued with new meanings, and may actually hamper meaningful communication if specific examples of intent or practice are omitted. For instance, historically the term "client" derives from a role of dependency. More recently it has come to mean "a customer," especially a recipient of professional services and particularly of legal or social services. In mental health consultation jargon, the term "client" is further extended. For purposes of this discussion, the term "consultant" shall denote a mental health specialist who consults with "consultees," who are professionals from other fields; often, the subject of consultation is the mental health aspects of their work with "clients." Thus, clients are the people served by the consultee in his professional role; they may be students if the consultee is a teacher, patients if the consultee is a nurse, parishioners if the consultee is a clergyman, and so forth.

In the recent literature there is evidence of a growing desire for clarity, precision, and, where possible, uniformity in terminology. There is also considerable impetus to order and conceptualize mental health consultation principles and practices in order to facilitate teaching and field application in a conscious professional manner. There is reason to believe that we may be approaching a generally acceptable and commonly understood nomenclature, significantly influenced by the writings of Caplan[4] and his colleagues in Massachusetts. However, there is much less consensus regarding underlying theory. There has not yet been time for validation of many of our working hypotheses, either by predictable repetition or by the experience of other investigators in a variety of settings. Until such critia can be met, mental health consultation must be viewed as an evolving specialty, in which any closure of the theoretical framework would be premature and ill advised.

Mental Health Consultation and "Preventive Psychiatry"

Since World War II, there has been increasingly widespread concern over the prevalence of mental illness, emotional disability, and the frequently related problems of economic dependency and behavior disorders. This concern has had several results. For one, mental illness has been designated the nation's number one health problem, which, in turn, has given impetus to the application of public health principles and practices to the field of psychiatry. There has been a marked increase in public and private support of studies on how to combat mental illness. The latest and most extensive of these, by the Joint Commission on Mental Illness and Health, strongly affirms the need for continuing research and better usage of existing knowledge and experience.[5] This study, as others before it, emphasizes the need to involve not only clinically trained mental health workers, but all basic community service workers, in programs aimed at the control and prevention of mental illness. Broad community involvement is one of the Joint Commission's major recommendations; mental health consultation is recognized as a primary means of implementing this.

Massachusetts, New York, and California were among the first states to promote community mental health centers which would provide not only "direct" diagnostic and treatment services, but also "indirect services." The latter include the following: (1) mental health consultation to nonpsychiatric agencies and professionals in the health, welfare, religious, educational, law enforcement, recreational, and vocational fields; (2) leadership in the development and coordination of facilities and services which contribute to the preservation of mental health; (3) direction and support for mental health education activities.

The rationale for these indirect services, and particularly for mental health consultation, derives in no small measure from insights provided by clinical psychiatry and psychoanalytic child psychology. Biologists have long been familiar with the phenomenon of critical developmental stages, at which time a differentiating organ or system is particularly susceptible to, and may be seriously damaged by, experiences which would have little effect on a more mature organism. Although first formulated in terms of physical growth and maturation, it is now generally accepted that there are critical periods in personality development as well. There is ample documentation of the importance of the early mother-child relationship, both insofar as the quality of protective nurturance and the consistency and continuity of such nurturance. At a later developmental stage it is important that the child be stimulated to undertake various activities, and that he achieve a fair degree of mastery over these activities. Limitations and frustrations should also be imposed in proper amounts, at the proper times. Thus, from earliest infancy, interpersonal factors are acknowledged as significant determinants in personality development, along with genetic and constitutional factors. In order to facilitate healthy ego development, the community mental health worker will wish to see such knowledge reflected in child rearing and socialization practices, and will use whatever educational, consultative, or administrative means are available to this end.

In addition, the concept of mental health as a balance of dynamic psychological forces, invites attention to social and interpersonal, as well as intrapsychic, factors. Just as there are critical developmental periods, there are also periods of disequilibrium throughout the life cycle which may result in a state of "crisis." Lindemann has focused on bereavement as one such critical period and emphasized the importance of grief work.[6] School entry, marriage, pregnancy, and retirement are some other critical life stages which have received special attention. Mental health clinicians are rarely called in at the time of these "normal" crises, although at a later date they may see some of the resultant casualities, when the critical issues were resolved maladaptively.

If one accepts the premises that a crisis is a time of disequilibrium and that generally people are more susceptible to influence while under stress, then presumably minimal intervention at that time may exert considerably greater influence than if applied after a new equilibrium has been attained. Thus, timely, sympathetic, and generally appropriate interventions by family physicians, nurses, clergymen, public welfare workers, teachers, or by whatever other knowledgeable supportive person is available, may make the difference between a healthy adjustment and various degrees of subsequent emotional disability. Therefore, community agencies and professionals who have significant contact with children or with people who experience severe emotional stress become important mental health resources which should be supported and strengthened through mental health consultation.

In the late 1940s, Lindemann and his colleagues at the Wellesley Human Relations Service,[7] Caplan in Israel,[8] and subsequently others who were interested in social psychiatry, began to experiment with mental health consultation and in-service training methods for selected nonpsychiatric professional personnel. Starting with case collaboration and psychiatric case consultation techniques, they began to develop modifications which appeared to be effective in strengthening the mental health aspects of their consultees' work. In the 1950s, there was a rapid burgeoning of interest in community mental health consultation. Its popularity has continued to increase as conviction has grown that it may be a reasonably efficient means of promoting and developing the mental health potential in the programs as well as the practices of a wide variety of community service organizations.

Hallock and Vaughan were probably the first to describe a

statewide community mental health program which included mental health consultation as one if its basic operating services.[9] They characterized mental health consultation as a service which might, at times, approximate the public health goal of "specific prevention" and developed a logical basis for this linkage. By the mid-1950s mental health center teams in Massachusetts had added mental health consultants to the familiar clinical triad, and mental health consultation was presented as an operation of central importance in community mental health practice.

By defining community mental health practice as a new public health field in which elements of the theory and practice of clinical psychiatry and public health are combined, mental health programming can be related to the public health concepts of disease and disability prevention. Through this linkage, mental health consultation and other indirect services are often loosely associated with the goals and methods of "primary prevention."[10] It should be noted, however, that there is no intrinsic or exclusive relationship between mental health consultation and primary prevention. Mental health consultation can be related to every level and aspect of prevention depending on the programs and professional roles played by the consultees. For instance, if a consultee's job affords opportunities to influence child care practices, and mental health consultation results in fewer traumatic mother-child separations, then one could reason that mental health consultation contributes to the promotion of mental health and avoidance of emotional disorder, and hence to primary prevention. Similarly, where consultation results in earlier recognition of a client's mental illness and prompt referral for effective care, then consultation helps to prevent further extension of the illness and thus contributes to secondary prevention. Finally, if consultation expedites the rehabilitation of a mentally ill person, thus preventing further disability, consultation can be related to teriary prevention. In summary, since the mental health consultant does not work directly with clients, it is only in relation to the professional programs and practices of consultees that mental health consultation can be categorized at any level as a "preventive" psychiatric service.

Mental Health Consultation Distinguished from Other Procedures in Community Psychiatry

This section and those which follow present our current definitions and working hypotheses regarding mental health consultation and those methods and techniques which have seemed empirically useful.[11] Although some conceptual models and basic nomenclature were taken from Caplan's early papers, there have been other significant influences. Thus, the theory and practice presented here represent a consensus, an eclectic synthesis, and are a reflection of our continuing pragmatism.

As mentioned earlier, no brief or simple definition of mental health consultation exists. A descriptive definition is offered, as follows: mental health consultation is a process of interaction between a mental health professional and one or more "consultees" for the purpose of increasing the consultee's awareness of, and ability to manage, the mental health components of his work. This goal is achieved by the consultant as he helps the consultee to clarify and find solutions for current mental health problems in relationship either to specific clients or to programs and practices of the consultee's organization as these influence the mental health of groups of clients. The process proceeds optimally when there is a positive relationship between consultant and consultee, based on mutual respect and trust. The nature of this relationship has been described as a "coordinate" one.[12] This emphasizes the fact that the consultant has no administrative control over the consultee and that each has his own area of competence. For this reason, it is frequently stated that consultation has a "take it or leave it" quality. However, the consultant does exercise the "authority of ideas" because of his professional expertness. His function is to offer his specialized knowledge, attidudes, values, and sometimes even his actual skills. It is the corresponding obligation of the consultee to make use of the consultant's help in a manner appropriate to his own professional role and particular work situation. If the consultee is able to generalize from a specific experience to other similar situations, then the consultant has provided some measure of education, as well as help with the presenting problem.

It is necessary to differentiate mental health consultation from other methods used in the mental health field such as supervision, in-service training, professional education, psychotherapy, and collaboration. In fact, there are many points of similarity among these methods as to goals, principles, and techniques. All these methods have in common the dual purposes of education and help, but with varying degrees of emphasis. All are rooted in the behavioral sciences, although some are more closely related to a particular field than others. For example, psychotherapy is related to clinical psychiatry and psychoanalytic psychology; professional education is related to learning theories, and so forth. All depend centrally on the professional use of relationship and on communication techniques. All may use some of the therapeutic techniques most consistently applied in psychotherapy such as support, suggestion, abreaction, manipulation, and clarification. Thus, when used in the mental health field, the differences in these methods are not so much determined by a differential knowledge base or the employment of differential techniques, as by the primary purpose of the transaction and other considerations such as setting, nature and degree of authority in the relationship, the nature of role relationships, and the defined limits of the shared task.

In psychotherapy there is usually explicit agreement between therapist and patient that their mutual task is to increase the patient's effectiveness in coping with his personal problems. Although in some instances the therapist may actively intervene to lessen stresses in his patient's environment or assume an authoritative role and tell the patient what to do, more often the approach is one of helping the patient to understand and solve his problems himself. It is generally accepted that any area of personal experience or feeling may be relevant and subject to scrutiny in the psychotherapy process. The duration and intensity of the relationship between therapist and patient are less definitive criteria than intent and personal problem focus, since some psychotherapy is very goal-limited and brief, as is usually true of mental health consultation. Insofar as the ego's capacity to deal with reality is strengthened, this process also has educational implications, but this is of secondary import.

The crucial difference between supervision and consultation lies in the administrative and authoritative aspects of the supervisory role. Supervision typically involves joint work problem solving but it also may have a major educational component. Where the supervisee is an experienced worker, the relationship may approximate consultation. However, supervision can never become synonymous with consultation, since the supervisor's administrative responsibilities are always explicit.

Professional education is the method by which the basic attitudes, values, knowledge, and principles of practice of a particular discipline are conveyed in an orderly and sequential fashion to a student who seeks to become a member of that profession. In contrast, in-service training utilizes educational techniques to maintain or improve competence in a job for which, presumably, the minimal requirements have already been met. When the purpose of in-service training is to improve a professional staff's knowledge and skill in handling the mental health aspects of their work with clients, then it may be very difficult to differentiate it from group mental health consultation. Somewhat arbitrary separation is possible, however, on the basis that in consultation the emphasis is on current work problem solving, whereas in the primarily educational processes there is an orderly, systematic coverage of the subject.[13]

Collaboration is a process in which two or more professionals share the responsibility for various aspects of the management of a case or for some other professional activity. The professionals may or may not be from the same organization, agency, or discipline. They may meet to share information, identify problems, or consider various plans for cooperative action. As in consultation the relationship is coordinate. The essential difference between consultation and collaboration is the direct line of responsibility borne by each collaboration in relation to the subject of their collaboration. Familiar examples of collaboration are the interagency family case conference and the increasingly frequent practice of collaboration between therapists working with several members of the same family. Collaboration which occurs between responsible community leaders and agency executives regarding community problems and program considerations, is usually called "community organization."

It has been pointed out that all these methods are employed in the mental health field. To varying degrees, they all have both problem-solving and educational aspects. Thus, it is necessary to recognize their basic differences if one is to choose the most appropriate method for a particular program objective.

Types of Mental Health Consultation

All mental health consultation is directed toward helping consultees to understand and cope with selected work problems. Hence, to a significant degree, all consultation is consultee-centered and task-oriented. Nevertheless, the proximate goals, functions, roles, and activities of a mental health consultant range widely. There have been various attempts to classify these activities into orderly categories. However, it is difficult to develop a typology that is operationally useful because consultation is a dynamic process in which there are shifts in content, focus, and activity. Classifications require conceptualizing the process in a static way. For example, a classification can be made on the basis of what is happening at a given moment, which is analogous to viewing a single frame in a motion picture. It is also possible to characterize the whole process by selecting the most representative or frequently occurring area of activity. Despite the difficulties, a commonly understood typology is desirable in order to facilitate communication, thus permitting the experiences of various consultants to be summarized and compared.

There are several criteria which can be used to determine the classification of mental health consultation—for example, (1) the method used (such as individual or group consultation); (2) the content of the work problems presented by the consultee (such as case material, program considerations, or administrative matters); (3) the problem area on which the consultant focuses (such as the problems of the client, the problems of the consultee in dealing with his client or with other professional tasks, or the problems of the organization in relation to policies and procedures as they affect the mental health needs of clients). Thus, one may speak of client-centered, consultee-centered, or program-centered mental health consultation. This particular categorization permits, under "consultee-centered consultation," the inclusion of work with staff, supervisors, and administrators who are using consultation for help with problems concerning clients, problems with personnel, or problems with service and program implementation. It does not classify the consultee according to his hierarchical position, since the consultation techniques used are essentially the same. In actual practice these categories overlap, since there are apt to be shifts in focus during the consultation process. Nevertheless, it is useful for the consultant to be aware of such overlap and shifts in focus, so that he may be clear as to his role at any given time.

In client-centered consultation the proximate goal is to promote change in a particular client, and the consultant concentrates on activities which will enhance understanding of the psychodynamics of the client's behavior. First, he will try to arrive at some diagnostic assessment. Subsequently, he may participate in plans for disposition or treatment. This might involve discussion of other community resources and what they have to offer, as well as how the consultee, himself, might work with his client. Such activities have been classified by Caplan as "case insight" and "action help."[14]

Generally, all data regarding the client is provided or transmitted by the consultee. He describes the client and his interaction with him, and reports other relevant information. Although, occasionally, the consultant may observe a client, such as a child in the classroom, direct interaction between the client and the consultant would alter the nature of transaction. When a psychiatric consultant does examine a client directly, in order to determine his mental status, he becomes a collaborator as well as a consultant. Such direct interaction between the psychiatric consultant and the client is typical of medical consultation, wherein the medical consultant often examines the patient before giving an opinion or advice. However, the medical consultant is often expected to put his recommended therapeutic regimen into effect. This is not the usual understanding and practice in mental health consultation where, if additional data is deemed necessary, the consultee may be encouraged to initiate steps to obtain it by referral of clients to appropriate clinical facilities. Quite possibly, the client would be referred to a clinic with which the mental health consultant was affiliated. The consultant might become the examining clinician and thereafter he might participate, on a collaborative basis, in a case conference about the client with his former consultee. In community practice, it is not unusual for a mental health consultant to play many professional roles. For semantic clarity, however, the connotation of "mental health consultation" should be limited and differentiated from other professional activities.

In consultee-centered consultation, the proximate goal is to enhance the consultee's professional functioning in order to strengthen his service to clients or his effectiveness in program development. In this type of consultation the consultant brings to bear all his clinical and consultation skills, including his knowledge of the consultee's agency and professional subculture. He must make a complicated appraisal of the consultee's difficulties in work problem solving and determine whether the difficulty is in the area of perception and understanding, action planning, or implementation. He also needs to determine whether the consultee's difficulty is related to any lack of knowledge or skill, or administrative limitations; and whether he might be blocked by personal factors. The consultant must then consider which helping measures would be appropriately within the boundaries of his role. The consultant is concerned with an evaluation of the consultee's personal or professional functioning only insofar as it bears on the problem presented, and then only as one aspect of his privately formulated diagnostic assessment.

The proximate goal in program-centered consultation is to influence the programs or practices of a consultee organization in order that the mental health needs of its clients may be consciously considered and met where possible and appropriate. Since a single administrative decision with respect to agency policy can affect large numbers of people, program-centered consultation may have far-reaching consequences. An example would be the decision to place preadoptive infants in subsidized foster homes, rather than follow the potentially more damaging procedure of placing them in institutional nurseries until they can be cleared for placement. In some program-centered consultation, the consultant's primary role may be to offer his professional opinions about general policy, rather than considering specific agency problems. In such instances, his own value system and leadership ability may properly be brought to bear more directly than in consultation which is primarily consultee-centered.

Although it is used with increasing frequency, program-centered consultation is still relatively rare in community mental health practice on the local level. By contrast, on other levels, various patterns of program-centered consultation have become familiar. At times, in his relationship with local, state, and federal agencies, the consultant in program development may combine his consultation functions with administrative and supervisory responsibilities. In other instances, a "purer" consultation pattern is maintained, based solely on the consultant's authority as an expert. This pattern would be typical for local level program-centered consultation. Such consultation might take the following form: Consultation with a pediatric ward staff about the separation problems of a young child might lead to consultation with the hospital administrator about regulations governing the frequency of parent visits. In the course of consultation with the administrator, the consultant might explain first how the current visiting regulations affected the mental health of the child about whom staff were presently concerned, and then generalize to other children and their experiences in other hospitals. Before he arrives at a decision to modify hospital policies or procedures, the administrator must, of course, consider many factors in addition to the mental health needs of patients. However, the mental health consultant will have fulfilled his goal if he has brought the mental health aspects of the situation into focus.

In the foregoing example, a request for program consultation grew out of other consultation activities in the course of which it became apparent that some program modification would be desirable for a particular client, and perhaps for many. A request for program-centered consultation may also be motivated directly by an administrator's desire to promote mental health in his organization. Thus a school superintendent might ask a local mental health consultation service to participate in curriculum development or reorganization of the counselling and guidance services. Before responding to such a request, however, the mental health consultant must ask himself whether he is really a technical expert in the area under consideration, and clarify his role and function accordingly.

The Mental Health Consultant

Mental health consultation in a local community program is practiced almost exclusively by professionals whose basic training has been in psychiatric social work, clincal psychology, or dynamic psychiatry.[15] The majority of these mental health consultants are recruited from those disciplines found in child-guidance or adult psychiatric clinics. Since client-centered and consultee-centered consultation are the forms of consultation utilized most frequently in local programs, the mental health consultant who functions at this level must have a high degree of clinical competence. Forstenzer suggests that the clincal skills and professional maturity of the community mental health consultant should be at least equal to the minimum requirements for a supervisory position in a psychiatric clinic.[16] The same degree of clinical competence may be desirable but is not always necessary for consultants whose primary concern is mental health programming, or health promotion, education, research, or administration, For such activities, personnel may be recruited from a variety of professional disciplines in the behavioral sciences and in the public health subspecialties.

Optimally, the community mental health consultant should be expert in two areas: first, in clinical knowledge and skills and in mental health programming; second, in the use of the consultation method. The latter would include knowledge and skill in the variable use of professional relationships, communication techniques, knowledge of the consultee agencies, knowledge of the consultees' professional subculture, and knowledge of community services and organization.

The problems and organizations which the mental health consultant encounters in the community, and the professionals with whom he comes into contact, will vary greatly. This may be true of the tasks he is required to perform as well. He must, therefore, be able to draw on a wide base of knowledge which should include the following: developmental psychology; individual and group dynamics; psychopathology; and psychotherapy, particularly brief, ego-oriented psychotherapy. He may also have to draw on knowledge from sociology, political science, cultural anthropology, and social psychology. In addition he should be familiar with a variety of methods used in mental health programming such as administration and community organization. Finally, he should know something about in-service training methods and supervision. Obviously, no mental health consultant can be equally knowledgeable and skilled in all areas. Some familiarity with all these areas is desirable; expertness in several areas is necessary, depending on the nature of the consultant's role and tasks.

At present, there are no commonly accepted standards or training requirements for community mental health consultants, beyond clinical training and experience. However, training programs in community psychiatry and community mental health which offer training in mental health consultation are currently being developed and should help to clarify these issues. In any event, although there is no precise agreement as to the educational or experiential requirements needed to facilitate the role change from clinician to mental health consultant, clearly, certain personal and professional factors should be operative. First, the consultant must be willing and able to shift the object of his primary responsibility from client to consultee. He must also alter his technique, so that he will put his knowledge and skill as a sensitive diagnostician into the service of helping to solve a consultee's work problem. He must avoid the twin temptations of dealing with a consultee's personal problems and of imparting clincal methods which would be inappropriate to the consultee's role. He must be able to tolerate the anxiety which departure from his familiar role as clinician may evoke, and to resist falling back on the clinical methods he employed previously in the face of uncertainty in his new role. If the consultant had been an administrator formerly, he will have to practice self-control, so that he will not be overly directive. If he was a nondirective therapist, he will have to make a conscious effort to order and structure his consultation sessions. Finally, he must be able to work toward long-range goals and to find professional satisfaction in the slow and sometimes imperceptible process of assisting others to achieve greater ease and competence in the mental health aspects of their professional work.

In due time, one can learn the facts about the structure of a community, its social organization, the function of its component parts, and the roles assigned to various professionals. In time, meaningful communication can be established in the "mother tongue" of a consultee system. Therefore, the crucial factor in the making of a community mental health consultant is not simply the acquisition of additional facts, but the desire to apply clinical knowledge and skills in a very different way and commitment to the broad goal of improving the mental health of the community.

Planning a Community Mental Health Consultation Program

A community mental health consultation program may originate as an extension of the services of an established mental health facility, or as one of the initial services in a newly constituted program. However, if his program is to function effectively, the administrator of the consultation service should take sufficient time to become thoroughly familiar with his own agency and the community he is to serve. He should have a detailed knowledge of what his immediate superiors expect him to undertake and to accomplish. To this end, he must be familiar with his program administrator's long-range plans and goals for the agency's indirect services and how decisions will be made as to the mode of service to be offered, be it consultation, in-service training, or increased case collaboration.

Thus, the administrator of a consultation service must accumulate the same kind of information about his own organization which, in due time, he must acquire with respect to his consultee agencies. These data will include the legal and administrative base of operation; the plan of organization and explicit and implicit power structure; the basic services rendered by the agency; the way policies and procedures affecting these basic services are determined; the level of training and competence of the staff; the nature of supervisory practices; the size of work loads; the nature of job frustration and satisfaction; the chain of communication and the degree of freedom of communication within the system; the degree of collaboration or competition which exists between this agency and other organizations which serve the same client groups; and the nature of the agency's previous experience (if any) with psychiatric or mental health consultation.

The administrator of the consultation service will then direct his attention to the establishment of priorities for service. Two major target groups most frequently selected are (1) those community agencies and professionals who have significant contacts with children; (2) those whose work brings them into professional contact with people who are experiencing several emotional stress. Within these two major target groups, further priorities are established by evaluating the following sets of factors: (1) factors pertaining to the client group served, such as numbers and types of clients served, age range, the frequency with which social and psychological problems are manifested, and opportunities in the agency's program to influence clients towards greater emotional stability and mental health; (2) factors relating to the agency or organization, such as the size of the agency, the number of subunits, the geographic area served, the number of potential consultees and their level of training, degree of psychological sophistication, expressed interest in mental health consultation as part of staff development activities, and the availability of consultation services from other sources.

In all probability, the administrator of the consultation service will not be able to deal with more than a fraction of the potential demand for consultation. Therefore, in addition to the general priority system, other factors may influence his initial selections. For example, he may wish to acquire consultation experience with specific kinds of agencies, or consider first those agencies which have initiated requests for service, provided they fall within the general high priority categories. Thus, if he has given the school system high priority, he may offer his services to all districts in his jurisdiction, but actively negotiate only with those districts in which key personnel have indicated receptivity and interest in helping to facilitate the development of a consultation program. Although opportunistic factors often determine the particular agencies with which such a relationship is initiated, the program administrator's long-range goals should include plans to make mental health consultation available to personnel of all those major professional organizations and agencies which provide basic community services.

Phases in Mental Health Consultation

In any mental health consultation relationship there is a sequential evolution of the process, which can be conceptualized as comprising four phases: preparatory, beginning, problem solving, and termination. These phases are not mutually exclusive, but frequently overlap. However, the accomplishment of certain tasks signifies the transition from one phase to another.

The main task of the prepartory phase consists of the implementation of administrative negotiations which lead to provisional understanding or "preliminary contract" for consultation services. The task of the beginning phase consists of the development of a mutually satisfactory consultation relationship between the consultant and a consultee or a group of consultees. The major task of the problem-solving phase, which is the most crucial in the consultation process, consists of cooperative efforts to understand a consultee's work problem and, if indicated, to formulate some plans for action. The termination phase usually follows the solution of a consultee's problem, although it may also be precipitated by the decision by either party to discontinue the relationship for administrative or personal reasons. The task of the termination phase, as of the preparatory phase, is primarily administrative in nature and should consist of joint evaluation of the service rendered and joint consideration of future services.

The administrator of a mental health consultation program must aim for long-term relationships with the high-priority community service organizations. His goal is to develop consultation relationships which can range freely in their focus from client, to consultee, to program; and, in contacts, from staff, to supervisors, to administrators. In contrast, the individual consultant usually aims attempts to limit his work with individual consultees in terms of time and goal. When, as frequently happens, the "individual" consultant is also the primary liaison with the agency administration, he must be able both to maintain long-term organizational contacts, and to meet specific requests for short-term consultation requests. In addition, he may be called on to perform other functions, which will require some modifications of his prescribed consultation role, such as assisting with in-service training or participating in some collaborative project.

An arrangement whereby the same mental health consultant must serve as liaison to administration and also as consultant to various levels of staff has certain advantages, as well as certain disadvantages. Advantages accrue by virtue of the fact that there will be more frequent and diverse contacts with the consultee agency. Thus, familiarity with and acceptance of the consultation service are expedited, which may lead to earlier requests for program or administrative consultation. The disadvantages stem from the fact that the ability to function effectively in this dual role requires an especially well-qualified and seasoned consultant who can empathize with the roles of supervisors and administrators as readily as with subordinate staff and who knows how to work at several levels within the system without role diffusion or contamination. In addition, when only one consultant is available to the organization, it can be anticipated that the beginning phase will be longer than usual. Under these circumstances, consultees at all operating levels need more time to satisfy themselves that the consultant is discreet and trustworthy—more precisely, that he will not divulge the content of their meetings, and will respect their confidences.

Regardless of who represents the mental health consultation service in the preparatory phase, the first step is to establish contact with the top administrator of the selected consultee agency. The administrator of the mental health consultation program may have laid the ground work by speeches or letters indicating the nature and availability of his services. He or his delegate follows this up by a personal interview in which he will introduce himself, describe his program, and encourage the administrator to discuss the activities, interests, and needs of the potential consultee agency. In the course of this discussion, the consultant will inquire about the mental health factors which may complicate the agency's work with its clients, and about those community or regional mental health resources which have proven helpful. Mental health consultation may then be introduced as another potentially useful service. In further explorations, the administrator of the consultation service will outline the specific services his staff can provide and indicate the limitations of a consultation service. For example, it must be clarified from the outset that consultation is not another form of direct patient examination and diagnostic service. Agencies can easily become confused by the overlapping functions of the consultant's agency, particularly when the consultant himself is already known to the agency in his role as clinician or if he has collaborated with them on specific cases.

If the agency administrator wishes to proceed with a consultation program he must give it his open sanction and support. It is usually best if he introduces the assigned consultant to his subordinate staff. The administrator of the consultation service or his delegate will then explain the nature of their services and obtain approval of the consultation program at all levels. The preparatory phase is completed when a "contract" for service has been agreed on mutually by the key personnel in the consultee agency. The contract states the purpose for which the consultant is to enter the consulteee agency, and stipulates what is required, in terms of specific activities of each party. It may be a verbal agreement, written confirmation of a verbal agreement, or a more formal document which includes such details as the mode of transfer of funds for service. Regardless of the degree to which the contract is formalized, there should be periodic review and evaluation of service, with renegotiation or reaffirmation of contractual details.

After administrative sanction has been obtained, the consultant moves into the beginning phase of work with various identified consultees or consultee groups. In both instances, a mutually satisfactory working arrangement must be established. This requires "refinement of the contract" by making explicit the details of the working relationship. The consultant should expect initial resistance, defensiveness, and anxiety at this point, which will be eased after the consultant's trustworthiness and usefulness have been demonstrated sufficiently. Even well-motivated consultees will evidence of such feelings. When consultees are more resistant, it may take months and even years before resistance and confusion disappear and a mutually satisfactory mode of working is achieved. In such cases, the consultant must take the initiative in developing the relationship and must make use of all opportunities for interaction even if such interaction does not immediately result in focus on work problem solving.

Moreover, the consultant must define his role and role limitations repeatedly, since the consultee will test these limits in various ways. With each consultee, he must demonstrate his awareness of those functions which are inappropriate to his role, both verbally and in practice. For example, he must consistently and assiduously avoid slipping into the role of therapist or supervisor. He must also be alert to possible countertransference problems which can distort his role. To illustrate, the consultant who enters an elementary school for the first time since childhood may experience a reactivation of old feelings and fantasies regarding school teachers and principals. Unless he is on guard, he may unconsciously overidentify with the school children instead of empathizing with his consultee.

The beginning phase is apt to be shorter if the preparatory phase has been slow and thorough. Again, if a consultee is greatly disturbed, that is to say "in crisis," his resistance and defensiveness may be minimal, and the problem-solving phase can be reached more quickly. Finally, the beginning phase may be bypassed completely when emergency consultation is requested for a problem which clearly demonstrates the need for expert advice on mental illness. However, implementation of the long-range goals of mental health consultation require the development of a working relationship in which consultees will seek consultation not only for their own crises or for their clients' emergency problems, but also for the typical mental health problems which their clients exhibit.

At any rate, the beginning phase is the most stressful for both consultant and consultee. The consultant must try to learn about the consultee organization and its professional subcultures while he is trying to find ways in which he can be most useful. Simultaneously, the consultees are looking him over, their natural curiosity tempered by many unexpressed expectations and fears. It may be helpful to compare an organization to a family in order to explain why the introduction of a mental health consultant predictably results in transient disequilibrium and stress. Organizations, like families, have genealogies and traditions, as well as goals and responsibilities. Its individual members, who possess individual skills and attitudes and sometimes personality problems, are united, by virtue of their related occupations, in an organization which is dedicated to the performance of specified tasks. In the hierarchical structure of an organization there are authority relationships which are reminiscent of parent-child relationships. There are also peer relationships which are reminiscent of sibling relationships. Only if a fairly stable equilibrium prevails can its members function optimally as a harmonious whole. Therefore, in even the healthiest system, the introduction of the first mental health consultant necessitates some realignment of forces and sometimes arouses disproportionate anxiety at all levels of the organization.

Anxiety and disequilibrium are particularly marked in the intermediate echelons, among supervisors or training officers. This may be attributed to the fact that the consultant's role and function does have some elements in common with other staff development methods. Unlike the top administrator, who can exclude himself from actual consultation after the initial contract, the intermediate staff cannot ignore a mandate that the service is to be used. Obviously, they may be expected to manifest less anxiety if they have had a prior positive experience with mental health consultation, and find that the present consultant is similarly benign. However, where consultation is entirely new to a system, the supervisory staff may have a greater need to control the functioning of the consultant. This must be understood and accepted by the consultant, who should be particularly careful to use measures which are nonthreatening and which build trust. For this reason, during the initial contacts, we prefer to invite the supervisory staff to attend consultation sessions with subordinates. Although there is some controversy as to the advisability of this practice, it facilitates getting acquainted professionally, puts the supervisor at ease, and helps to orient the consultant to agency policy and procedure. In the interest of long-term relationships, it is more important to become known and trusted by top administrative and supervisory personnel, then to push one's way through to staff. The hope is that ultimately the staff who work with clients will be given free access to the consultant's services.

Mental health problems may be discussed during any phase of the process, of course. However, it is during the problem-solving phase that presumably the relationship has developed to the point where energy can be devoted mainly to the task of joint work problem solving. During this phase, the procedure might follow a general formula. It consists of realistic perception of the problem, systematic consideration of the various possible solutions, and decision to follow through on a chosen course. To this end, the consultant listens to whatever is present, and tries to understand and define the central problem and the core anxiety. More precisely, he attempts to assess the consultee's dilemma in regard to the work problem and to identify the reality as well as the personal factors which contribute to it. He must ask himself why the consultee is presenting this situation for consultation at this time, to identify the stage at which the consultee's own problem-solving skills became ineffective, and to draw inferences regarding the possible reasons this occurred before he can offer assitance discriminatingly. If he is to obtain relevant and confirming data, the consultant must guard against premature interventions which might assuage the consultee's anxiety and curtail further discussion. He must be particularly attentive to the consultee's initial presentation, to which he will respond by attempting to define and clarify the manifest work problem. At the same time the consultant is also aware that the manifest work problem may derive from more personal, unexpressed conflicts. He is therefore attentive to cues which suggest the existence of such related problems. However, the personal problems are almost never dealt with directly, even though they may be of central importance to the consultee's difficulties in realistic problem perception, definition, and solution.

The consultant's ability to pick up such cues will depend on his senses and cognitive processes. As in psychotherapy, he uses himself as a diagnostic instrument. If he cannot get a clear picture or a logical sequence of events even after seeking clarification, he must assume that the problem is vested in the consultee, or that the consultee's present confusion stems from his relationship to him. After the consultant has ruled out factors of countertransference, lack of sufficient understanding of the consultee role or the organization of the consultee agency, and other factors which might contribute to distortions in his own perception, he tries to ascertain what might be interfering with the consultee's perception and understanding. Regardless of whether the consultee's difficultues are in the area of perception, action planning, or implementation, the consultant must determine whether the consultee has considered all the obvious approaches to problem solution, whether he has arrived at any decision or embarked on a course of action, and if not, why not. There are various possible answers to these questions: (1) the consultee may lack the special knowledge or skill needed to obtain relevant information or to evaluate available information in order that he may attempt to arrive at a solution; (2) administrative factors may limit his efforts in this connection; (3) the personal factors involved may be of sufficient intensity to interfere with his perception and understanding of the problem.

The consultant should be clear about which particular aspect of the work problem is the focal point of the difficulty. If the major difficulty is related to insuffiicient knowledge, then the consultee may need information and clarification of psychodynamics. If the consultee has perceived and understood the problems and needs of his client correctly but lacks skill or assurance as to how to develop a plan of action, then the consultant may offer several alternate plans for consideration. Sometimes a consultee may have some tentative plan for action in mind and may wish to present this to the consultant for support and approval. In the process of presentation, the steps necessary for implementation of his plan may become apparent to both consultant and consultee, in which case only a simple affiirmtion by the consultant would be required.

If the major difficulty is related to administrative policies or practices, then a review of the consultee's professional role and function may clarify the appropriate course of action. For example, if the consultee is seeking permission and encouragement to try an unusual approach or technique, the consultant must be clear as to whether such actions are consonant with the usual role of the professionals in that agency, and whether the action is consonant with the agency policy and procedure. Although it is rarely part of a conscious plan, a consultee may be trying to manipulate the consultant into supporting some position which is contrary to that taken by his supervisor or to agency policy. Therefore, in helping him to formulate plans for disposition or treatment, the consultant must scrupulously avoid any impulse to contribute to diffusion of the consultee's professional role. It is particularly important that a clinically trained mental health consultant recognize his obligation to assist the consultee within the framework of the consultee's usual professional role, and not to urge him to undertake unfamiliar and possibly inappropriate clinical techniques.

If the major dificulty is related to personal factors, then the consultant's task is a more delicate one. His legitimate concern is only with those problems which are manifest in the consultee's professional role. Work problems may manifest themselves in a myriad of idiosyncratic ways, of course. However, they tend to express themselves through some frequently observed patterns. One problem which is commonly encountered is the loss of professional objectivity by the consultee due to his overidentification of the client with important people in his past. A similar problem may arise when some aspect of a client's behavior has activated or aggravated comparable poorly resolved conflict in the consultee. In general, the consultant deals with identification problems and derivative conflicts only indirectly. His primary purpose is to support the consultee's ego functioning, especially his capacity for reality-based perceptions and actions. This approach is similar to that used by child guidance workers who often deal with limited aspects of a parent's latent problem through the medium of discussing the child's overt behavior in the same problem area. In this approach the guidance worker attempts to impart a deeper understanding of the meaning of the child's behavior which, in turn, may enable the parent to achieve greater mastery or control in the area of reciprocal conflict. Similarly, after the consultant has emphasized the understandable and manageable aspects of the client's behavior, the consultee usually experiences a decrease in anxiety and an increase in mastery. The consultant, like the guidance worker, also hopes that a positive transference will lead to identification with some of his attitudes and values for the purpose of reducing the consultee's anxiety and guilt. This method can result in more effective ego functioning without ever exposing the consultee's core problem and arousing his resistance and defensiveness.

Occasionally the consultant will encounter a consultee whose work problem has not been precipitated in response to a client or by limiting administrative factors, but who has severe emotional problems which have affected large segments of his professional functioning. Wherever possible, the consultant will work with the derivatives of the central problem as outlined above. Customarily, if a consultee is markedly and overtly disturbed, either he or his supervisor will ask for help. If the consultee initiates this request, the consultant may advise him how to obtain necessary professional services. If the supervisor initates the request, the consultant helps the supervisor arrive at an independent judgment based on his own observations. Although conceivable, it would be most unusual for the mental health consultant to initiate such considerations.

Termination of the relationship with any given consultee is by mutual agreement generally after the particular work problem of the consultee has been solved. Although the mental health's consultant's relationship with the consultee agency may be on a long-term basis and consist of regularly scheduled visits, his consultation with an individual consultee or single consultee group is usually limited to a few sessions for each case or problem. Consultation is terminated when the consultee has arrived at a decision regarding his future management of the case in question. When the case or problem was of critical concern to the consultee, there is often feedback to the consultant through reports of further developments or outcome. The relationship then lapses until the consultant is called back for further consideration of that or some new situation. Where there is more prolonged contact with a particular consultant or consultee group, the consultation process may approximate more closely in-service training or supervision. Under such circumstances transference and countertransference factors may become operative, which could foster an undesirable degree of dependency, or become a rather expensive substitute for other types of on-the-job training. Therefore, it is desirable practice to review and renegotiate consultation services annually, at the least. As consultees become more experienced in the use of consultation they tend to become more discriminating and to request consultation only for unfamiliar or more complicated situations. This enables the consultant agency to free mental health consultation time for new groups and projects.

Problems in Evaluation

The attempt to evaluate any aspect of mental health consultation poses formidable problems, as is the case whenever the objective is to measure psychosocial change. It is extremely difficult to evaluate psychotherapy, yet psychotherapy is considerably less complicated than mental health consultation, which operates within a much wider field of forces. At this time, the difficulties in evaluating mental health consultation are compounded because it is a new and evolving specialty. Even elementary descriptive studies are hampered by lack of a commonly accepted and understood nomenclature. Recording and reporting systems are similarly hampered; therefore, statistics, even if available to date, would be essentially meaningless for cumulative or comparative purposes.

However, the greatest impediment to evaluation stems from the fact that the goals of mental health consultation have not been defined in terms which lend themselves to research investigation. It is difficult to pinpoint what one aims to change through mental health consultation, and how the success of one's efforts can be measured. The ultimate goal of mental health consultation is to improve the mental health components of services to clients. The immediate goal is to strengthen and improve the knowledge and skill of the consultee. While it might be easier to determine whether the knowledge and skill of the consultee had indeed been improved, we can only presume that his enhanced functioning will result in better service to clients. In the face of manifold variables in the social field, causal relationships would be hard to validate. Nevertheless, despite the difficulties indicated, efforts should be made to devise more structured evaluation procedures within individual programs, and to achieve greater clarity regarding the nomenclature, objectives, and procedures of mental health consultation, in order to develop a more useful cumulative body of knowledge. Several research and evaluative studies, which should shed light on possible methodologies, are currently in process.

Notes

1. C. Towle, "Workshop on Consultation Process, School of Social Service Administration" (unpub. MS, University of Chicago, 1951).
2. C. G. Backcock, "Some Observations on Consultative Experience," *Social Service Review,* XXIII (1949), 347–58.
3. I. N. Berlin, "The Theme in Mental Health Consultation Sessions," *American Journal of Orthopsychiatry,* XXX (1960), 827–28; G. Caplan, *Concepts of Mental Health and Consultation* (Publication No. 373 of the U.S. Dept. of Health, Education, and Welfare, Social Security Admin., Children's Bureau; Washington, D.C.: Government Printing Office, 1959); G. Caplan, "Dynamics of Mental Health Consultation" (unpub. MS, Harvard School of Public Health, 1954); G. Caplan, "Principles of Mental Health Consultation" (unpub. MS, Harvard School of Public Health, 1954); B. Parker, *Psychiatric Consultation for Non-Psychiatric Professional Workers* (P.H. Monograph No. 53, P.H.S. Publication No. 588 of the U.S. Dept. of Health, Education, and Welfare; Washington, D.C.: Government Printing Office, 1958); B. Parker, "The Value of Supervision in Training Psychiatrists for Mental Health Consultation," *Mental Hygiene,* XLV (1961), 94–100.
4. Caplan, "Dynamics of Mental Health Consultation" and "Principles of Mental Health Consultation."

5. Joint Commission on Mental Illness and Health, *Action for Mental Health: Final Report* (New York: Basic Books, 1961).

6. E. Lindemann, "Symptomatology and Management of Acute Grief," *American Journal of Psychiatry,* CI (1944–45), 101–41.

7. D. Klein, "Consultation in the Framework of Preventive Psychiatry" (paper read at the American Orthopsychiatry Association meeting, San Francisco, 1959).

8. G. Caplan and J. M. Rosenfeld, "Techniques of Staff Consultation in an Immigrant Children's Organization in Israel," *American Journal of Orthopsychiatry,* XXIV (1954), 42–62.

9. A. C. K. Hallock and W. T. Vaughan, "Community Organization—A Dynamic Component of Community Mental Health Practice," *American Journal of Orthopsychiatry,* XXVI (1956), 691–706.

10. In the public health field, the concept of "prevention" has been considerably extended from the traditional medical usage in which the connotation was limited to the prevention or prophylaxis of disease. In public health terminology "prevention" now frequently encompasses limitation of disability as well as actual avoidance of illness. Methods leading to avoidance of illness are subsumed under "primary prevention"; those that limit the disease process are termed secondary; and those that lessen disability following disease, tertiary. This extended conceptualization of "prevention," although useful, is widely but not universally accepted, nor is it universally understood. In recent years this extended concept of prevention has been applied to the mental health field in an attempt to categorize its activities in accordance with the three levels of prevention.

11. Mental health consultation techniques, as developed and practiced in the San Mateo County Mental Health Program, are described in detail in V. Kazanjian, S. Stein, and W. Weinberg, *An Introduction to Mental Health Consultation* (P.H. Monograph No. 69, P.H.S. Publication No. 922 of the U.S. Dept. of Health, Education, and Welfare; Washington, D.C.: Government Printing Office, 1962), p. 11.

12. M. H. Gilmore, "Consultation as a Social Work Activity" (unpub. MS, School of Applied Social Sciences, Western Reserve University, Feb. 1962).

13. It may be argued that in group consultation the consultee who presents a case is receiving consultation whereas the others in the group are receiving in-service training. Such refinements are not only impossible to categorize or report statistically for program recording, but are based on a misunderstanding of the use of groups in consultation. The example cited represents a frequent pattern of service. However, it cannot properly be classified under group consultation unless it utilizes the dynamics of group process for problem solving.

14. Caplan, *Concepts of Mental Health.*

15. However, psychiatric and public health nurses may also be trained to serve as mental health nurse consultants.

16. H. M. Forstenzer, "Consultation and Mental Health Programs," *American Journal of Public Health,* LI (1961), 1280–85.

8 Advanced Education for Practice in Community Mental Health

Current developments in social psychiatry, new mental health legislation, and new modalities in the practice of community mental health have given rise to the claim that we are in the midst of a third revolution in the mental health field. A great demand for specialists in various mental health disciplines has been created. Social workers are expected to take on new, broader, and more complex responsibilities that extend beyond traditional clinical roles. It is our thesis that advanced practice in community mental health requires additional educational preparation and that, at this time, such education needs to find its place at the post-master's level.

It may be considered a bit of a luxury, if not an outright presumption, to write about advanced education for community mental health practice when the concern of the field is so largely fixed on the necessity for staffing the unmet personnel needs with people who possess the basic minimum professional credentials. Nevertheless, the field has great need for competent personnel at all levels of education. There is a need particularly for personnel capable of moving into leadership positions and bringing about the social change necessary to implement mental health goals.

Current Practice Needs in Community Mental Health

It is important that advanced education in social work be taught on the basis of demands dictated by evolving professional practice, the character of which is only beginning to take shape. It is our point of view, however, that practice in community mental health should not be equated with practice in the community mental health centers program, for it transcends the specific

Source: Written with Robert Z. Apte. Reprinted, with minor changes, from *Social Work Education Reporter,* XVI (Dec. 4, 1968), 24–65. Used by permission.

programs and structures thus far devised. It needs also to concern itself with problems on regional, state, and national levels, as well as with issues related to broader social policy.

The current manpower shortage and the special needs of experienced, often older, workers returning to the position of learner dictate a sense of urgency that the educational pathway be clearly illuminated toward those roles and functions that have both community sanction and salience. Yet, when one directs this dictum to training for community mental health, this pathway does not have the desired degree of clarity. Indeed, the overall view obtained leaves a confused image that lacks the specificity we desire. Neither the mental health movement nor the profession of social work has come to any firm consensus as to the most fruitful course to follow in regard to both education and practice.

Some community mental health experts hold that we must put our major effort into the area of primary prevention by creating a climate that will sustain or develop those aspects of community, group, and family life that are health promoting, and will utilize a variety of broadly based techniques to protect predetermined populations from known hazards. Other community mental health proponents hold that we know far too little about primary prevention to be effective in reducing the incidence of mental illness. Their argument states that our major thrust should be in the area of working with the already defined population of emotionally disturbed individuals to prevent them from becoming chronically handicapped and institutionalized, and towards fostering their social adaptation in, or readaptation to ,the community. Although these are examples of extreme positions on the continuum of prevention there are many other suggested conceptual models with their concomitant practice approaches for promoting community mental health. Part of the confusion is related to the fact that we are going through a period in which the definition of mental illness is being broadened, while simultaneously our recognition of the multiple factors associated with it is increasing. As a field of practice having its roots in the individual approach of the psychiatric social worker, we have had to increase our awareness of these factors and their interrelationship to encompass the family, the group, and the community.

As an outgrowth of this broadened perspective, the traditional roles and functions of those in the mental health disciplines have been changing, while at the same time there is an emergence of new roles and functions, including those of subprofessional and nonprofessional. Not only is there a change in the actors, but also a change in the scenes and locations of their activities, as demonstrated by the amount of experimentation with and the development of new structures and patterns of service. It should be recognized that we are just beginning to enter this intriguing but frustrating era of change, and that it is too soon to define any definite patterns for practice. From one geographic area to the next, the roles being assumed differ in content and complexity. Many of the new positions require the community mental health worker to carry multiple roles based on skills in several social work methods. In addition, there are now several major trends which will sharply influence the direction of future practice: the Community Mental Health Centers Act, the break-up of the traditional mental hospital and its extension into the community, Medicare, inclusion of the coverage of mental illness in the health insurance package, and the urban renewal and model cities programs and their implication for socioenvironmental design. It may be a decade before the full impact of these trends will be realized. Because of these factors, it is neither desirable nor timely to foster closure on professional roles for the sake of crystallizing training.

These programs of social change provide the mental health worker with a major challenge to continue to experiment with and to develop innovative approaches previously not considered. The main goal should be in the direction of leadership in social planning rather than in repetition of earlier patterns of service, which fulfilled mainly those residual functions not taken on by other professional disciplines or social services. Certain patterns in this direction are already becoming discernible, as social planning skills are now being utilized at significant points. It is noteworthy that one out of every four staff directors of statewide comprehensive planning efforts in community mental health is a social worker.[1] Other relevant examples could be cited of social workers engaged in prominent administrative, research, community organization, and consultative roles. Unfortunately for newcomers entering practice, there are still far too few of these important role models in community mental health.

Skills Needed in Community Mental Health Practice

What are the needed skills and role expectations of a social worker in this complex and evolving field? He is not likely to be the recent MSW graduate, but more apt to be a worker, seasoned in practice and steeped in various patterns of experiences, who has, in addition, prepared himself through continuing or advanced education. He would be a social worker who has been able to master multiple skills and to define clearly each of his numerous roles and the tasks appropriate to them. He would be able to shift from one role to another easily, and comfortably carry widely differing roles simultaneously. He would, therefore, have to be able to deal constructively and unanxiously with such uncertainties in the work situation as role blurring, role diffusion, and role expansion.

Although guided by personal and professional value systems, this worker should be able to maintain an objectivity similar to that of the cultural anthropologist, to bring out for examination those cultural discontinuities so prevalent in our pluralistic society. In his search for the appropriate techniques to employ in social change, he should be able to keep in proper balance an awareness of the individual and the complex social matrix in which he moves. As the responsibilities of this worker widen in the community beyond those of clinician, his training should have prepared him to maximize his use of observations, professional contacts, and case or situational examples in order to function at the broadest and most influential level of intervention. The change-agent role may require a shift in the worker's ideology, self-concept, and reference group, particularly as some of the activities may penetrate into fields previously considered inappropriate for social workers.

The community mental health worker needs to develop the capacity to work in less rigidly structured settings, often without supervision or professional direction. The gratification from his work will have to come from efforts directed at long-range goals rather than from daily endeavors. He will have to learn to accept and deal with resistance or hostility from community groups as he participates in wider community activities. He has to accept a tempo of work which is different from the pace of clinical work and which yields results of a different magnitude. He also has to resolve any tension arising from conflicts as to where to focus his efforts, to consider group versus individual needs, and resolve this through incorporating a broader philosophy of serving larger groups of populations at risk.

A different set of team relationships has to be developed, broader than that found in clinical practice. Professions new to this extended team will have to define their roles, while traditional team members are forced to redefine theirs. This is a difficult task, since the roles and functions are even more nebulous here than in traditional clinical practice. For all these tasks and responsibilities, the requisite practice skills can best be obtained through a period of academic study, although practitioners also can, and often do, develop their later abilities in other ways.

Patterns of Advanced Education

There are many possible patterns for continuing education beyond the master's level. Institutes, workshops, and seminars of short but intensive duration are constantly offered under university or professional auspices. Such programs offer a refresher-type education, providing channels for new information and stimulation. Staff development and in-service training also contribute to upgrading practice in agencies. These programs are usually geared to immediate agency practice demands but may provide a broader perspective, if educational resources are available.

The third-year program offered in many schools of social work is another pattern of advanced education. It developed in response to acute needs in the mental health field for personnel to assume leadership roles.[2] Although financed largely by NIMH, personnel produced by this program were engaged in other fields of social work practice as well as in mental health.[3] The educational objective of the clinical third year was to help practitioners achieve special or superior competence to enable them to move into advanced or independent practice, as well as into supervisory and administrative positions. To some extent, in its early days, it served as a kind of remedial education to fill gaps in areas not covered by the master's education. It also tended to be a terminal year. More recently, however, it has become a pathway to doctoral study, where advancement of knowledge and preparation for teaching and research are major objectives.

Objectives of Advanced Education

To some extent, as mentioned earlier, advanced education is, in part, remedial, to make up for what knowledge and skill could not be acquired at the MSW level. It is also remedial in the sense that, after the acquisition of the MSW, there may be professional growth, but there also may be attrition. Sometimes there is a loss of knowledge and skill; for example, many social work practitioners, now limited to practicing the casework method, will admit to having forgotten the content of group work and community organization courses to which they were once exposed. There is also attrition if the level of practice experience is not particularly high. As Charlotte Towle forthrightly pointed out, "breakdown in learning occurs with the vicissitudes to practice."[4]

Advanced education also fulfills another important objective. Both the technician and the professional in today's society are very soon faced with the danger of professional obsolescence. This situation has arisen because of the rapidity in the development of new knowledge, methods, and techniques, and in the sheer amount of information that becomes available. To some extent, it is possible for the alert practitioner to keep up with aspects of the information output, but periodically time must be allotted for special study and absorption of new knowledge and ideas and their implication for contemporary professional practice.

Refresher or remedial objectives, however, are not in themselves enough for an advanced educational program. From a more positive viewpoint, advanced education affords the opportunity to renew the habit of orderly thinking, to engage in retrospective thinking for the purpose of developing a new perspective by drawing on hindsight for the attainment of foresight. The learner on the advanced level should be able to absorb larger systems of ideas and engage in more prolonged abstract thinking. He should be able to tolerate the kind of tension generated in taking in new knowledge, not only for immediate but also for later use. He should also be able to engage more broadly in the transfer of learning from the specific to the general and the reverse. Advanced education should lead to rediscovery as well as to new discovery; it should meet the requirements of breadth and depth to avoid developing only skilled technicians. It should also help the learner develop new responses to the new demands of the profession. Advanced education gives the learner an opportunity to revive and reaffirm his identification with the profession and its social purposes. The crystallization of professional identity is an important task, especially for the worker in the community mental health field who practices in a multidisciplinary arena, which can readily lead to identity diffusion and uncertainty.

Specifically, what are the objectives of an advanced, nonclinical, third-year program in community mental health? This type of education is conceived as a way of developing a specialist both in the social problem area of mental illness and health and in the use of specialized methods. The primary objective is to help the clinician-practitioner make the transition from clinician, a specialist within a narrow framework, to community mental health worker, a worker engaging in a broadly based, multifaceted operation.

Motivation for Advanced Education

It might be asked what motivates the practitioner to return to the university for nondoctoral advanced education. It is clear that there are people so motivated, though it is impossible to estimate the extent of the potential demand, which depends, in part, on the availability of quality programs and scholarship support. Those choosing to engage in nondoctoral advanced education are motivated entirely from within, since, at this time, little status, credit, or reward is available either by way of formal recognition or financial gain. There are various reasons for the desire to return to school. Many practitioners have been pushed prematurely into advanced positions and new roles because of acute manpower needs. Some can acknowledge that they do not find themselves ready to carry out these roles. They are perceived as experts in a wide area of practice but do not, in fact, feel they possess the necessary expertise. They operate intuitively, by trial and error, often without sufficient support and supervision. They have a conviction that knowledge and skills acquired through advanced education would enable them to function more effectively.

For some practitioners, going back to the university affords a needed professional moratorium. Many reach a point in their career when a need for change is felt. An educational program offers the opportunity to explore new problem areas, new knowledge, and new methods, with the possibility of reaffirming old or making new commitments. Some hope to stave off a feeling of professional obsolescence by immersing themselves systematically in new knowledge. For others, advanced education affords the opportunity to get some distance from practice, in order to renew their objectivity and develop a new and broadened perspective. In essence, formal education provides time in which to reflect and integrate new learning with prior professional competence. Some seek the opportunity to do this systematically and under the guidance of teachers and mentors, rather then relying on more casual or haphazard opportunities.

Guiding Educational Principles

Several philosophical and educational principles guide our thinking in the matter of advanced education. It is our view that, at the present time, preparation for specialist roles is a function of advanced education. This stems from the current position regarding the MSW program, which is conceived of as generic preparation for social work practice. This view may once again shift as different educational patterns begin to emerge within the master's program. We are already moving away from the tight uniform package conception of social work education and are beginning to experiment with other patterns and processes for preparation for a variety of career goals—as exemplified by the developments in the community organization sequence of specialization. It seems evident that a different type of student elects this option, one who has a different philosophical and value base in regard to goals, interests, and approach to social problem solving, and who differs markedly in career goals, temperament, and intellectual stance from the students committed to the direct service methods.

It is our bias that the community mental health practitioner, by virtue of the specialist roles he will have to assume, must be grounded in clinical knowledge and practice in order to be truly effective in other roles. The community mental health worker must have an astute capacity for self-appraisal and self-awareness, and also a great sensitivity to interpersonal process. He would be less likely to develop this if he began to train for a specialist role on the master's level and by-passed the direct role in working with people in need. This is simply a point of view which cannot, at present, be substantiated by any empirical evidence. In fact, it is sometimes argued that a grounding in clinical knowledge and skills makes for "trained incompetence" in nonclinical roles, since they call for different values, objectives, and modes of operation. We would maintain that a more richly endowed professional emerges when the specialist roles are built upon a sound clinical base. The person without this knowledge, or with a need to negate its values, tends to be more abstract, sterile, and simplistic in his views and less able to grasp the necessary complexities involved in problem solutions. Community mental health goals would be strengthened by practitioners who are neither disillusioned with nor avoiding the direct service role, but who are able to maintain a "binocular vision," encompassing the needs and problems of the individual and community and holding in view both the psychodynamic and sociological dimensions.

As far as possible, advanced educational programs should be tailor-made to meet individual interests, aptitudes, and career goals. Trainees entering such programs bring with them a richness of experience and a capability in advanced clinical practice. Experience and talent are quite variable among trainees. This demands extra attention on the faculty's part to the process of educational diagnosis in order to assess the trainee's professional strengths and to delineate the areas of weakness or gaps in knowledge and skills. Only out of such an ongoing assessment can one then design an individualized academic program and field experience.

The field experience, in particular, is important for the trainee, who needs to test himself in new roles. It should be designed in such a way as to call for the exercise of several roles, some of which may be more clearcut and more readily assumed, while others must be defined and relevant tasks developed. The field experience should provide opportunities for experimentation without the serious and long-range commitment that a job would require. It might be added that these trial-run endeavors provide opportunities both for achievement and for possible failure. However, in this instance, failure does not risk any penalty, since it can be transformed into a learning experience as the trainee tests for himself the range of his professional abilities.

The assumption of the student role brings with it numerous stresses. The older the student and the more professional self-dependence he has achieved, the greater the likelihood that return to the student role would be stressful. He experiences a distinct loss of status; the student role at any level is inevitably accompanied by anxiety in learning and by the risk of regression. A one-year academic program with high demands for productivity cannot afford the usual, even limited, regression that takes place during the initial period of returning to school. Therefore, a program should have built into it all measures possible to minimize anxiety and avoid a regressive adaptation. One way is to give the student maximum responsibility for his own learning and maximum choice in the content and design of his experience.

The measurement of growth and movement also must be individualized. We have no solid norms of performance on the master's level. In an educational endeavor to prepare for practice in an evolving field, there are even fewer firm guide posts regarding standards or norms of expected performance. The trainees enter with differing levels of professional sophistication and competence. Therefore, the trainee's progress can best be evaluated in terms of his growth from his baseline, rather than by comparison with his peers.

The faculty member has a distinctive role in advanced education. The trainee wishes to view him more as a colleague, which is a legitimate and appropriate desire. Learning through the structure of small seminars, with maximum responsibility on the trainees, and learning through interaction in tutorials can encourage a more informal and egalitarian relationship. Faculty members should also serve, in part, as relevant role models. They are perceived primarily as people dedicated to the advancement of knowledge and learning. It is desirable, for many reasons, that faculty be involved in research and project activities of their own and be active in community mental health affairs. Aside from the contribution to knowledge, such activities can provide possible opportunities for the trainees and faculty to work together as collaborators; this can also serve as another aspect of identification with an appropriate role model and can provide an egalitarian relationship.

The Community Mental Health Training Program at the School of Social Welfare, University of California at Berkeley

The post-master's program at the School of Social Welfare, University of California at Berkeley, is one experimental model in advanced education in community mental health—a model in which the previously mentioned objectives and principles have, for the most part, been incorporated. The objective of our program is primarily to add to the pool of highly skilled community mental health workers by preparing seasoned clinicians to take on the responsibility for leadership and specialist roles; second, to join with practice in the discovery and development of new knowledge and techniques in community mental health; and third, to experiment with a new educational format and method of training in social work on the advanced level.

The criteria for admission to this nine-month program, for

which academic credit is given, are an MSW degree plus at least three years of post-master's experience in a clinical setting. We require that the trainee have a high scholastic record, the personal qualities of creativity, flexibility, and capacity for leadership, and that he demonstrate successful mastery of casework or group work skills. In addition, it is expected that he show curiosity about the broader factors affecting community mental health, and have a definite commitment to influencing social change.

The program was designed to recruit trainees with a wide range of interests in community mental health activities, which include career goals in social planning, community organization, administration, consultation, and research.

Considerable attention is given to creating a stimulating and productive learning environment in which the trainees can study the problems and methods in community mental health. We try to develop an atmosphere in which competition is kept to a minimum and in which learning is measured by the individual's own pace and progress. In order to diminish resistance to learning and to prevent regression to a dependent role, the relationship of the community mental health faculty to the trainees is as egalitarian as possible. An individualized education plan is developed by ascertaining the trainee's choice of methods, the problem areas in which he wishes to concentrate, and his career goals. This plan encompasses both academic course work and field projects.

Academic course work falls into three main areas: (1) social work methods, (2) social and behavioral science theory, and (3) the philosophy of community mental health, its knowledge areas, and concepts. Courses from all departments of the university are open to the trainees, and elective courses can be taken that are commensurate with career goals.

In the methods area, there are courses in mental health consultation, community organization, social planning, administration, and research. In the area of social and behavioral science theory, there is a growing body of knowledge considered valuable for community mental health practice. This includes social system theory, bureaucratic theory, human ecology, cultural anthropology, small group theory, reference group theory, theory of planned change, communications theory, and so forth.

Since our trainees are preparing for practice, it is important to select those theories and concepts that have special relevance for community mental health practice. The task of pulling together relevant theories for integration into practice is sizeable—one which has not yet been successfully achieved in the community mental health field. To meet this need, our trainees take a course in the behavioral sciences in which the content has been adapted to mental practice.

In the field of community mental health there is, as yet, a paucity of knowledge which is identifiable as its own. Here, community mental health resembles public health and criminology, which are also essentially eclectic, all borrowing from wide and diverse disciplines. The knowledge to be taught is dictated by practice demands in the field. In order to pull together the philosophy, theory, and knowledge relevant to community mental health practice, an integrative seminar extending over the entire academic year has been designed. In this seminar, emphasis is placed on public health philosophy, knowledge, and concepts. The seminar proceeds with an examination of the social, cultural, and environmental factors affecting mental health. Major epidemiological and ecological studies are reviewed. Also emphasized is preparation of the trainees to study and analyze community mental health problems from several social perspectives, taking into consideration multiple-stress factors and their relation to individual, group, and community phenomena.

Throughout the year, the trainees are given increasingly more responsibility for conducting the seminar by preparing and presenting material from their own concurrent field projects, research, and readings, in order to maximize their opportunity to incorporate new knowledge and concepts into their professional understanding. The seminar also provides a place for an appraisal of the present state of knowledge in the field, in order to question the validity of many of the concepts and assumptions that frequently pass for theory.[5] By the end of the year, the trainees are also expected to produce a paper of professional quality based on empirical or bibliographic research, to serve as another tool to integrate the theoretical knowledge and field experience and to foster the discipline of professional communication and writing.

Field Work

The basic purposes of field work are to help the trainees master the methods being taught and to experience the changing work roles in contemporary community mental health practice. Our model has some unique features that depart from the traditional field work model. These features are found in the nature of the assignments, which are developed in several settings; the nature of supervision; and the concept of the field as a laboratory.

The trainees are assigned to specific field projects, which have special learning components for them. The assignments are highly individualized and geared to expanding the trainees' skill in the methods of their choice. Two types of field settings are used for each trainee: first, mental health settings, which have an articulated community mental health philosophy and a broad range of services of a direct and indirect nature following the community mental health center concept; second, settings that are nonpsychiatric in nature, but in which the service has implications for the mental health of its clientele. In the second type of setting, a mental health specialist can make a major impact on the system or on its clientele by influencing the administrative process or structure, program policy, or coordination of services, or by carrying out program demonstration or research. Examples of such settings are public health, urban renewal, economic opportunity council programs, public schools, recreation departments, neighborhood houses, welfare services.

In the first of the two field assignments, the task to be performed is relatively well defined in advance and allows the trainee to become quickly involved in providing an indirect service. In the second assignment, the role to be developed and the problem to be solved are purposely left relatively undefined. Such a state is frequently characteristic of situations in which a worker will find himself in actual practice.

The supervision of the trainee's field experience is split into administrative and educational aspects. The agency maintains administrative responsibility, while the educational components of supervision are assumed by the teaching faculty, in the form of weekly individual and group tutorials that ensure an integrated approach to both course work and field work. The tutorial method of field supervision provides the opportunity for a high degree of conceptual teaching, and enables us to use settings for field projects which do not have social work supervision available. In order for faculty members to perform this kind of tutorial teaching, it is necessary for them to become thoroughly acquainted with the agency, its staff, functions, and policies. Furthermore, through their ties with the field, they are in an ideal position to recognize current practice problems, issues, and trends, and to bring these into the classroom for examination and discussion.

It is obviously too soon to evaluate any facet of this program. We cannot even affirm with hard evidence that this type of program meets a current educational need. We believe that it does. It is very hard to predict the long-range developments of such specialized programs. It may be that some aspects of knowledge and skill will be absorbed into the master's program, while other aspects may be suitable for and be incorporated into the doctoral program. However, at this point in time, a specialty program of the sort we have described seems to be valid and useful for practitioners who wish to make a commitment to a career in community mental health and who wish to prepare for such a career by means of advanced education.

Footnotes

1. Bertram Brown, M.D., "The Community Mental Health Center Movement: Its Impact on Social Work Practice and Education" (unpub. paper presented at the annual program meeting of the Council on Social Work Education, New York City, Jan. 25–27, 1966), p. 9.

2. Eleanor Cockerill, "Advanced Education for Social Work Practice—Its Nature and Purpose," *Social Work Education in the Post-Master's Program, No. 1, Guiding Principles* (New York: Council on Social Work Education, 1953), p. 65.

3. There are other educational patterns midway between staff development, refresher courses and academic education. For example, the Center for Training in Community Psychiatry of the State Department of Mental Hygiene, located in Berkeley, offers theoretical and informational courses in a sequential curriculum which can be taken part-time while the worker remains on the job. See Portia B. Hume, M.D., "Principles and Practice in Community Psychiatry: The Role and Training of the Specialist in Community Psychiatry," *Handbook of Community Psychiatry,* ed. L. Bellak, (New York: Grune and Stratton, 1964). The joint training program of NIMH and NASW offers periodic seminars to potential leaders in community mental health in Chicago, with provisions for some continuity of learning between seminars.

4. Charlotte Towle, "Aims and Characteristics of Advanced Education Differentiated from Master's Degree Education," *Social Work Education in the Post-Master's Program, No. 1, Guiding Principles* (New York: Council on Social Work Education, 1953), p. 15.

5. We concur with Dr. Gerald Caplan, who maintains that "an

educational program must be organized within a framework of pioneering practice." This enhances the possibility for creative innovation and theory building, and avoids what Dr. Caplan calls the risk of a trainee's becoming "a technician or a conforming disciple." See Gerald Caplan, M.D., "Community Psychiatry: Introduction and Overview," *Concepts of Community Psychiatry: A Framework for Training*, ed. Stephen E. Goldston (P.H.S. Publication No. 1319, U.S. Department of Health, Education, and Welfare; Washington, D.C.: Government Printing Office, 1963), p. 15.

IV

Social Work and Family Planning

9 *The Social Work Role in Family Planning:* A Summation

The Present Status of the Problem

Let us begin with our present status and where we are now in the field of family planning. We begin further with those areas where we have been able to establish some reasonable consensus. The most heartening fact is that family planning, seen as a vital need for which services are required, has, within recent years, achieved wide sanction and legitimacy through public opinion and legislative and judicial processes which have removed important barriers and moved the field away from the margin of illegality where it was poised for so long. Family planning is now part of national social policy, vigorously affirmed by numerous governmental and voluntary health and welfare agencies and by related organized professional groups. It is being viewed essentially as a basic health measure which should be available to all, particularly those previously deprived—the so-called "poor" and "near-poor." From social work and other perspectives, family planning is conceived as a basic right of the individual and the family, linked with the concept of health and well-being as enunciated in the broad WHO definition, and with those basic rights, and their extension, which are the essence of the democratic state. Rights of access are considered equal with protection of rights to self-determination, freedom of choice, and self-expression in this most private area of individual and family life. These rights need affirmation because there are numerous examples of violation by departments of welfare and the courts which have issued dicta which are coercive and punitive in the extreme, and perhaps unconstitutional as well. The impressive changes in public policy, however, . . . have not led, across the board, to a policy shift by

Source: Reprinted, with minor changes, from *Family Planning: The Role of Social Work,* ed. Florence Hazelkorn (Garden City, N.Y.: Adelphi University School of Social Work, 1968), pp. 144–59. Used by permission.

agencies, many of which have not as yet responded with renewed energy to the possibilities, or even to the mandates. . . . Less than one-third of local health departments and one-fifth of hospitals with large maternity services provide any kind of family planning services for the medically indigent. According to one unpublished study, only 50 per cent of the hospitals in San Francisco and Philadelphia offered family planning services.[1] A recent study by Frederick Jaffe gives a wealth of detailed data on uncovered needs.[2]

Major Target Groups

The main concern at present is how to make contraceptive measures increasingly available to populations other than those who, by virtue of ability to purchase private medical care, have had ready access to information and contraceptive help. The major target group appears to be the so-called medically indigent—the nonwelfare clientele—who live on the margin of poverty, and for whom private services are out of the question (although such referrals are frequently made), and for whom government-subsidized services are at best fragmented and complicated by a wide range of excluding eligibility policies. It is calculated that only 700,000 of 5.3 million women of child-bearing age are currently being served (about one-third of them by Planned Parenthood clinics). Of this number only about fourteen per cent are recipients of welfare for whom contraceptive information and referral, if not service, is more readily available; the remainder fall through the regular health and welfare nets. . . . It is important not to structure policy and service as though women in need of service can be reached via departments of welfare since this approach would miss the larger target.

Organizational Problems of Service Delivery

As indicated, the chief problem today is one of implementation and organization of programs and services. There seems to be a consensus that, ideally, family planning should be part of comprehensive medical care and should have a place in the spectrum of curative and preventive services. The ideal does not seem to be realizable in the near future. Furthermore, medical services now, to both indigent and near indigent, are a patchwork or tangle of services. . . . The comprehensive approach, while sound in the long run, is not sufficient for present purposes. Therefore, family planning proponents feel that such programs should have vigorous, specialized present visibility and vigorous promotion. . . .

From all that has been said, it would seem that there is a need at present for variable patterns of service, in the public and private sectors, which would serve as a network in reaching populations that are in various life stages in family life and child bearing. Thus, services need to exist as part of obstetrical and gynecological clinics, in maternal and infant care projects, in pre and postnatal programs, in Planned Parenthood clinics, in storefront clinics, in mobile units, whether under OEO or health department auspices, and so on. . . . There will be many women not covered in this patchwork of agencies due to complex and more stringent eligibility definitions, whom such services as Planned Parenthood could and must serve; moreover, such agencies have established a tradition in their ability to push at the boundaries of present acceptability and legality, and to respond to pressing needs in line with contemporary realities. Thus, for example, such an agency can explore and face the tremendous needs and demands of the unmarried teenager.

. . . . Overall planning needs to be governed by the likely responses to services by populations who have previously been deprived of services and not by considerations of the special needs of the so-called "intractable families" or what is referred to as the hardcore, multiproblem families. . . . The multifaceted needs of this group, so much a concern and responsibility of the social work profession, should not be ignored, and family planning help needs to be made more available to them as well.

Family Planning and Poverty

Relating problems of poverty with the need for successful family planning is not a new linkage. . . . Workers in each look towards the other: family planners look at impoverished groups with large families as a relevant and high-risk target group; poverty fighters look at family planning as one means of breaking out of the poverty cycle. . . . One of the announced goals of family planning is the reduction of poverty.

Some feel that concerted family planning can make real inroads in helping poor families to break out of the poverty cycle. Others—economists, sociologists, and even family planning specialists—maintain that problems of poverty have to be fought with other means, largely economic and social in nature, which are more relevant to the problem of poverty in an industrial society. The two points of view are pithily expressed by those who believe the cause of poverty is large families with large numbers of children (since those are indeed found most frequently among the poor), in contrast to those who maintain that the cause of poverty is simply lack of income. . . . Some argue that family planning cannot be offered as an antipoverty policy except as a prescription for individual families where it can contribute to maintaining a better balance between family income and family responsiblities. But it will not cure poverty. We are told further that family planning should be located in the range of those services which are needed for, and are supportive of, family life and family well-being.

In recent American social thought, we have moved from the myth of an egalitarian, classless society to a recognition of the importance of acknowledging and identifying relevant social class and ethnic factors. We now recognize the "poor," or "culture of poverty," with their well-identified value system and orientation, behavioral patterns and life style. However, many voices have warned against new stereotypes[3] and untested hypotheses about the poor. . . .

Frederick Jaffe . . . maintains that there are two basic dichotomous approaches to problem solving in poverty and in family planning, one an environmental approach, the other cultural.[4] The environmental view, put baldly, is focused on strategies of outreach programs tied to service networks to ensure that tangible assistance is forthcoming. The cultural approach "attempts to restructure values and to strengthen the presumably deficient motivation of the poor for family planning" and emphasizes counselling and family life and sex education.[5] Jaffe cites Lee Rainwater's comments that his early findings of his study of the attitudes of the poor towards contraception (pre-pill study) have been misread and misunderstood and have been used to buttress official resistance in places by implying the poor did not really *want* to limit their families.[6] Jaffe also states that the cultural advocates equate the poor with the multiproblem family. The environmentalists explain difficulties in family planning by factors of availability and accessibility of services and prevalence of misinformation uncorrected by successful peer group experience. The culturalists tend to attribute failures of institutions and of programs to the inadequacies of the recipients of their service.

The life style of the poor is often cited as an obstacle. He puts it bluntly that the "culture of poverty" concept has become a new "cop-out" in public policy and in family planning. This controversy, I am sure, reverberates in the social work field, which is also beset by similar dichotomous views.

More recent research has pointed to the fact that the poor have similar aspirations to the middle-class in regard to ideal family size. (This is not altogether accurate and needs to be corrected for such factors as ethnicity. For example, a study in our local community showed a sizeable difference in family-size aspirations between Mexican-American families, who approached their ideal and exceeded it, and other lower-class families.[7] But this fact needs to be examined more carefully in relation to possible post hoc rationalizations.) As James Lieberman puts it, lower-class women have "helpless motivation" towards family planning not realizing they have a choice about child bearing.[8] When adequate help comes in the way of available services, this motivation is transformed into adequate coping with family planning. This could be supported by further studies, such as the experience in Mecklenburg, North Carolina, where lower-class families responded positively to newly available family planning services.[9]

Family Planning and Population Policy

. . . Family planning . . . is embedded in the contexts of democratic process, self-determination, and control of privacy when it comes to making decisions regarding fertility. Professor Shlakman is concerned with the social consequences of such private decisions. She cautions against hiding antinatalist policies under the guise of family planning, particularly in regard to certain population groups, such as the Black Nationalists, whose response to family planning in the Negro ghetto is already inflamed with accusations of genocide. She wisely counsels, and I wish to emphasize her point and my agreement with it, that family planning *not* be discussed in the context of population issues until we can advocate a population policy on its own merits.[10]

A much stronger position on this issue is taken by the demographer and sociologist Kingsley Davis.[11] . . . According to Davis, the terms "population control" and "population planning" should not be used synonymously with family planning. He defines population control as "deliberate determination of all aspects of human demography, including geographical location and movement, age-sex structure, mortality, fertility, and total size." His thesis is that family planning does not provide for fertility control but provides only for a reduction in fertility. Family planning devotes itself to couples having the number of children they want and with questions of child spacing and, indeed, according to its declared purpose, with problems also of infertility. The assumption has been that family planning will lessen population growth. But millions of individual private reproductive decisions do not automatically control population for society's benefit. Family planning can therefore reduce fertility only by the margin that unwanted births constitute all births.

If it is decided that the creation of new human beings is too fundamental in society to be incidental, then there needs to be built into human relationships a system of rewards and punishments which further need to be related to economic and personal interests. This means alteration of the social structure and of the economy in order to create fundamental, even painful, social changes. These changes would have to be basic enough to affect reproductive motivation, such as altering the family, the status of women, and sexual mores. Such changes could be effected by giving economic advantages to the single over the married; to small versus large families; paying people for sterilization or abortion; taxing marriage licenses; requiring illegitimate pregnancies to be aborted; not giving maternity leaves or tax exemptions to parents, etc. More positively, women could be encouraged into careers rather than into idealized motherhood by inducements of equal pay and greater opportunities.

Davis says that a prescription for a government policy of low fertility reads like a chamber of horrors: squeezing consumers by taxation and inflation; making housing scarce; forcing mothers and wives to work because of inadequacy of male incomes; no provision for day care of children; increasing congestion in the cities; preventing immigration, etc. No government would institute all such hardships. Therefore, attractive substitutes should be developed for family interests.

In a similar vein, a recent report by Dr. Paul Erlich, a specialist in problems of population biology at Stanford University, advocates extraordinary measures which he acknowledges will outrage American public opinion. He would make birth control education mandatory in the schools, abolish income tax deductions for children, and tax infant supplies and foods as luxuries.

He would cease exporting foods to foreign countries like India, where fair analysis indicates food population unbalance hopeless. He would cease foreign aid to a nation which cannot convince us it is doing all in its power to limit population. Dr. Erlich expresses graphically his view of the world situation: "Saying the population explosion is a problem of underdeveloped countries is like telling a fellow passenger, 'your end of the boat is sinking.' "[12]

I offer these strong positions of advocacy of the adoption of a positive population policy on ly to highlight the larger problem and some proposed remedies, and place the family planning movement in its proper perspective. And, as I indicated, the time may soon be upon us when these views will be taken out of the studies of the academicians, and be opened to public debate. Social work will then have to take a searching look at its value commitments.

Preventive Mental Health and Family Planning

Mental health, and, more specifically, community mental health, has widened its scope and responsibilities from strictly clinical concerns into the arena of social problems, all of which impinge on the emotional stability and well-being of populations. It conceptualizes its tasks and operations increasingly within the public health philosophy and framework, with increased emphasis on preventing mental disorders or lowering their incidence. The essential congruence of the philosophical bases of public health, community mental health, and family planning is striking. All three are committed to the goal of promoting positive health and well-being, and to the concept of prevention. Community mental health addresses itself to the enhancement of effective social functioning of populations. Family planning offers a means of helping people develop competence and control over an extremely important area of their biological functioning. Through its modern technology, it has opened up for people a new sphere of environmental mastery. Achievement of mastery in one area of functioning can have profound effects on the possibilities of mastery in other areas of ego-functioning.

Up to now, mental health insights have not been applied to any great or systematic extent to some of the problems in family planning. It is true that the priority claims of attention have had to be on pushing ahead on three fronts—on developing birth control technology, social policy, and the delivery of services.

These matters require vigorous energy and effort now. However, it is not too soon to begin to examine some of the more subtle psychological and psychosocial aspects in family planning.... For example, we need investigation of and research into such areas as failure in consistent usage of contraceptives and maladaptive behavior in attempts to regulate fertility. We also need, at the other end of the mental health continuum, information regarding the effects on family life and family styles of contraceptive usage, both as to positive aspects and occasional negative factors. We have had attitudinal studies of a survey type in general as to views regarding contraceptive usage, and less on attitudes regarding sexuality. We need some depth studies in these and similar areas, as well as some longitudinal studies that would tap attitudes as a function of the developmental aspects of the family.

In addition to the mental health concepts and knowledge that might guide some of the needed research, the mental health field can also contribute substantially to issues of family planning counselling. We have not begun to explore what the counselling needs might be and what design or format they might take. Here, for instance, social psychiatry and ego psychology can contribute relevant concepts from crisis theory which can serve as guides to preventive intervention. Dr. Grete Bibring's work on pregnancy and birth as normal crises is also relevant here. . . . The ecological systems approach, as I understand it, is a more sophisticated version of the "person-in-situation," which we have not been able to conceptualize in holistic terms. The question of the need for counselling in family planning seems controversial in itself, and seems to be seriously neglected. To some it is unnecessary on the basis that a "normal population" is being served, or that it is considered a luxury. According to others, it should be a built-in feature for designated subpopulations especially at risk and be a part of more comprehensive care. Others have argued that we should delay having family planning services unless we can have the rounded complement of services. Here, then, are three different positions.

I was interested to discover only recently and through the literature that the Planned Parenthood Federation today sees itself as supporting a fourfold program: conception control, treatment of the infertile, education for marriage, and marriage counselling and research.[13] Just from a cursory view, I did not find much ongoing activity either in fertility problems or in counselling. At the very least, there certainly is a need for experimentation in this area.

Social Work Responsibility and Family Planning

It has been said that social work has been out of the family planning field for so long because it has not been concerned, until more recently, with the broad issues of social change, or because it seeks to avoid controversy. I do not think this a fair judgment. The history of the social work profession demonstrates that it has been responsive to changing social needs; in fact, one of the inherent strains in the profession is its ever-widening commitment to increasingly greater areas of social problems and social maladaption. There are some professionals who maintain that we have spread ourselves too thin.

As to the avoidance of controversy, this might be negated to some extent by reference to the profession's history of social reform. Nevertheless, it is true that social work, until rather recently, has played a tangential and passive role in family planning. One piece of evidence suffices: a literature search . . . has found that content on family planning has appeared in professional social work journals only within the last two years.[14] Only two articles appeared during the fifteen years between 1950 and 1965. But rather than dwelling on what *was,* we can assert that we have an opportunity and a mandate to play a vital role *now.* Social work and the family planning field have much to contribute to one another. It should be an easy alliance because the value bases of both are congruent. The central concern of social work is to enlarge people's opportunities for choices and fulfillment, and to enhance personal and interpersonal competencies in the direction of free and alternative choices. Family planning offers this in one vital area of social functioning.

Social work can contribute to family planning in numerous ways, with all its methodologies playing a role. It certainly must contribute toward social policy development and its refinement, and to program planning. It might also conceivably play a role in social administration. The knowledge and know-how of the community organization specialist is very relevant and necessary in relation to current developments in the field, and to the need for concerted planning in many communities. I also see a vital role for the two direct service methods—social group work and social casework. The techniques of group work can make important contributions to educational and informational needs, and casework to counselling efforts. Both group work and casework could have a remedial function, but, more important, both could provide preventive functions.

. . . Many current attacks on casework see its contribution as irrelevant, or at least very limited. Casework has never been a method devoted exclusively to remedial work or to dealing with pathology. My concept has always been broader. It is primarily a method which has the means of individualizing services, essential to the presentation of family planning services, which, from both a medical and a psychosocial point of view, deals with a most sensitive and intimate aspect of behavior. We are not yet at the point of offering a vaccine in a sugar cube or putting a birth control equivalent to fluoride in the water supply. Seen in this light, social casework has a potential contribution which we have only begun to explore and to exploit fully. We also have a significant role in transferring the knowledge we have of social factors and psychodynamics to other professionals and helping agents.

Professional Education in Regard to Family Planning

It has been noted that the profession of social work has not been at the forefront of leadership in regard to furthering the cause of family planning, either in terms of social policy development, or in terms of programmatic developments. Except in rare instances, it has not employed an aggressive outreach appraoch, which it has developed in other social problem areas, to the area of family planning in reaching certain target groups. When we look at universities and, particularly, schools of social work, it becomes even more evident that this whole human problem area has been relatively neglected. It does not have high visibility simply because it is not studied as an important part of relevant content. . . . For example, Planned Parenthood is not used as a field work placement. I understand that some schools of social work have field placements for casework in this area, and several other schools do for community organization. In making a quick check at Berkeley, I found that one second-year course in programs and policies in child and family welfare deals briefly with the topic. However, only fifteen students (about 10 per cent of our second-year enrollement) are enrolled in this course. In the basic first-year course on social organization, only one community case study was used (in this instance the New York City experience in the late 1950s), and that to show city hospital practices and the impact of public opinion and pressure groups in getting policies and practices changed in such hospitals. (This has now been discontinued as outdated, and some issues raised by the Moynihan report are used instead.) Family planning may also come up tangentially in casework methods courses in relation to particular cases.

To my knowledge, we have never had a student research project in this area and, of course, no field work. It is a dismal record and I fear my school is not atypical. In our new third-year program in community mental health, we are currently working with Planned Parenthood. We have at present one advanced student experimenting with group work services to clients under twenty-one, considered a vulnerable group which might profit from some form of counselling. Dr. Goldman and I are engaged there in research as well as service through consultation and help with in-service training of volunteer interviewers, chiefly in order to sensitize them to the social problem and mental health needs of their clientele.

The record of professional schools preparing personnel in other health sciences and helping professionals is also not impressive. Schools with public health programs generally do include informational and social policy content on family planning and population control. However, I did not encounter any such content in the school of public health which I attended. That may have been coincidental or a function of selectivity on my part, or a product of the social climate in Massachusetts seven years ago. Schools of nursing also have a long way to go, but more disturbing is the fact that medical schools give scant attention to human sexuality and to family planning. It is hard to imagine such a state of affairs. Lieberman states that there is "serious omission and misinformation in regard to sex and marital problems in medical practice and in teaching medical students."[15] I might mention that at the time I attended a school of public health, the library of the first-rate medical school nearby kept books and information on sexuality and birth control on locked shelves. This, hopefully, has been changed by now.

These remarks point to the conclusion that we will get needed professional interest and competence in this area only if the professional schools will carry out their responsibilities in developing relevant and needed content. You may be disappointed that I do not spell out what the relevant content might be, but it seems to me that this is a job to which we must all address ourselves soon. It may be that the impetus for this will have to come from those dedicated professionals already in the field who can exert pressure as well as lend assistance in the collaborative endeavor of curriculum development and teaching.

Research and Family Planning

There are innumerable areas and unanswered questions in the complex field of family planning and conception control that urgently need to be clarified and explored through research before informed policy and programs can be developed. . . . The social work profession has a definite role to play here. To some of the research investigations, social work can contribute through interdisciplinary participation, but some questions should be investigated by other disciplines. There are still other areas for research that fall within the specific competence of social work.

There has been considerable investigation of motivation and attitudes to family planning. However, we could use more refined studies of the psychosocial factors that influence family planning. The reverse of this also needs research; namely, what the psychosocial effects are on the family who make use of family planning. . . . Research in a narrower segment—the influence of the husband on the wife's decision to practice contraception—is needed. We also need to know more about the use and nonuse of contraception on marital stability and relationships. There is an amazing amount of contradiction in the literature on family planning. For example, among recent things I have read, there were admonishments to involve men more in family planning efforts, as well as conclusions that the husband's role in contraception is negligible and that therefore he need not be taken into account in large-scale family planning efforts. Even the "machismo" theory is raised and buried by various investigators and writers. . . .One can only conclude that we operate with less than certain knowledge.

If we are to become interested in questions regarding population policy, which, it seems to me, are as important as issues of war and peace and conflict resolution, we need research on how to bring about value changes regarding ideal family size, and how to strengthen alternatives to the life career of motherhood. In her recent study on an analysis of national population surveys since the mid-thirties, demographer Judith Blake Davis concludes that "no major social or economic group has considered a small family (two children) to be desirable; that proportionately more lower income and less educated respondents consider families in excess of three children to be desirable than do the more affluent and better educated; and that men typically want somewhat smaller families than women, thereby casting doubt on the widely held belief that, in exceeding a two-child family, women are merely complying with their husband's wishes."[16]

We need follow-up research on users, non-users, and drop-outs. We also need work on establishing psychosocial factors and cues that would serve as predictors for nonusers in order to build in more supports for such groups. . . .

There are the unmet needs of special problem groups that have long been in the purview of social work concern and action. For example, we need to consider more actively the special needs of the mentally retarded and the mentally ill. We need to experiment with more effective approaches to the so-called hard core and multiproblem families and to gather better data as to the failure in family planning among this group. The special problems of teenagers can no longer be ignored. . . . The latter suggests contraceptive help is available for college students, but this is by no means universal and is especially absent in publicly supported universities. Even in most Planned Parenthood clinics the ticket for admission for an unmarried minor is an illegitimate pregnancy. . . . We also need information and understanding about the needs and strategies involved in meeting the needs of older groups.

We often hear of one of the numerous "revolutions" about us. . . . —the one in sexual behavior, especially among the young and unmarried. We are losing great opportunities to gather data on changing sexual mores simply by not inquiring about this subject in our own encounters with people seeking contraception. In fact, it is most striking to a novice like myself in the family planning field who first encounters the literature and finds that virtually no attention is paid to complex areas of sexual feeling and behavior, and that contraception behavior is treated as if divorced from sexuality. Brewster Smith supports this: "The neutral language in which family planning is discussed scientifically and professionally should not let us forget that we deal here with sex and the marriage bed, around which surely are woven some of the strongest and least rational motives, the most intimate and private relationships and the firmest institutional norms and taboos known to man."[17]

Sex education in the schools is another front that social work should support and help promote with programs and needed evaluation. There is a great urgency to prevent unwed adolescent pregnancies, which seem to be on the increase. A recent article on the "Pedagogy of Sex" points out that current sex education in the schools is offered as reproductive biology and is presented in strongly nonhuman imagery; or it is presented as if managing sexuality involved only managing boy-girl social relationships.[18] It seems that even when dealing with sex directly we still manage to avoid discussion of sexual feelings, urges, and needs, something that is part of *experience,* rather than something that simply happens. . . . We want to develop in young people responsible sexual relationships and not only offer notions of abstinence. . . . We have found in our brief experience and observations numerous virgins, eighteen or younger, who appear on the doorstep of Planned Parenthood and who seem to want to prepare for sexual experiences. They are met with confused and conflicting adult responses which confirm for them adult hypocrisy. They are actually preparing responsibly for an experience, but, in effect, are penalized for this. This, then, is another ideal group for both study and counselling. . . . There is a need to study the kinds of counselling services that ought to be offered, and I would expand this to include all informational, and educational, and preventive approaches.

The complex subject of abortion . . . deserves some mention here. As state laws change in the direction of legalizing abortion for health and mental health reasons, such as recent legislation in some states, mental health personnel increasingly will be called upon to make judgments. Psychiatric justification for abortion is by no means simple, largely because, despite all our knowledge, our capacity for predicting human response is so poor. We ought to begin to gather data on these cases. We should also watch for what I predict will happen—namely, that even legal abortion will clearly emerge as an avenue of availability for the middle-class and educated who know their way around psychiatric clinics and personnel. . . .

In summary, I see the central responsibility of social work in family planning is to close the gap between the impressive changes in expressed public policy as against actual prevailing public policy, and to address its energy to modifying the behavior of social institutions and creating new social institutions, taking into account not only societal but also individual human needs. It is the commitment to this bifocal view—or ecological approach—which can be the unique contribution of social work.

Notes

1. Jane Castor and Pamela Sue Hudson, "Social Workers and Fertility Regulation: The Circumvention of Community Inertia" (unpub. mimeo., Langley Porter Neuropsychiatric Institute, San Francisco, May 1966).
2. Frederick Jaffe, "Closing the Gap in Subsidized Family Planning Services in 110 Metropolitan Areas with More Than 250,000 Population" (unpub. mimeo., Department of Program Planning and Development, Planned Parenthood-World Population, Oct. 1967).
3. Jerome Cohen, "Social Work and the Culture of Poverty," *Mental Health of The Poor,* ed. Frank Reissman, Jerome Cohen, and Arthur Pearl (New York: Free Press of Glencoe, 1964), pp. 129–38; also in *Social Work,* IX (Jan. 1964), 3–11.
4. Frederick Jaffe, "Family Planning and Public Policy: Is the 'Culture of Poverty' the New Cop-Out?" (paper presented at American Sociological Association, San Francisco, Aug. 29, 1967).
5. *Ibid,* p. 9.
6. Lee Rainwater and K. Weinstein, *And the Poor Get Children* (Chicago: Aldine, 1960).
7. Laura Keranen et al., "Analysis of Attitudes towards Family Planning in Three Oakland Populations" (unpub. mimeo., Division of Research, State Department of Public Health, Berkeley, Calif., 1966).
8. James Lieberman, "Preventive Psychiatry and Family Planning," *Journal of Marriage and the Family,* XXVI (Nov. 1964), 472.
9. Elizabeth Corkey, "The Birth Control Program in the Mecklenburg County Health Department," *American Journal of Public Health,* LVI (Jan. 1966), 40–47.
10. See Vera Shlakman, "Social Work's Role in Family Planning: Social Policy Issues," in *Family Planning Readings and Case Materials,* ed. Florence Hazelkorn (New York: Council on Social Work Education, 1971), pp. 66–81.
11. Kingsley Davis, "Population Policy: Will Current Programs Succeed?" *Science,* CLVIII (Nov. 10, 1967), 730–39.

12. Quoted in the *San Francisco Chronicle,* Nov. 17 and Nov. 20, 1967.

13. Sophia J. Kleegman, "Planned Parenthood: Its Influence on Public Health and Family Welfare," in *Abortion in America,* ed. Harold Rosen (Boston: Beacon Press, 1967), p. 261.

14. Castor and Hudson, "Social Workers and Fertility Regulation," p. 7.

15. Lieberman, "Preventive Psychiatry," p. 473.

16. *University Bulletin of the University of California,* vol. XIV, no. 16, Nov. 27, 1967.

17. Brewster Smith, "Motivation, Communications, Research and Family Planning," in *Public Health and Population Change: Current Research Issues* (Pittsburgh: University of Pittsburgh Press, 1966), pp. 70–89.

18. William Simon and John Gagnon, "Pedagogy and Sex," *Saturday Review,* Nov. 18, 1967, p. 76.

10 *Education and Training of Social Workers for Roles and Functions in Family Planning*

This paper is concerned with the need for relevant education and training for social workers to prepare them for significant roles and functions of family planning activities. Social work is new to this area and has developed little experience and expertness, with some rare exceptions. Our task is to explore ways and means by which we may move ahead responsibly through educational development to give the necessary impetus, knowledge, and competence to practitioners at various levels of practice.

Basic Definitions of Terms and Implicit Issues

Semantic confusion in behavioral and social science areas and in applied fields of practice is not an unusual phenomenon. In the field of family planning and in population dynamics, the need for scientific clarification is crucial if we are to move ahead in a rational manner. Until recently, because of societal taboos, non-respectability, and illegality, various terms have been used which, in essence, are euphemisms. These constraints no longer operate, however. The persistence of euphemisms and semantic looseness hides basic motivation and intention and therefore obscures what we are about. We need clarification of terms and intentions in order to contribute honestly to the necessary dialogue about issues of social policy in regard to population problems. Clarity is also needed for interprofessional communication in order to move toward a more scientific perspective and to communicate with paraprofessionals and the target groups we are trying to serve with health and welfare programs.

Semantically, during this century, there has been a shift in such

Source: Reprinted, with minor changes, from *Journal of Education for Social Work,* VI (Fall 1970), 27–38. Used by permission.

terms as birth control to contraception, to family planning, and now these are intermingled with problems of population dynamics and population control. Each term has a different intention, purpose, possibility, and limitation, both technical and social. Basically, we refer to three areas of control: *conception control,* which includes all methods of a mechanical, chemical, or surgical nature for preventing conception (e.g., sterilization); *fertility control,* which aims at the prevention of births and includes all measures of conception control plus such measures as the so-called "morning after pill" and abortion; and *population control,* which is directed to the rate of population growth and takes into purview fertility control plus the relation between fertility and mortality, migration, and problems of economic and social development, and so forth.[1]

The term "family planning" is a more recent phrase. One writer states that "it is intended to be so homey, inexplicit and inoffensive as to find universal acceptance, and this has almost happened."[2] Family planning as a field of endeavor has many basic concepts built into it. One key concept is the regulation of fertility by preventing unwanted pregnancies, by spacing the number of children desired. This gives families mastery over their reproductive functions and enlarges their capacity for choice and self-direction in individual and private family goals. Self-determination, choice, and effectiveness in family planning are important ethical and behavioral considerations. "Every child a wanted child" is the popular slogan. Family planning is also embedded in the health matrix and seeks to make an impact on foetal wastage, prematurity, maternal mortality and morbidity, and child health. It is also rooted in concepts of social and psychological well-being in its emphasis on strengthening the quality and stability of family life; thus, it becomes a measure for positive mental health. Family planning objectives include not only conception control but also help with problems of infertility, although this dimension is underplayed in actual practice. Thus, family planning deals with the promotion, postponement, and prevention of conception. The development of programs and services are expressions of the concept of the basic right to access to information and service for all as part of the broad human right to health and well-being with equal protection of rights to self-determination and freedom of choice. In essence then, family planning deals with the vital concern of fertility control via individual and family behavioral acts which will help produce wanted and planned children.

Historically, the family planning movement has been motivated by numerous opinions and purposes from liberating and protecting the social rights of women to advocacy of population control and eugenic selection. Professor Shlakman pointed out that "the attainment of official sanctions for fertility control has probably been facilitated by an unofficial or tacit coalition of diverse interests and the argument marshalled in support of different approaches persuaded different publics. This has left us with a residue of confusion which can hamper effective policy developments."[3] From the policy declarations within the family planning literature she identifies thirteen divergent purposes, one of which is to control total population. I concur with her when she cautions against hiding antinatalist policies under the guise of family planning.

It is highly undesirable, for many cogent reasons, to use the growing movement and practice of family planning as a way of backing into the complex problems of population control. One reason is that family self-determination and population control clash sharply where they intersect. Another reason is in regard to target groups to be served—such as the poor and certain ethnic and racial groups—which tend to be singled out for emphasis. The need to equalize services to enhance family planning opportunities is different from expressed concern about excess fertility in these groups. We are going through a historical period characterized by a great self-consciousness in different class and ethnic groups linked with a growing pride in identity, with affirmation of self-determination and a movement towards the concept and practice of community control and self-help. Some have labelled these trends as aspects of a social revolution. It therefore becomes urgent that professionals in the population field be very clear about purposes and goals as well as means. The charge of genocide has emanated from some segments in the black community; such a charge may have its distorted and self-destructive overtones from one point of view, but it is understandable from the perspective of the insider, the racially oppressed ghetto dweller who has been the recipient of lifelong cumulative discriminatory and oppressive practices. Any propensity to distortion or to group paranoia is reinforced by policy and programs which single out the poor and specific ethnic groups, especially if they are then reinforced by coercive and punitive practices which unfortunately have been known to exist in some public welfare departments and even in our legal system. Social justice becomes a primary issue. Population policy and family planning programs must be beamed at the society as a whole with scrupulous avoidance of practices which might contribute to the politicalization of necessary efforts. Here we might cite Margaret Mead, who stated that "we have to have an ethic on the subject of population control that is worldwide, that includes every one, where class, ethnic, and racial difference will not confuse the issue."[4]

The problem of rapid population growth is an increasingly urgent concern. The issues involved need to be dealt with separately, seriously, and honestly as problems in national and social policy and deserve much careful thought, study, and public debate in regard to means and consequences for the whole society. The problems of overpopulation are a high-priority concern for both developing and highly industrialized nations. The United States seems at the brink of moving into such an arena of public policy considerations, stimulated by growing popular concern regarding broader aspects of physical and social ecology and further stimulated by recent presidential pronouncements and legislative activities.

Population experts, demographers, and other social scientists who are fundamentally concerned with population problems tend to see family planning efforts, even if widespread and comprehensive, as nonsignificant means of reducing the population. This is a controversial area. To put forth this position, the demographer and sociologist Kingsley Davis is cited at length. Davis contends that the terms "population control" and "population planning" should not be used as synonyms for family planning. According to Davis, population control is "deliberate determination of all aspects of human demography, including geographical location and movement, age-sex structure, mortality, fertility and total size."[5] He maintains that family planning provides not for fertility control but only for a reduction of fertility. To say that family planning will lessen population growth is to ignore the fact that millions of individual private reproductive decisions will control population for society's benefit only by the proportion that unwanted births represent of all births. Dr. Franklin Robbins states that family planning is but one facet of population control and might be considered to relate to it much in the same way the private practice of medicine relates to public health.[6] Another demographer, Philip Hauser, asserts that "it is doubtful that family planning programs, as conducted at present, can significantly reduce population growth rates during, at least, the remainder of this century."[7]

Direct rather than oblique approach to overpopulation requires fundamental social and economic changes in society which may be painful and politically or morally unacceptable. The changes would have to be basic enough to affect reproductive motivation and behavior powerfully. Davis, in the article previously cited, enumerates many of these measures, some of which he himself characterizes as a chamber of horrors. However, there can be positive inducements as well as deterrents and constraints. In a recent paper, Bernard Berelson offers a most lucid and comprehensive statement as to the kinds of proposals and measures that might have to be undertaken and the obstacles likely to be encountered if a serious population control effort were to be instituted as part of social policy.[8] Such measures need to be explored, studied, and debated in the public realm, separately, and unlinked from family planning programs.

A similar unfortunate linkage, related to the above and affecting the profession of social work in particular, has been the linkage of family planning to the efforts to eradicate poverty. To state the issues briefly here: there are proponents who feel that concerted family planning can make real inroads in helping poor families break out of the poverty cycle. Others—mainly economists, sociologists, and even some family planning experts—maintain that problems of poverty have to be fought with other means, mainly economic and social in nature, which are more relevant to problems of poverty in an industrialized society. Just as family planning cannot be offered as an antinatalist policy, similarly it cannot be offered as an antipoverty measure, except as a prescription for *individual* families where family planning can contribute to the maintenance of a better balance between family income and family size.

Some Impediments to Social Work Practice and Curriculum Building in Family Planning

It is a fact that the profession of social work in the United States has not been at the forefront of leadership in regard to furthering the cause of family planning, either in terms of broader social policy development or in terms of programmatic development and service delivery. Indeed, this whole human problem area has been seriously neglected by the social work profession. This situation is particularly strange in view of the fact that this profession generally has moved very quickly in response to many challenges for service with various defined population groups and newly emerging social problem areas, and specifically in view of the fact that the goals of family planning are not charged with conflict or dissent for social work. Florence Haselkorn rightly points this out and notes the compatibility of the value base of family planning and social work in regard to the right to opportunity for self-realization and the right of self-determination regarding freedom of choice in decisions affecting one's own fate.[9] Furthermore, there is great compatibility between social work and family planning at a level of more instrumental values in regard to enhancing, strengthening, and preserving of family life, which are central concerns to social work.

Several reasons which have contributed to this state of affairs might be identified. One is the lack of a firm tradition in this country, with some exceptions, for the profession to operate at a level of social policy development. Currently we are striving to emphasize this area. A related reason is the often noted function of social work in our society, which is designated as residual in contrast to an institutional function. Basically, that means that the profession is largely concerned with problems of social breakdown and with social disorganization, dealing with residual problems caused by social and cultural lags in institutional development.

Social work has not developed a strong role in prevention, either on the level of provision of services as institutionalized for the entire society or on the level of promotion of health and well-being. We have operated largely in the realm of secondary and tertiary levels of prevention (as defined by the field of public health), which means in remedial and rehabilitative efforts. We tend to deal with populations already identified as problematic or "sick" and are less responsive to working with populations potentially indentifiable as "at risk" or healthy populations in need of basic services. In contrast, family planning has a strong preventive perspective and institutional dimension. Therefore, social work, by its tradition, has not grasped the opportunity of making impact there. This becomes even more paradoxical in view of the fact that "family planning has a far reaching potential for preventing and reducing the incidence of many of our most plaguing problems."[10]

Another possible reason for the lack of high social visibility and activity in family planning is due to the fact that family planning is generally conceptualized as a basic health measure and is offered in a spectrum of health and medical services. Although medical social work is an old and respected specialty area of practice, it is a relatively small part of total social work practice. Furthermore, where social work has been in an "ancillary" position (we have often changed the words but not the position)—in this case a paramedical professional—it has rarely been able to exert strong initiative and leadership. For years the enabling and facilitating function and role of social work in so-called secondary settings has been conceptualized. This role suggests the image of smoothing over, filling in gaps, and raising the quality of service on an individualized basis—a not unimportant task. But we have been slow to grasp the potential for social work to lead, develop, and promote institutional and service delivery change.

The overall compatibility of basic values between social work and family planning should not obscure the fact that there are other serious complex value issues which may have contributed to the relative professional passivity of social work in the family planning field. The most obvious issue concerns human sexuality and the changing mores in regard to premarital, extramarital, and adolescent sexuality. Scientific knowledge in regard to the effects of such change on people and on the social fabric is lacking; this forces professional practitioners in all service fields to fall back on their personal beliefs, attitudes, and mores. The whole area of sexuality is still highly charged. Social workers cannot deal comfortably with this subject despite frequent denials to the contrary. The paradox has been pointed out that professional social workers are knowledgeable and comfortable with psychosexual development knowledge and the unconscious aspects of sexual drives, needs, and even aberrations, but are uncomfortable with conscious sexual behavior, feelings, and practices. To quote Haselkorn again, "One can only speculate why, despite social work's unique access to the most private feelings and experience of people, there is no evidence that it has acquired a body of empirical observation about sexual behavior."[11] It should be noted that other health professionals, including doctors and nurses, unless specially trained and prepared for family planning functions, also have observable difficulties. Much of the literature dealing with family planning by-passes human sexual feelings, needs, and responses. Contraceptive behavior is most often dealt with as separate from sexual behavior. Furthermore, much of what passes for sex education for young people is essentially reproductive biology represented in nonhuman imagery. Brewster Smith underlines this observation: "The neutral language in which family planning is discussed scientifically and professionally should not let us forget that we deal here with sex and the marriage bed, around which surely are woven some of the strongest and least rational motives, the most intimate and private relationships and the firmest institutional norms and taboos known to man."[12]

Other value issues that contribute to complexity and uncertainty, in addition to the discomfort with the subject of human sexuality in all its more raw forms, have to do with dilemmas such as the invasion of privacy and the need to safequard it and individual freedom as opposed to the need for social responsibility and the professional's role in the exercise of social controls. These are technical as well as philosophical issues around reaching-out approaches which can border on the verge of the aggressive; however, they can only be indicated here as areas in need of further clarification.

An examination of the impediments to curriculum development suggests a whole host of other difficult problems that are not only specific to content of family planning. We are in an important period of transition and change, almost in the nature of an upheaval. The growing complexity of social problems has brought a profound sense of urgency for more and better problem-solving efforts in a wider area of social need. We are confronted with many conflicting demands, a reordering of priority efforts, and a demand for "relevance" which is defined differently by various sectors of our constituency. There are, therefore, many competing areas for content inclusion. For example, we are continually pushed to the growing edges of practice in social problem areas such as delinquency control, mental retardation, geriatrics, alienated youth, drug abuse, alcoholism, racism, urban decay, and disorganization. We are also pushed toward new methodological approaches which are often too readily espoused without requisite testing, selection, and validation. At the same time we are struggling to define the nature of the core curriculum, to determine what is basic for all learners and practitioners. If we cannot define our core character we become chameleon-like, without a central identity. When the pressures and demands become inordinate, we retreat to a defensive position and aver that we cannot be all things to all men nor spread our resources so thin that there is no hope of being effective in any arena.

The problems of curriculum saturation, the wish to avoid curriculum construction via the additive method, the balance between generic education and specialization of content and its timing, and the commitment philosophically to a holistic approach are certainly not unique to social work education. They are equally troublesome, for example, to medical education.[13] They are inherent in the nature of professional development, in the fact of rapidly expanding areas of knowledge and in ever-widening areas of social responsibility and societal expectations. To keep up with these dynamics, professional education must engage in a constant effort of curriculum design and revision and must build into the learner and practitioner a concept of life-long study for the profession through various mechanisms of self-development and more formalistic continuing education.

Another impediment is the lack of ready visibility of social work roles in family planning. Curriculum changes usually come about through community pressures to develop new programs with a clear social service component or social work role. Although schools of social work tend to see themselves in leadership roles and on the growing edge of practice, in fact most tend to lag behind the actualities of practice. There simply has not been the demand for highly trained social work manpower in family planning in contrast to other well-defined manpower needs. On the service level in family planning programs run by the traditional medical team, there is often the spoken or unspoken question, "What do we need a social worker for?" This implies that social work has to sell itself by demonstrating its competence and potential contribution. However, where qualified social work manpower has existed, it has been used extremely effectively. We are now beginning to have social work role models in family planning who are utilized in a wide variety of tasks and roles and who clearly do make a significant contribution. Increasingly, work in family planning can become a viable career choice for the professionally trained social worker.

There are pioneering social workers who have been operating in primary family planning settings, in a range of direct and indirect service roles, though not in sizeable numbers. They have been able to do this without having any special educational preparation because of the ability of social workers to transfer and build on basic social work knowledge skills. The activities on the direct service level have been in clinical settings such as in Planned Parenthood Clinics, special Maternal and Infant Care projects, obstetrical wards and gynecology clinics, medical teenage clinics, public health clinics, clinics under the auspices of the Office of Economic Opportunity, and so forth. Direct service functions are connected with screening, intake, counseling, referral to community resources, follow-up and out-reach programs. Other roles, indirect or facilitating, are frequently taken—administering local programs, executive functions, consultation to other health personnel, health educator roles, community organization roles, staff development and in-service training, and research.

Social workers are already working with various high risk groups—such as unwed mothers, the mentally ill, the mentally retarded, child protective services, well baby clinics, etc.—on both preventive and, more often, rehabilitative levels. They already have a mandate and responsibility for the care of such patients as part of more traditional practice. This large core of social workers could be more consciously directed to help those clients and others obtain family planning services as part of the overall social services being given.

Potentialities for Curriculum Building

An examination of current curriculum offerings in schools of social work indicates lack of substantial content on family planning and population problems. The difficulty lies in opposite approaches to curriculum development: the additive versus the integrative approach.

In order to develop a new specialty area some new knowledge and information must be added or built into existing courses. Adding new knowledge and information as such is relatively simple, except for the competing areas of interest, which all vie for curriculum time, and the question as to the appropriate level and timing. More cogent is the issue of the rapid obsolescence and change in knowledge and the need to help the practitioner continue to acquire knowledge as a lifelong quest. In the integrative approach, knowledge, issues, and problem-solving approaches are dealt with in the context of a broad range of social problem areas. There is less opportunity to build cumulative knowledge and to develop specialist sophistication in any one social problem area.

Some chronic and plaguing questions confronting curriculum builders are as follows: What is essential knowledge; from what sources should it be drawn? How should the rapidly changing nature of knowledge and its obsolescence be dealt with? What aspects of knowledge are in the nature of general education and what needs to be selected out for professional uses? Which levels of education should provide for what kinds of knowledge—for example, should knowledge of demography, population dynamics, basic concepts of family organization and family functioning, reproductive biology, and contraceptive technology be part of undergraduate or graduate professional offerings? What happens if it is not available in the undergraduate curriculum? At what level of specificity or concreteness should knowledge be presented in a contrast to the degree of abstraction and conceptualization as a means of generalization and transferability of use?

Haselkorn deals with these issues lucidly, making a strong case for the presentation in professional schools of interface concepts with emphasis on linkages in knowledge and technique for transferability in learning. She argues essentially for an integrative approach, while recognizing that certain issues of a value nature, social policy considerations, legal questions and the implications of the rapidly changing nature of contraceptive technology as to physiological, medical, phychological, and service delivery aspects do need special attention and are specific to family planning and population problems. However, the selection of knowledge in the foundation courses in a graduate professional school should be geared toward a special perspective of complexity and problem focus to move the learner to an emphasis on problem solving. The task in the presentation of knowledge is to sensitize a student to and increase his awareness of an issue and to provide him with basic conceptual tools for analysis. Basic information courses, it can be argued, belong in an undergraduate curriculum.

Given this perspective, the basic sequence on human growth and the social environment should contain content on biological and psychological aspects of sex, reproduction, pregnancy and childbirth, and contraceptive technology. Family structure and evolving roles within the family life cycle and the impact of family size in regard to family functioning should be examined in the context of class and ethnic cultural variables. Sexuality at all developmental stages should be taught in terms of achievement of identity, autonomy, mastery and capacity for choice and self-direction. Factors in development that lead to maladaptive responses and psychopathology that diminish capacity for choice and mastery need to be identified.

The social policy sequence can easily be reordered in its priorities to give central attention to world population issues, population patterns, and the reciprocal effects of great social trends such as economic development, attempts to eradicate poverty, industrialization, automation, urbanization, environmental pollution, war, migration, growing ethnic self-determination, the changing role and status of women, entry into the labor market and its effect on family structure and family relationships. The social implications of a national policy for population control should be explored with attention to political and moral issues, anticipation of social consequences and an examination of the social work profession's stance and role in policy formation. Legal constraints against abortion and sterilization can be explored with examination of the effects of changing legislation. Against this kind of backdrop, social welfare programs and health care services with particular attention to maternal and infant care can be examined as to general population served, with particular attention to the needs of special population groups at high risk and with equal attention to preventive as well as remedical services.

All methods employed in problem solving in social work are relevant to the family planning enterprise. The direct service methods, casework and group work, still receive heavy emphasis in the professional curriculum. They could readily be geared for application in family planning work. Group work approaches are particularly applicable to educational and preventive goals and can be directed to special interest and problem groups such as former mental patient, the mentally retarded, unwed mothers, welfare recipient mothers, etc. Group work techniques can bring greater sensitivity and personalization to the whole enterprise of sex education for youth.

The casework method is essentially geared to the individualization of services. This is a much broader conception than its equation with psychotherapy. Some family planning strategists emphasize that all energies should go into the basic provision of services to that motivated part of the population which is not served at present but would be competent users with ready access to service. Although such a priority should be stressed, it does not negate the fact that for many people effective contraceptive usage involves complex feelings and behavior which they cannot manage unaided and which may need some clarification, support, and reinforcement. Indeed, social work has a special commitment to those who are less effective in social functioning. Haselkorn elaborates forcefully on this controversy: "Conventional wisdom tells us that there are some women who are unable to take advantage of opportunity for reasons of limitation in capacity and motivation. It is precisely when motivation and capacity are obscured by an interplay of intellectual, social and emotional factors that the one-to-one relationship is the social work method of choice. Nor will adequate institutional arrangements, when we ever finally achieve them, eliminate the need on the part of some for mediating help to locate and utilize and persist in the use of family planning. Follow-up of the drop-out cannot easily be handled by community approaches."[14] She sees the purpose of casework as a clarification of life goals for people uncertain of their wishes and plans relating to family size and spacing, and for those who need to clarify their fears and confusions regarding contraceptive usage. On a more complex level, individualized services given by more sophisticated clinicians are also needed for people who have suffered more severe ego damage and whose total approach to living tends to be chaotic and disorganized. Casework may not be able to reverse the process or alter the character structure, but it can help people to use services more effectively when impediments are reduced to a minimum and supports are maximized. It is unfortunate that polarities have been engendered by many, both in social work and family planning and outside the field, as to where the major thrust of the professional efforts needs to be. Frederick Jaffe talks of the environmental view, which is geared to outreach programs and service networks, versus the cultural approach, which locates the deficiencies in people and calls for remedial action through counseling and education.[15] The polarity is artificial and reductionist. The uniqueness of social work is precisely its prescription to both views in what I have called a "bifocal point of view." Haskelkorn supports this point, stating that the so-called "environmentalist and cultural approaches coalesce in social work's psychosocial approach."[16]

Community development and community organization is growing rapidly as a significant method of intervention by social workers. Strategies for social change—including political action—receive major attention. Community organization on the neighborhood level geared to self-help efforts and the development of local services and programs is another level of intervention. Both these levels of action are relevant for and can be taught as applied to the family planning enterprise.

The so-called facilitating methods such as supervision, consultation, and administration at present get only limited attention in the graduate curriculum. They are generally geared to more experienced students whose early career goals involve roles which make use of these methodologies. Supervision and other methods of teaching and training are of great use for the development of nonprofessional (and professional) personnel. Administration and program development is more often an acquired skill rather than an area for which there has been intellectual and experiential preparation. Consultation is a newer method of problem solving which has a growing body of theory that can be taught systematically, particularly to the more experienced student. A good part of the work in the family planning field calls for skills in consultation to personnel within the agency and, much more likely, to other community agencies, professionals, and nonprofessionals. Collaboration is also a method of working, generally in an interdisciplinary context, but aside from exhortations, it usually gets scant attention. Family planning clearly requires an interdisciplnary team approach. At the very least there should be content regarding the subcultural value orientation of other professional disciplines and knowledge of and respect for each other's competence and contribution.

The field work practice experience could provide students with almost unlimited opportunities for some aspect of family planning work. Student training could make much greater use of already existing family planning services for work with individuals, groups, and communities and for development of skills in direct patient services and in a whole host of roles previously discussed. In addition, on the direct service level, almost all work in agency settings lends itself to attention to the family planning needs of clientele.

The research sequence provides great opportunity for engaging student interest in the exploration of many unanswered questions in family planning where there is a vital need for knowledge in a relatively new field. The focus of research should be related to social work practice issues and should also take advantage of the kind of access and intimate relationships the social worker has with this clientele group. For example, survey research, such as epidemiological and demographic data collection, does not need the insight and understanding which are unique to the social work profession. Several areas are natural for social work research efforts: (1) program evaluation in regard to the effectiveness of services in achieving program goalsand objectives, evaluation of experimental approaches of an out-reach or preventive nature including health education and sex education efforts, assessment of demonstration-type programs geared to new population groups or high-risk groups such as teen-agers, evaluation of qualitative aspects of services given by nonprofessionals and the use of differential manpower in general, and so forth; (2) follow-up studies of ineffective users, drop-outs, and effective users for understanding of differential variables making for effective usage, and follow-up studies of high-risk groups; (3) studies of a qualitative nature to yield insights regarding attitudes and motivation in use of family planning by different population groups, more subtle analysis of the impact of family planning on family well-being, mental and physical health, family life styles, marital roles and adjustment, and teenage sexuality and behavior; studies on the effects of pregnancy testing and pregnancy and abortion counseling; studies of failure to regulate fertility among supposedly informed and motivated women in relation to maladaptive or ineffective coping and life styles. The qualitative studies could yield insights which could generate hypotheses for systematic study and testing; they could also yield insights for greater capacity for prediction of behavior and need which could serve as feedback for program design. Many of the areas of inquiry indicated above can be started and carried out by social work students with faculty supervision and by social work practitioners. Some studies fall within the specific competence of social workers; some they can contribute to through interdisciplinary participation; other types of inquiries are more logically investigated by other disciplines.

Training for Service Roles

A bare sketch of the present curriculum areas in graduate schools of social work with potentialities for training for work in family planning by no means is a sufficient indicator for the multiple training needs or possibilities of the field. It leaves many questions unanswered, particularly the problem of training and education for different levels of practice. These can only be touched on briefly here.

Specialist roles in family planning are emerging which require either more concentrated education in graduate school or for which some advanced education and practice is required. Education for specialists should draw from a broader interdisciplinary base. It may have to be fashioned from offerings in advanced programs in schools of social work, schools of public health, and centers for the study of population problems. The roles may be geared to policy development, program design, and implementation, administration, evaluative research, and program and administrative consultation.

The practitioner emerging from a professional school who has acquired the knowledge of family planning objectives, problems, and programs should be able to apply this knowledge in family planning programs and services. He should be equipped to operate with reasonable self-direction and independence at least in the direct service roles applying clinical skills in the individualization of services. He should be alert to the needs of special problem cases and to be able to participate in the development of new services, including education, and information out-reach programs, and be able to develop group approaches to designated populations. He should also be able to help with the training and supervision of volunteer staff and community aides or new career workers as part of their orientation and contiuing work.

The worker who has a general education on the college level but is lacking in professional education is increasingly called on to play a very direct role in family planning. He is to be found primarily in the basic public welfare services and in health agencies and other voluntary services. The college-educated but professionally untrained worker has needed a good deal of training through various means of staff development and in-service training for all phases of his work. To make him effective in the role of initiating discussion of family planning services for his clients, sensitive discussion of attitudes and feelings, enhancement of motivation, and effective referral and follow-through, he will need a good deal of systematic knowledge in this area that the agency will have to provide. At this point, the agency will need expert outside help in designing content and teaching methods for such staff development programs. The first emphasis may be on training the supervisory and in-house training staff in order to provide a cadre of personnel who can continue to train new staff and to lend active and continuing supervision to sustain such an effort. Useful training materials and experimental teaching approaches to conveying content with opportunity for working through of anxieties and ambivalent attitudes, such as through methods of role playing, are increasingly available.[17]

The use of social service and health aides who are members of local communities and of the ethnic population to be served—the so-called indigenous worker—is a fast-growing means both of providing necessary manpower and of opening up new career opportunities for previously unemployed or underemployed individuals. It has great potential if roles and tasks are clearly defined and specified, and if adequate training and continuing supervision and support suitable to the needs and abilities of this group is provided. Health and social service aides are being used successfully in many types of agencies, including family planning clinics. They often make a significant contribution and are effective by functioning in ways that the professionally trained social worker cannot, mostly because of the problem of social and professional distance from the client group to be served. The aides are used in out-reach programs to specific neighborhoods, in one-by-one case finding, in referral to various community resources, in supportive relationships through the family planning clinic procedures, and, most important, in supportive relationships which help to sustain the follow-through effort. They are also very helpful in follow-up work. They play a central role with ambivalent clients who lack knowledge or are fearful about services and who may have multiple health and social problems as well as personal or family crises which need attention. Without a comprehensive approach, the family planning effort made by these families becomes sporadic or ineffective because of other pressing, unsolved, and overwhelming problems. The aides become a key resource in identifying, mobilizing, and sustaining resources and motivation fortified by the back-up services of other more highly trained or specialized personnel.

Training for social service and health aides is still evolving and is probably of an uneven quality and effectiveness with much trial and error experimentation and not enough synthesis and building on known successful approaches. Often the staff in training and supervisory capacities is not sufficiently schooled in educational techniques and approaches. In this area, as with staff development programs for the college-educated social worker, consultation by social workers competent in educational methods through teaching and supervision is needed to help with design of content and, more important, with training and supervisory formats and methods that can be geared to staff and which is appropriate to their level of educational and cultural background and learning styles.

From the foregoing discussion it can be concluded that education and training for the great variety of roles and tasks in family planning is needed on a broad spectrum of educational levels. Ways and means of developing relevant content in professional schools is one task. Staff development and in-service training methods, including the use of supervision and consultation, are the most obvious and traditional means of reaching our greatest manpower pool—the partially trained and completely untrained workers. The mechanisms of continuing education, either under professional or university auspices, is becoming a more important device for up-dating professional knowledge and skill as well as introducing new areas of knowledge and practice. It could become a central means of reaching personnel at all levels of education and experience. Continuing education under university auspices has better access to scarce resources of skilled teaching personnel and specialists. The content as well as the patterns by which it is offered can be variously designed to reach the different manpower levels. Courses can be offered to the social work community at large or on a contract basis to large agencies to meet their staff needs. Such educational programs need to be promoted and, because experimentation with content and format is an important feature, built-in evaluative research in regard to effectiveness in reaching educational objectives should be fostered. No one segment of the educational enterprise can meet the educational needs for manpower in family planning. All levels of training and education need to be engaged with continuing clarification of the relevant levels of education for the changing and differing roles and tasks in practice.

Notes

1. Philip Hauser, "On Non-Family Planning Methods of Population Control" (unpub. paper presented at the International Conference on Family Planning, Dacca, Pakistan, Feb. 1969).
2. Rev. Don C. Shaw, "Barriers to Fertility Control," with Special Reference to Low Income People," *Family Planning-An Option for All People* (Chicago: National Federation of Settlements and Neighborhood Centers, 1969), p. 3.
3. Vera Shlakman, "Social Work's Role in Family Planning: Social Policy Issues," in *Family Planning: The Role of Social Work,* ed. Florence Haselkorn *(Persepctives in Social Work,* vol. XI, no. 1; Garden City, N.Y.: Adelphi University School of Social Work, 1968), pp. 70–71.
4. Margaret Mead, "The Need for an Ethic," *Family Planning and Medical Education, Journal of Medical Education,* vol. XLIV, no. 11 (Nov. 1969),p. 2, ch. 4, p. 32.
5. Kingsley Davis, "Population Policy: Will Current Programs Succeed?" *Science* (Nov. 10, 1967), pp. 730–39.
6. Franklin Robbins, "Population: A Hopeless Case," in *Family Planning and Medical Education, Journal of Medical Education,* vol. XLIV, no. 11 (Nov. 1969),p. 2, pp. 14–19.
7. Hauser, "On Non-Family Planning Methods."
8. Bernard Berleson, "Beyond Family Planning," *Studies in Family Planning* (publication of the Population Council), no. 38 (Feb. 1969).
9. Florence Haselkorn, "Value Issues for Social Work in Family Planning: An Introductory Note," in *Family Planning: The Role of Social Work,* ed. Florence Haselkorn *(Perspectives in Social Work,* vol. XI, no. 1; Garden City, N.Y.: Adelphi University School of Social Work, 1968), p. 8.
10. Florence Haselkorn, "The Responsibilities and Opportunities for Social Work in Family Planning" (unpub. paper delivered at University of North Carolina Seminar Nov. 21, 1969), p. 2.
11. Haselkorn, "Value Issues," p. 10.
12. Brewster Smith, "Motivation, Communications, Research and Family Planning," in *Public Health and Population Change: Current Research Issues,* ed. Mindel C. Sheps and Jeanne C. Ridley (Pittsburgh: University of Pittsburgh Press, 1966), pp. 70–89.
13. George James, "The Role of the Medical School in Family Planning," in *Family Planning and Medical Education, Journal of Medical Education,* vol. XLIV, no. 11 (Nov. 1969), part. 2, ch. 10, pp. 115–23.

14. Haselkorn, "Responsibilities and Opportunities."

15. Frederick Jaffe, "Family Planning and Public Policy: Is the "Culture of Poverty' the New Cop-Out?" (paper presented at the American Sociological Association, San Francisco, Aug. 29, 1967.

16. Haselkorn, "Responsibilities and Opportunities."

17. Miriam Manisoff, ed. *Family Planning Training for Social Service* (New York: Planned Parenthood/World Population, 1970).

Index